GENDER, CULTURE, AND POWER

GENDER, CULTURE, AND POWER

Toward a Feminist Postmodern Critical Theory

BEN AGGER

PRAEGER

Westport, Connecticut
London

Library of Congress Cataloging-in-Publication Data

Agger, Ben.
  Gender, culture, and power : toward a feminist postmodern critical theory / Ben Agger.
    p. cm.
  Includes bibliographical references and index.
  ISBN 0-275-94700-9 (alk. paper)
  1. Feminism. 2. Power (Social sciences) 3. Critical theory.
  4. Sex role. I. Title.
  HQ1154.A37 1994   93-14119

British Library Cataloguing in Publication Data is available.

Copyright © 1993 by Ben Agger

All rights reserved. No portion of this book may be reproduced, by any process or technique, without the express written consent of the publisher.

Library of Congress Catalog Card Number: 93-14119
ISBN: 0-275-94700-9

First published in 1993

Praeger Publishers, 88 Post Road West, Westport, CT 06881
An imprint of Greenwood Publishing Group, Inc.

Printed in the United States of America

The paper used in this book complies with the Permanent Paper Standard issued by the National Information Standards Organization (Z39.48-1984).

10 9 8 7 6 5 4 3 2 1

For Sarah and Beth Anne

Contents

Acknowledgments		ix
1	**Critical Theory and Postmodernity**	1
	Third-Generation Critical Theory	1
	Transitions in Postmodern Capitalism	7
	Fast Capitalism: Toward a New Theory of Ideology	11
	Is a Totality Theory Possible?	16
	The Politics of Totality	21
	Theorizing Postmodernity	27
2	**Postmodernism and the End of Politics 1: New French Theory**	31
	The Aversion to Grand Narratives	31
	Postmodernism, Post-Marxism, Neoliberalism	36
	Derrida, Foucault, Baudrillard, and the Frankfurt School	42
	Modernism, Postmodernism, and Cultural Studies	46
	Postmodernism and the "End of Ideology"	52
3	**Postmodernism and the End of Politics 2: Feminist Theory**	57
	Lacanian Feminism	57

	Difference Theory, the Celebration of the Feminine, and the End of Politics	66
	The Problem of the Postmodern Feminist Subject	73
	Theorizing Feminism: The Text Is a Woman	77
4	**Producing Reproduction: The Logic of Feminist Postmodern Critical Theory**	83
	Retaining the Concept of Structural Primacy	83
	Beyond Poststructuralism	88
	Production over Reproduction	94
	Essaying Critical Theory	98
	Totality, Relationality, Transformationality	104
5	**Critical Theory and Everyday Life 1: Against Economism**	109
	Transcoding the Logics of Domination	109
	Postmodernism and the Discourse of Imagination	116
	Feminism and the Valorization of Reproduction	121
	Critical Theory for and against the Popular	126
	Transcoding the Transcoder	131
6	**Critical Theory and Everyday Life 2: Desire, Discourse, and Domination**	137
	Desire: Can Men Be Feminists (and Write Feminist Theory)?	137
	Discourse: Cracking the Code	143
	Domination: Negating Negative Dialectics	150
	Who's Left?	154
Bibliography		159
Index		169

Acknowledgments

I would like to thank the following people:

John Dings—for useful comments on the manuscript.
Kate Hausbeck—for editorial legwork.
Anne Kiefer—for signing this project.
Ross D. MacKinnon—for supporting my career in every way.
Diane Spalding—for good production values.

GENDER, CULTURE, AND POWER

Chapter One

Critical Theory and Postmodernity

THIRD-GENERATION CRITICAL THEORY

My aim in this book is to develop a third-generation critical theory, surpassing but learning from the first-generation critical theory of Horkheimer, Adorno, and Marcuse and the second-generation critical theory of Habermas. The next generation of critical theorists needs to confront challenges from feminism and postmodernism in order to address postmodern capitalism adequately (see Jameson 1991). Although Frankfurt critical theory, postmodernism, and feminism are often viewed as divergent, I will develop an argument for synthesis, outlining what I call the logic of feminist postmodern critical theory (Chapter 4). I then apply this logic to particular social, political, sexual, textual, and cultural problems of today (Chapters 5 and 6). I develop this logic of a new critical theory through readings of postmodernism (Chapter 2) and feminism (Chapter 3), preceded by this opening stage setting (Chapter 1), in which I lay out the relationship between critical theory and postmodernity and argue for the priority of critical theory's totality theory over the antitotality perspectives of postmodernism and feminism, albeit learning from them.

I suggest a version of critical theory incorporating the most politically acute insights of postmodernism and feminism. In this project, I risk hierarchizing nouns like *critical theory* over the adjectives (e.g., *postmodern* and *feminist*) qualifying them. All such exercises in naming are political in their implication of priority and must be recognized as such. I am interested in combining the best insights of theories that embrace total social explanation (e.g., Marxism) and that refuse total explanation (e.g., postmodernism and feminism). Some readers may accuse me of reconciling the irreconcilable—Lyotard with Adorno, Kristeva with Marcuse, Foucault with Habermas, Derrida with Horkheimer, Baudrillard with Jameson. Exercises in synthesis typically fail because they integrate incommensurables, or they are exercises in what Jameson (1991) calls named theory, putting new labels on yesterday's theoretical vintages. By acknowledging these risks I hope to avoid them, especially where my aim is to develop a critical theory of society that serves distinctive purposes.

From feminism I draw the very powerful insights that the personal is political and the political personal. Social change must involve the minds, bodies, and intimate lives of people lest the product of change sacrifice the process of changing to various authoritarian expedients. There are no legitimate excuses for oppressing people in the name of distant future liberation. Indeed, as Marcuse (1969) crucially shows, changes in our daily lives prefigure as well as reflect larger structural changes; thus they must be conducted with the attitude of what he calls the "new sensibility" in order to ensure that the choices we make today emerge in qualitatively new institutions. Once we separate the personal from political, everyday life from overarching institutions, we defuse the dialectic bridging present and future and hence subvert democracy.

Feminism has understood this much better than Marxism. There are certain remarkable parallels between critical theory and feminism in this regard. Horkheimer, Adorno, Marcuse, and Habermas both anticipate and overlap the feminist understanding of the politics of everyday life, albeit without theorizing sexuality and the household as important political venues in their own right. One may ask how the Frankfurt theorists could miss the politics of sexuality when they understood the politics of subjectivity so clearly. Sadly, they were male supremacist, defending paternal authority as the source of childhood ego autonomy. But I contend that the Frankfurt School's sexism can be negated within the basic framework of their critical theory, extending it both empirically and politically.

This effort to refurbish totality theory from within the Marxist perspective of the Frankfurt School will immediately put feminists and postmodernists on the defensive. Most efforts at totality have ignored women, people of color, all sorts of "others." But I believe that a new totality theory can avoid male supremacy by carefully rethinking its own critique of domination in such a way that feminism is no longer considered an appendage but informs and transforms the very logic of critical theory. Nancy Fraser (1989) has begun this effort in her sympathetic critique of Habermas's system/lifeworld theory. She argues that Habermas does not theorize the lifeworld (everyday life) as a contested terrain and thus he does not produce a critical theory that adequately addresses male supremacy.

Feminism's challenge to male critical theory is considerable. To meet this challenge requires more than simply acknowledging it or adding a "feminism" chapter to critical theory books. The feminist critique of patriarchy as a world-historical logic of domination must be integrated into critical theory from the beginning. Indeed, as I hope to demonstrate in this book, feminism's understanding of the devaluation of reproduction, notably domestic labor, is central to my version of feminist postmodern critical theory. The issue of the hierarchy of nouns and adjectives ultimately determines how people react to what I call a feminist postmodern critical theory (as opposed to a postmodern critical feminism). I modify critical theory with the words *feminist* and *postmodern* because I contend that the Frankfurt School's critical theory is the most totalizing in intent. This does not deny that feminism and postmodernism can generate readings of totality in their own right. That they can is precisely why I am writing this book. But to make *critical theory* a noun and *feminist* and *postmodern* adjectives is politically contentious precisely because critical theory—indeed, Marxism generally—has been a male modernist discourse, missing crucial issues of oppression made thematic by radical and socialist feminists and by postmodern theorists like Foucault.

My theoretical synthesis intends deconstructively to reverse the tendency of nouns to take priority over adjectives, thus preventing the subordination of feminism and postmodernism to male critical theory. I address squarely what it means for men to write feminism. That will be a discussion in which I argue not only that men can and should write feminism but that what it means to write feminism is an unresolved issue. I not only claim feminism; I argue that my version of critical theory so fully integrates feminism as well as certain radical postmodern insights that these adjectives and nouns blur to the point of indistinguishability. Why, then, retain nominal differentiations that, as Derrida understands, tend to become hierarchies? My answer is that differentiations are useful and inevitable, highlighting areas of divergence as well as convergence. They cannot be avoided where we recognize that language is a prison house, imposing its own meanings on us.

Someone is going to be rendered adjectival in any theoretical synthesis, which raises the risk of subordination. We must do our best to prevent adjectival status from becoming a mark of political inequality. The first will be last only if we are disingenuous in our attempts to forge an integrated social theory that blends the analytical logics of feminism, postmodernism, and critical theory. My argument for the priority of critical theory is that the Frankfurt theorists develop an interdisciplinary materialism that seeks to comprehend the whole sweep of world history. Whether it has been successful in achieving this panoramic perspective is debatable. But the Frankfurt School theorists urged the reconstruction of original Marxism in a way that addressed the civilizational logic of Western and world society and not simply the particular features of nineteenth- or twentieth-century European capitalism. In deepening Marxism in their book *Dialectic of Enlightenment*, Horkheimer and Adorno (1972) opened the way for further deepenings and broadenings of critical theory, making this study possible.

As critical theory enters its third generation, it needs to reground itself in a reading of history and society that stresses *the politics of everyday life*, the *possibility of postmodern progressivism*, and *cultural studies as critique of ideology*. These are the respective contributions of feminism, postmodernism, and nonmandarin cultural studies inspired by the Frankfurt School; I combine these influences into a feminist postmodern critical theory. This rearticulation of Horkheimer and Adorno's critical theory confronts the feminist and postmodern challenges in a way that strengthens their own critique of the dialectic of enlightenment. In Chapter 4, I reformulate their original dialectic-of-enlightenment argument in my analysis of the dialectic of production and reproduction which, appropriately interpreted, allows itself to be applied locally by feminists, postmodernists, and culturally oriented critical theorists. Thus, a feminist postmodern critical theory that rests on a critique of the primacy of production as an axial critique of all hierarchy leads to particular regional applications of critical theory in the sites of contestation heretofore associated with feminism, postmodernism, and critical theory as differentiated theoretical practices.

The integration of feminism, postmodernism, and critical theory allows me to theorize the possibilities of *the liberations of women and household labor*, *the imagination*, and *the popular*, the respective aims of these three social theories. A feminist postmodern critical theory integrates these perspectives without effacing their different nuances and intellectual priorities. My version of critical theory suggests that women and household labor, the imagination, and the popular have been equivalently devalued by male supremacy, a modernist philosophy of history, and cultural mandarinism, respectively. I argue that these three "causes" of domination are, in fact, one, requiring us to rethink theoretical separability and territoriality in creative ways—the aim of this book. Feminism politicizes the household and sexuality; postmodernism interrogates the modernist philosophy of history; and the Frankfurt School theorizes the culture industry politically. Within these three venues of politics and power people actively resist their own domination, working imaginatively and courageously to create vital spaces of what Gramsci called counterhegemony.

This interpretation of the logic of civilization calls into question critical theory's relationship to Marx. The original Frankfurt theorists and then Habermas have attempted to show that Marx's particular critique of the alienation of labor can be extended into a critique of domination. In this book, I make explicit their implicit critique of all hierarchies that devalue activity regarded merely as reproductive. Whereas Marx theorized the alienation of labor and the Frankfurt theorists theorized domination, I theorize *productivism*—a logic involving but going beyond alienation and domination that produces the fateful hierarchies of men over women, capital over labor, white over colored, straight over gay, First World over Third World, and society over nature. A critical theory appropriate to postmodernity can elaborate this critique of productivist hierarchies by *valuing* people and activities heretofore viewed as reproductive, demonstrating that women, labor, people of color, and nature are secretly productive in their own rights.

This revaluation was begun by Marx where he argued that the uncompensated surplus labor of workers is the source of capitalist profit. He showed that the seemingly valueless, labor power, produces value and should be compensated adequately. Feminists extend his particular critique of what I am calling productivism by valorizing the realm of household labor (including sexuality) buttressing patriarchal capitalism. Feminists draw attention to Marx's male supremacy, arguing that he missed the contribution of women's unpaid household labor to the formation of value. They extend his critique of the market to the nonmarket, hence broadening his critique of civilization. This exercise has paralleled the Frankfurt School's effort to reformulate Marx's critique of economic exploitation as a critique of all domination.

My version of critical theory integrates the Frankfurt critique of domination with the feminist critique of male-supremacist assumptions about productivity. Productivism is conceptualized as the underlying source of economic exploitation, domination and male supremacy, which are seen as interstitial moments of value's generic hierarchy over the allegedly valueless. Interestingly, the critique of productivism that I am developing in order to ground my feminist-postmodern reformulation of critical theory was already foreshadowed in the Frankfurt School's own critique of instrumental rationality, which they derived from Nietzsche, Heidegger, Weber, and Lukacs. This connection is rarely made inasmuch as the Frankfurt theorists, like Weber and virtually all Marxists before them, were simply not interested in sexism as a meaningful social phenomenon. But they could well have applied their immanent critique of productivism and instrumental rationality to the various manifestations of male supremacy.

A feminist critical theory is eminently possible, as this book will demonstrate (also see Benjamin 1988). Postmodernism further informs this version of feminist critical theory by developing a critique of modernity that salvages the emancipatory project of modernity while jettisoning the more ideological aspects of modernism, which even Marx uncritically accepted. It is important to theorize postmodernity as a stage beyond "late" capitalism (see Mandel 1975)—a horizon of possibilities not adequately charted on the eschatological tableau of modernity theory, both capitalist and socialist. Habermas's (1984, 1987b) attempt to retheorize domination in terms of system/lifeworld dynamics belongs to this effort to theorize postmodernity in politically relevant terms. Although his communication-theoretic reformulation of critical theory fails to develop a notion of intermediate or interstitial critical theory connecting system and lifeworld, he valuably moves the dialectic-of-enlightenment argument a crucial stage beyond the original Frankfurt theorists' critique of modernity, which was phrased in overly fatalistic terms.

A radical conception of postmodernity holds open the door of possible social change but does not derive this dynamic from the teleology of modernity theory, plotted originally by the *philosophes*, Comte, and even Marx. But neither does it renounce the project of modernity which, in its best sense, embodies the telos of rationality. We need to theorize the possibility of social rationality outside of the deterministic coordinates of both evolutionary and revolutionary modernity theory. In other words (see Huyssen 1986), we need to theorize postmodernism itself as a radical moment of modernism that points beyond the present toward new modernities—postmodernities—embodying reason and justice. It is clear that Horkheimer and Adorno (1972) supported generic enlightenment, with a small *e*, if not the particular Enlightenment of early-bourgeois Europe, which, they argued, betrayed enlightenment by conflating it with scientism. It is transparent that the Marx of *Capital* was a modernist, recognizing that capitalism broke with premodernity and thus inaugurated the era of the modern.

We need a critical philosophy of history that somehow distinguishes between the possibility of social rationality, on the one hand, and the particular projects of capitalist and state-socialist modernization, on the other. Postmodernity can be viewed as the possible next stage of social history in which we relinquish modernist eschatologies, which reinforce fatalism ideologically ("social laws"), and yet retain a modernist social activism—modernist in the sense that this activism aims to bring about a better world governed by reason. It is difficult to conceive of this dialectical philosophy of history within the framework of postmodernism because postmodernism is so often read as antirationalist. But postmodernism can be radicalized so that it rearticulates the most emancipatory features of modernism, which ambivalently contains both reason and unreason, enlightenment and myth.

I contend that postmodernism can best be radicalized through critical theory itself, which in many respects (e.g., see Jay 1984a) is remarkably similar to various postmodern social theories such as those of Foucault (1977) and Baudrillard (1975, 1981, 1983, 1985). Postmodernism becomes a critical theory where it advances the notion of a reconstructed history, not only the antifoundational sense of historicity. Foucault (see Fraser 1989) and Baudrillard (see Kellner 1989b) do not have room for social change, even though their writings are amply, even thickly, historical. They lack a philosophy of history, which in its Marxist version they dismiss as naively modernist. But it is crucial to disentangle bourgeois and Marxist modernisms in a way that fulfills the project of modernity within a noncapitalist framework. The dismal failure of state socialism only underscores the need for this sort of philosophy of history. In its absence, a quiescent, ironic postmodernism obliterates critique, replacing explicit ideology with the cynical world weariness of Western cosmopolitanism and consumerism.

A feminist postmodern critical theory fights certain enemies within, notably the left's right. This left authoritarianism surfaces among Marxists, critical theorists, feminists, and postmodernists. The left's right gives up on the emancipatory project of modernity, instead endorsing various species of irrationalism and authoritarianism. The contemporary furor over so-called political correctness reflects liberal and conservative anxieties about the authoritarian left, which fights a rear-guard action in the university. Although claims about the leftist domination of the academy are hysterically inflated, affiliation subverts independent thought on the left, where small-mindedness prevails as never before. This is why in claiming critical theory, feminism, and postmodernism I must be careful to put distance between their authentic versions and secretly neoliberal imposter versions. Habermas (e.g., 1981a, 1987a) has indefatigably defended the emancipatory project of modernity against both antimodernist and postmodernist critics. He shows the way for those of us who value reason, enlightenment, and social justice as the central values of critical social theory, even if he has not sufficiently appreciated feminism and postmodernism as possible companion versions of critical theory in their own right (see Fraser 1989; Poster 1989).

TRANSITIONS IN POSTMODERN CAPITALISM

Jameson's 1984 *New Left Review* article on postmodernism as the cultural logic of late capitalism (expanded into a 1991 book) suggests the direction of my analysis. He periodizes capitalism in very useful ways, even if he has not adequately developed a systematic version of critical social theory, something that he may be unable to do from within the framework of literary theory. I agree with him that we can usefully talk about postmodern capitalism as a stage somehow beyond *and* continuous with what the Frankfurt School and Mandel (1975) had earlier called "late" capitalism. I am less concerned with taxonomic refinements than with framing a third-generation critical theory in historically appropriate terms.

Whereas Horkheimer, Adorno, and Marcuse developed the Frankfurt Institute for Social Research's critical theory in the 1930s to address phenomena somehow unanticipated by Marx in *Capital*, especially regarding state intervention in the economy and the rise of the culture industry, Habermas (1984, 1987b) deepened their deepening of Marx's original critique of bourgeois political economy in his two-volume *Theory of Communicative Action*. In particular, he argued that the "paradigm of consciousness" retained by Horkheimer and Adorno (1972) in *Dialectic of Enlightenment* needs to be abandoned in favor of a "paradigm of communication," outlined in his universal pragmatics of discourse. Habermas's attempt to develop critical theory as a communication theory allowed him to reformulate Marx's capital/labor motif in system/lifeworld terms, thus enabling him to theorize "new social movements" that spring creatively from the lifeworld and thus can be further mobilized.

Although Habermas's reconstruction of Marxian historical materialism has been ambitious and instructive, it falls short, notably in its lack of attention to a postmodern philosophy of history, a critical cultural studies, and feminist concerns. His new social movements theory, however suggestive in its generous heterodoxy, does not adequately integrate the concerns of feminist theory, which, as I argue here, go significantly beyond the women's movement as a social movement. I put feminism to work as a critique of the domination of reproduction, which, I argue, should be the foundation of critical theory today. So what I am calling third-generation critical theory needs to move beyond Habermas's reconstruction of the original Frankfurt School's own reconstruction of Marx's critique of political economy. Integrating influences like postmodernism and feminism, this theoretical move would allow us to develop *an interstitial critical theory that moves back and forth between system and lifeworld and thus produces a politically-relevant philosophy of history, a critical cultural studies and a politics of sexuality and gender*.

A contemporary critical theory needs to learn from feminism and postmodernism without exhibiting defensive male-modernist territoriality. In the process, critical theory will be transformed, perhaps appearing barely recognizable to its first and second generations. This is necessary where critical theory, like Marxism generally, has been abandoned by feminists and postmodernists convinced that it has little to offer apart from a certain antiquarian interest. Clinging devotedly to their dog-eared copies of *Capital*, orthodox Marxists do little to serve the cause of theoretical revision and political consolidation. But even the Frankfurt School theorists and their followers fall into similar orthodoxies based on hallowed texts like *Dialectic of Enlightenment* and *Negative Dialectics*, which become objects of interpretive cultivation and not theoretical elaboration.

Critical theorists have been remarkably slow to apply critical theory to contemporary social problems (for exceptions, see Forester 1985; Luke 1989). They lack the interstitial theory necessary to bridge the sweeping but important abstractions of negative dialectics and the lifeworlds identified as politically relevant by proponents and theorists of new social movements. I develop a lifeworld-grounded critical theory here that mediates between large-scale social structures and everyday life by conceptualizing and mobilizing socially and politically reconstructive activities (or, in an older language, bridging theory and practice). I contend that the most relevant cultural, political, economic, and sexual resistances occur at the interstitial level somehow interposed between deep structure, on the one hand, and quotidian existence, on the other. Critical theory can best connect system/structure and lifeworld/experience by delving intermediately into culture, politics, economics, and sexuality. That is to say, critical theory needs to conceptualize ways in which everyday resistances can blossom into, and be informed by, large-scale social movements. Feminism and postmodernism make this intermediate theorizing possible, affording perspectives on the politics of sexuality, cultural studies, and the philosophy of history, three theoretical topics explored further in Chapters 5 and 6, where I suggest concrete applications of feminist postmodern critical theory in these three interstitial regions.

Postmodern capitalism is characterized by an implosion of centrifugal forces unleashed with unprecedented power in the late capitalism of the "authoritarian state" (Horkheimer 1973) identified by the original Frankfurt School. This is not to deny that we should attempt to theorize totality but rather to suggest that totality cannot be reduced to singular principles that manifest themselves equivalently in spheres of existence already defined as separate—think of the class, race, gender trinity. Having said that, I will promptly go ahead and propose a new principle of totalization in postmodern capitalism!—what I am calling the domination of reproduction (Chapter 4). But this theoretical logic, as I will demonstrate later, has the advantage of flexibility and thus preserves what postmodernists call difference and Adorno called nonidentity. A feminist postmodern critical theory addresses a postmodern capitalism characterized by a self-differentiating principle of totality that conceals the underlying sameness of difference in order to simulate plurality and democracy—thus totalizing domination ever more effectively. This postmodern logic of totality that masquerades as difference is captured best by an encompassing critical theory that traces the domination of reproduction to its multiple manifestations (which often appear to be contradictory in their own right, such as the class/gender relationship).

In postmodern capitalism domination, as Horkheimer, Adorno, and Marcuse call it, is regionalized, differentiated, and deconstructed inasmuch as system, in Habermas's terms, colonizes the everyday lives of people everywhere. Upon casual inspection, these differential instances of domination appear to stem from separable sources—capitalism, patriarchy, racism. But once we understand their common source in the hierarchies of production over reproduction, as I conceptualize them in this book, then we can theorize a complexly integrated postmodern capitalism that only appears to proliferate healthy difference at every turn. Difference, like plurality, is marshalled ideologically in order to demonstrate the system's openness and fairness.

This is not to ignore that the system is always open, precisely Foucault's point where he argues that power is ubiquitous, encoded in various protean discourse/practices that resist co-optation. Such openness is the essential possibility of radical social change. But openness—historicity—can only be exploited through a theory and practice that address the complexly interrelated hierarchies that, on the surface at least, seem irreducible to each other. Only by deconstructing the appearance of political and social difference as fraudulent can we create real difference—autonomy via social freedom. *What is unique about postmodern capitalism is the way in which differentiation reproduces homogeneity and hegemony, hence blocking world-his-*

torical transformation. Whereas the original Frankfurt School correctly understood domination to be a totalizing logic of bureaucratic-capitalist administration that erases all difference—Weber's rationalization—today, in a postmodern stage of capitalism, administrative domination has been differentially regionalized in order to conceal and extend its even deeper colonization of people's everyday lives.

In its affirmative version (e.g., Lyotard 1984), postmodernism updates the earlier pluralist affirmation of capitalism (e.g., Bell 1973). Postmodern theory valorizes difference as a way of arguing for the existence of difference—democracy—today. But as Best and Kellner (1991) have convincingly shown, this version of postmodernism abets late capitalism where it deflects attention from the self-same logic of capital that, now as before, is colonizing, dominating, and reifying. The challenge for me in this book is to reconceptualize what Marxists have traditionally called the logic of capital in a way that empirically addresses its contemporary manifestations, plumbs them for possible resistance, and theorizes their connection to other moments and forces of resistance. To do this, I need to distinguish carefully between the project of modernity as it has been postured by modernists who favor the colonizing logic of capital and the project of modernity as it has been conceived by radicals who favor reason, freedom, and justice.

Postmodern capitalism is a quantitative and qualitative extrapolation of an earlier "late" capitalism, which emerged since the Depression and World War II. (As I discuss later, people periodize the dawning of postmodern society in different ways; e.g., see Harvey 1989, for whom postmodernity began with the destruction of the Pruitt-Igoe housing project in St. Louis.) Postmodern capitalism regionalizes domination in order to conceal its emanation from the common axis of what I am calling the generic hierarchy of production over reproduction or value over valuelessness. A disaffirmative postmodernism functions as critical theory where it resists the notion that some activities (people, groups, etc.) are more valuable than others, building on Marx's classic analysis of the sources of value hidden in workers' labor power. Postmodernism distinctively theorizes "otherness's" subordination by a superordinate term, subject, group.

In this sense, Marx's analysis of the exploitation of labor power outlined in volume 1 of *Capital* is the first postmodern address to the hierarchy of production over reproduction, even if Marx failed to theorize unpaid household labor, service work, and caregiving, which remain crucial in explaining the domination of houseworkers and people employed in the informal sector of the economy. Although Marx clearly supported the emancipatory project of modernity, including science, his formulation of the hierarchy of value over apparent valuelessness as a civilizational logic was importantly postmodern. This is another way of understanding how fluid is the boundary between the modern and postmodern—how, indeed, the postmodern is merely the most recent stage of a modernity that has yet to be completed in Marxist and feminist terms.

Postmodern capitalism needs to be "mapped" (Jameson 1984, 1991) as a world in which we suspend our timeworn assumptions about the separability of regions. In fact, the map of postmodernity would reveal not only the interconnection of places but their virtual identity. Everybody has been colonized, hence marginalized—the Third World, proletarians, gays, houseworkers. There are no worlds apart in postmodern capitalism, if there ever were in earlier capitalism. But this is difficult for the left to swallow at a time when the assertion of difference—especially "multiculturalism," the new slogan of academic neoliberals—is echoed frequently. It is assumed that the world is a plural place and that we can no longer piece together the large stories in which the parts are somehow smaller than the whole. Postmodernity produces precisely this illusion as ideology, trying to thwart cartographic exercises that would reveal difference to be a sham, when in fact people are hierarchized everywhere, and for the same reasons.

FAST CAPITALISM: TOWARD A NEW THEORY OF IDEOLOGY

What I (1989a) have called fast capitalism and Baudrillard (1983) has called hyperreality are other terms for postmodern capitalism, which I periodized above. Postmodernism functions as ideology where it promulgates the notion of a plural, decentered world impervious to totalizing mappings. It checks efforts to tell the large stories in which the particular players are all connected by their participation in the global logic of capitalist modernity, which is not postmodern at all in the sense of being beyond modernity. This is fast capitalism in which the deceptive images traditionally used to conceal or invert reality are now dispersed into the world itself, preventing their careful scrutiny and facilitating their thoughtless enactment. Money, science, edifice, and figure have become the new ideologies, supplementing older ideological treatises like religion and bourgeois economic theory.

These new postmodern forms of ideology are nearly impossible to refute counterfactually; after all, they make no apparent claims. Advertising has sunk so deep into the commodity that we no longer treat it propositionally but consume it as commodity itself. Whereas Pepsi formerly purported that it was better than Coke (e.g., that more people liked it), today Pepsi ads make few claims about the product but transform its acquisition into sheer experience—what sociologists call lifestyle. Michael Jackson dances for Pepsi and Paula Abdul dances for Coke; the "message" is that by drinking these beverages we will dance, if not literally like Jackson and Abdul then in the sense of becoming stars of our own lives—and all this from drinking the beverage of choice!

Baudrillard calls these images simulations, capturing the ways in which they formulate reality and hence become real. I characterize dispersed ideologies as endemic to fast capitalism because I stress the speed with which the economic and cultural reproduction process hums along, further preventing mediating, meditating readings, rebuttals, and rejoinders. Postmodern capitalism creates capital out of images and images out of commodities, utterly blurring the boundaries between the real and imaginary. Indeed, the notion of a solid "reality" is anathema to postmodernists who have capitulated to the phantasmagoric conflation of the real and imaginary and indeed celebrate it (e.g., see Kroker and Cook 1986).

A "fast" postmodern capitalism requires demarcating activities that pry apart the real and imaginary in order to subject simulations to the test of validity. This must not be done in a positivist vein lest concepts only seek to reproduce the reality to which they are nonidentical (see Adorno 1973a). There can be nonpositivist cognitions, as the Frankfurt theorists (e.g., Marcuse 1969; Agger 1976) have argued from the beginning. These "new sciences" would retain the traditional epistemic differentiation between the real, on the one hand, and images and concepts, on the other. This would empower thought, speech, and writing to take issue with the political imaginary of postmodern capitalism, refusing the ideologizing claims made about the rationality of reality.

Above all, this deconstructive strategy would translate the imaginary into discrete discursive claims, thus allowing it to be falsified. The Coca-Cola company's implication that lives will be transformed by Coke needs to be narrated, put into words, so that it can be rebutted by counterfactual claims. We need to be able to show that stars are created by the culture industry, that commodity consumption does not set us free, and that Coke is not good for our health. The Michael Jacksons and Paula Abduls are themselves simulations, as gossipy fan-magazines clearly show. Jackson faded from black to white. Abdul was assembled by the technical wizards of rock video, having been "discovered" as a professional basketball cheerleader. There are so many levels of deception here that we barely know where to begin with the deconstructive work of cultural studies, which I regard as one of the three central activities of a postmodern feminist critical theory, as I outline in Chapter 6.

Above all, we need to turn the imaginary back into a text, which it has long since ceased to be. Advertising agencies begin with discourse and figure where they plot the campaigns that turn commodities into heroic, fantastic existences. We must be able to read the simulation of commodities as the texts they really are, disgorging the claims encoded in them and then dispersed into the sentient world as pieces of postmodern civic furniture. This is largely, but not entirely, a story about the media. It is equally important to deconstruct science as a persuasive text (e.g., see Agger 1989b) that is mystified in the figural discourse of quantitative analysis, a central feature of positivism in the social sciences. By deconstructing figure and number as rhetorical devices that drive the implication of ironclad social lawfulness, we challenge their hold on people's everyday experiences.

This is politically radicalizing where it is no longer easy to challenge ideologies in postmodern capitalism. Books—textual interventions—are found everywhere but in bookstores and libraries. Old-fashioned textuality has been nearly eclipsed, except in the rarefied university world, in which struggling assistant professors attempt to publish their arcane dissertations and thus earn the sinecure of tenure. Even university presses, formerly outlets for specialized scholarly monographs, are feeling the pressure to publish trade books for general audiences, causing discourse to decline still further. Jacoby (1987) has demonstrated that the critique of the decline of intellectuality in this "age of academe" is not the monopoly of conservatives like Bloom (1987). Arguments for basic and cultural literacy are radicalizing in the sense that they position themselves in a discussion of the role of textuality in postmodern capitalism.

In traditional Marxist terms, the critique of ideology is politically important inasmuch as Marx understood that human relations are thoroughly mystified under the regime of wage labor. Commodity fetishism was discussed in *Capital* as the tendency for alienated human relationships to appear naturelike in their inevitability. In the hyperreality of fast postmodern capitalism, the degree of commodities' fetishism has expanded exponentially, as Lukacs (1971) and the Frankfurt School initially argued through their analyses of reification and domination. Today, the eclipse of reason (Horkheimer 1974) proceeds via the dispersal of sense into sentience, texts dispersing into social nature as simulations. The critique of ideology now needs to be deconstructive, burrowing from within images, figures, and discourses to show the hidden authorship and arguments underlying naturelike reflections of a fixed cosmos. This ideology critique subjects the commodifications of culture to rigorous readings that narrativize the value claims they conceal in the encodings of cultural expression today.

Old-fashioned Marxists double over with hilarity at the notion that ideology critics today need to deconstruct videos, shopping malls, sociology textbooks. Surely, this is dilettantish epiphenomenal work, inferior to union organizing. But orthodox male Marxists are equally skeptical about the women's movement and environmentalism as valid political projects, thus only revealing their obsolescence as well as gender defensiveness. Whether or not we deem our age to be distinctively postmodern, it is clear that pre–World War II Marxism is hopelessly out of date. I share with traditional Marxists significant skepticism about postmodernity theory especially where it is suggested that postmodernity is somehow postcapitalist. This is still capitalism, now as before, albeit on an unprecedented global and psychic scale. But our capitalism *is* postmodern in the sense that it utilizes new modes of interconnection and infiltration simply unknown in earlier stages of development. The internationalized state intervenes in the economy as never before. Similarly, the culture industry is crucial in establishing taste, coercing conformity, and diverting attention. Although Horkheimer (1972) recognized these interconnections in his agenda-setting 1937 "Traditional and Critical Theory," many Marxists have been slow to revise original Marxism. Instead, Marxology has been stalled (e.g., Althusser 1970) in scholastic disputation about Marxian economic determinism, an issue that had been settled by the Frankfurt School in the 1930s.

Since the revisionist projects of Lukacs, Korsch, and the Frankfurt theorists, little has happened in traditional Marxism to help us better comprehend contemporary capitalism. Indeed, traditional Marxists have dug themselves into insular defensive positions from which to fend off non-Marxist and post-Marxist attackers, notably including feminists. Admittedly, concerted attacks on Marxism have become stronger, not weaker. We in the United States are in the midst of a new McCarthyism targeted by neoconservatives on people of color, women, entitlement programs, leftist academics, gays, and many others who threaten the dominant American ideology. In this context, it is perhaps understandable that Marxists reaffirm the faith, protecting it against feminist and postmodernist detractors. But I would argue that this posture has tended further to fracture the left, making it doubly difficult to resist the hegemony of neoconservatism.

I retain the notion that the global social totality is above all capitalist, thus grounding my version of critical theory squarely in Marxism, albeit vastly different in inflection from Marx's Marxism. Marxism cannot be bypassed because capitalism cannot be bypassed. No amount of theoretical casuistry will efface the fact that capitalism remains an extraordinarily powerful structuring force in all of our lives. Feminists respond by suggesting that patriarchy is an equally powerful structuring force, and of course I agree. But patriarchy, like capitalism, is a moment of a larger hierarchizing system that manifests itself in the realms of both market and nonmarket activities, the respective domains of traditional Marxism and feminism. I am not suggesting that we bypass feminism, either; indeed, Marxism needs feminism as much as the other way around. An overarching critical theory can embrace both Marxism and feminism if we translate Marxism into feminism and feminism into Marxism via a unifying theoretical logic, a mutual translation that is very far from being accomplished given the intense territoriality on both sides.

Fast capitalism is a better term for the postmodern/capitalist/male-supremacist conjuncture than is Baudrillard's hyperreality, which threatens to unravel into idealism. My notion of the domination of reproduction (Chapter 4) does more work than Baudrillard's "simulations" inasmuch as it connects the realms of productive (market) and reproductive (domestic) activity, thus embracing the traditionally bifurcated concerns of Marxists and feminists while also theorizing postmodernity in useful ways. Postmodernists like Baudrillard and Foucault are absolutely correct that traditional Marxism lacks a viable theory of ideology that can be applied to the deconstructive reading of dispersed ideologies in postmodern capitalism. But both Baudrillard and Foucault tend to conflate the ideal and material in such a way that we can no longer reliably distinguish between the two, hence losing epistemological criteria with which to sift true from false—ever the aim of the Marxist critique of ideology.

The Baudrillard of simulation theory might respond that we no longer enjoy the luxury of having clear criteria of validity in hyperreality, or what I call fast capitalism. Yet hyperreality and reality are still separable inasmuch as capitalism, however "late" or "postmodern" it may be, now as before requires systematic deceptions—Gramsci's hegemony—in order to function. If Baudrillard's point in *Simulations* (1983) is simply that it is increasingly difficult to separate true from false, I would agree. But his concept of hyperreality loses the historical specificity of the Marxist critique of ideology by essentially abandoning the totalizing aim of critical social theory (see Kellner 1989a). "Reality" is still real—it is grounded in historical structures of domination that can be unpacked, to use a popular deconstructive phrase, around the axial principles of their structure and function. Thus, we can comprehend the deliberate way in which false consciousness or hegemony both reproduces and is reproduced by the systemic requirements of sustained deception.

Simulation theory denies people the ability to separate true from false or real from hyperreal. Postmodernists position themselves against Marxist Archimedeanism because they want to avoid the Bolshevist outcomes of theoretical, hence political, vanguardism (a theme I take up below). I believe that the Frankfurt theorists have shown convincingly that one can develop comprehensive social theory, along with a standard of ideology critique, without losing a sense of ironic reflexivity about the problematic grounds of one's own truth claims. This is precisely the point of productive contact that I see between critical theory and postmodernism: The latter provides the former with a sense of the deconstructibility of all discourse, while the former grounds postmodern deconstruction squarely in comprehensive social theory that maps the world in a nuanced and differential way. One can make epistemic and evaluative judgments without pretending a positivist worldlessness and stancelessness.

The Frankfurt theorists have done important work by broadening traditional Marxism into a generic critical theory of domination. I extend *Dialectic of Enlightenment* and *One-Dimensional Man* in a feminist and postmodern direction via my theory of fast capitalism (Agger 1989a), which emerges in this book as a critique of all hierarchies of value over valuelessness. Whereas the Frankfurt theorists broadened Marx's concepts of exploitation and the alienation of labor into the category of domination, hence explaining aspects of structured social inhumanity unanticipated by Marx, I enrich their notion of domination with insights into its discursive and male-supremacist components. In formulating domination's generic tendency to hierarchize superior and inferior persons, groups and practices as productivism, I open the way for a critique of ideology that valorizes activities heretofore regarded as useless and articulates their interstitial potential for social transformation. The rearticulation of domination as hierarchy helps capture the ongoing struggles by people *to lay claim to value*, an enduring feature of class society in its many varieties.

This rearticulation of critical theory through feminism and postmodernism helps enrich the critique of domination, which tends to become static and monochromatic in Adorno's phrasing. A more dynamic perspective on fast capitalism stresses its differential, non-identical nature (leading, for example, to Habermas's new social movements theory) while preserving Marx's brilliant attempt to grasp society as an extraordinarily interrelated system that thwarts self-determination at every turn. This synthesis, which I call feminist postmodern critical theory, avoids idealism and determinism at once, showing the powerful inertial tendencies of capitalism while also demonstrating the many ways in which people attempt to remake their lives and the world in the open space between system and lifeworld.

IS A TOTALITY THEORY POSSIBLE?

It is ambitious to propose a totality theory that preserves Marx's emphasis on structure and at the same time holds open the possibility of ground-up social change. My aim in this book is nothing less! The postmodern attack on Marxism has been so powerful that many wonder whether critical theorists can ever again theorize totality and thus act politically in credible ways. I am not among those skeptics, although I recognize the need to address this skepticism, especially since I want to recuperate postmodernism for leftist political purposes. This need not be a contradiction in terms if we can somehow reconcile postmodernism's critique of totality theory with critical theory's totalizing agenda. I submit that this is possible if we regard totality not as an aprioristic abstraction but as an empirical reading (e.g., Jameson's cognitive map or Fraser's big empirical story). Indeed, this is the notion of totality that has animated the Hegelian-Marxist tradition (see Jay 1984b), especially the work of the Frankfurt School.

Let me anticipate a criticism of my approach here: Agger simply substitutes a new reductionist theoretical logic—hierarchies of value over valuelessness, also called productivism and heterotextuality—for prior theoretical logics like alienation of labor, reification and domination. Thus, his theory is as insensitive to "difference" as all other modernist male totalizations. My aim in this book is to offer a comprehensive theoretical logic that not only protects difference but relies on it for its political and intellectual energy. There is nothing about the world that compels us to explain and criticize different groups' oppressions in necessarily different terms. It is precisely my contention that postmodern male-supremacist capitalism subordinates difference to the rule and regime of productivist heterotextual hierarchy—terms that I explicate in the course of this work. At the risk of offending certain postmodernists and feminists, I defend a unifying theoretical logic on empirical grounds—as what "really" happens to marginal people and groups today. I do not apologize for my theoretical unification but celebrate its explanatory sweep (and hence its potential for political unification and mobilization at a time when many abandon politics as futile).

Lyotard's (1984) critique of Marxist Archimedeanism is leveled at Marxist economic reductionism. In itself, this is nothing new, resembling earlier critiques of Marxian economism. Like many of these critiques, Lyotard's postmodernism suggests a liberal pluralism that decenters Marxist class analysis and blunts its radical transvaluation of capitalist economic and social relationships. Lyotard, like other postmodernists (including Foucault), conflates the critique of Marxian economism, which the Frankfurt theorists share, with a rejection of totality theory. This is unfortunate because it blocks the development of a comprehensive critical theory that joins the concerns of Marxism, feminism, and postmodernism—my project here. Lyotard is certainly right to indict positivist and economistic Archimedeanism, which pretends that the Marxist epistemological subject can somehow stand outside of history in plotting its preordained developmental course. But he is wrong to suppose that all Marxisms, all transformational critical theories, require the idealist postulate of a transcendental theoretical subject. The Frankfurt School's critical theory demonstrates convincingly that one can fashion a totality theory sensitive to the ironies of the theorist's own participation in, and hence transformation of, the world. This was very much the theme of Horkheimer and Adorno's (1972) *Dialectic of Enlightenment*, in which they argued that positivism wrongly exempts itself from its own critique of mythology, hence becoming more mythological for all that. *Dialectic of Enlightenment* is postmodern *avant la lettre*, as Ryan (1982) and I (1989a, 1990, 1991) have argued. Adorno's (1973a) *Negative Dialectics* is a sustained deconstruction of Kantian and Hegelian idealism, paralleling the deconstructive effort of Derrida, as I explore later.

These deconstructive decenterings of idealist and positivist knowledge are important aspects of the critique of ideology in fast capitalism. They are compatible with a comprehensive critical theory if they are understood to be critiques of ideology. Unfortunately, Lyotard, Foucault, and Derrida's deconstructive efforts go untheorized; they do not contribute their decenterings of Western logocentrism to an interrogation and undoing of postmodern capitalism. The theorization of capitalism, whether early, late, or postmodern, goes the way of all totalizing theory, which is relegated to the dustbin of modernist narratives. Baudrillard comes closer to a theory of fast capitalism, especially in his (1981) earlier book *For a Critique of the Political Economy of the Sign*. By the time of *Simulations* (1983), however, he had largely replaced his political economy with a notion of hyperreality that renounces the project of historical materialism, however flexibly that project is conceived.

Deconstructive insights into the undecidability, or lack of closure, of theoretical discourse help sensitize language to its own perspective and pitfalls. But these insights need to be theorized if we are to deploy deconstructive strategies in the immanent critique of the disguised codes of fast capitalism, including science and theory themselves. It is one thing for deconstructors to lament the impossibility of epistemological clairvoyance. It is another thing to use deconstruction in order to clarify and enlighten—the project of left and feminist deconstructors. The postmodern critique of theoretical grand narratives rarely leads to new theory; it only disqualifies existing theoretical statements. This is very much the problem with the antiscience posture of positivism's critics. These critics inflate their critique of positivism's dogmatic insistence on its own superiority to dogma into a critique of all knowledge. Although language can be deconstructed to reveal its omissions and aporias, some language is less arrogantly representational than others. In other words, truth is always possible, albeit not an incontrovertible version impervious to deconstructive implosion.

For Marxists this "truth" is not the positivist "truth," which freezes the social universe into inert nature. Indeed, postpositivist philosophers of science recognize that nature itself is not inert, deconstructing the Vienna Circle's attempt to reduce science to mathematics. I (1989c) have argued that the positivist model of presuppositionless representation produces ideological outcomes when imported into the social sciences, notably in the way that it emerges discursively in concepts and hence practices of social lawfulness. I argue that these alleged "laws" describing the invariance of capitalism and patriarchy are intended to produce conformity with them, hence making them come true. Marxism is the most important critique of positivism, although Marx problematically gave the impression, especially in later work, that his critique of political economy was virtually a law unto itself, thus giving rise to a pernicious theoretical and political tendency within Marxism to "outpositivist" the positivists. It was not until the advent of Western Marxism (e.g., Lukacs 1971; Horkheimer and Adorno 1972) that Marxists exorcised the demon of positivist presuppositionless representation from Marx's own ambiguous legacy, thus producing the basis of an ideology critique of what Marcuse (1964) called one-dimensionality—a stage of capitalism in which positivist fact fetishism becomes the dominant ideology, disqualifying all attempts at critique, especially from within everyday life itself.

Ironically, a Marxist positivism reinforces positivism at large, hence distancing Marxist theory from Marxist practice. Unfortunately, in their desire to undercut Marxist scientism (which helped legitimate Stalinist terror via the official state ideology of Marxism-Leninism in the USSR), postmodernists dismiss the original aims of the critique of ideology. The historical project of reason is rejected, not only its positivist version—

which, as Horkheimer and Adorno (1972) knew, was no version at all. For their part, feminists reject the critical theory of the Frankfurt School because the Frankfurt theorists defended patriarchal familial authority as the source of ego autonomy. Marxism in general missed male supremacy as a legitimate social problem, or worse endorsed it, causing many feminists to reject Marxist social theory in total. Certain left feminists, discussed in Chapter 3, have laboriously attempted to correct Marxist male supremacy with the feminist project of the politics of the personal, an effort joined by my project here.

It is remarkable and lamentable that many proponents of the postmodern theory of culture and the feminist theory of gender, which parallel the Frankfurt School's critical theory in many respects, have turned against the project of total social theory. In the case of postmodernism, the aversion to totality is matched by an aversion to Frankfurt mandarinism, which is certainly notorious (see Agger 1992a). Postmodern cultural studies theorizes the popular in order to identify resistance points and projects ignored by the Frankfurt School's high-culture theory. People such as Baudrillard (1983) clearly build on the Frankfurt School's culture-industry thesis, while departing from the Marxist political program of the Frankfurt School. Feminist stress on the relationship between the personal and political is highly reminiscent of the lifeworld politics of both Marcuse (1969, 1972) and Habermas (1984, 1987b). My own argument for a lifeworld-grounded critical theory is developed throughout this book. I contend that the Frankfurt School's totalizing perspective on postmodern capitalism requires buttressing by postmodern cultural theory as well as by the feminist critique of gendered everyday life in order to address the present adequately.

Without these buttresses, critical theory will remain mired in Horkheimer and Adorno's hopeless dialectic-of-enlightenment position, Marcuse's (1955) Freudianization of Marx, which ushers in the notion of a "rationality of gratification" and "new sensibility" (Marcuse 1969), or Habermas's (1981b) new social movements theory. None of these perspectives adequately grasps the oppositional opportunities available today because all lack a sufficiently totalizing perspective. They require theoretical resources "from without," notably from postmodern cultural theory and feminism. I argue emphatically that this integration can be conducted within the frame of reference of original critical theory. In my opinion, only critical theory attempts, even if it fails to achieve, a totalizing analysis of the social world; it eschews precisely the pluralist perspectivity that disables both postmodernism and feminism. The crucial question is whether postmodern cultural theory and feminism will make themselves available to be integrated—that is, whether critical theory does not engage in a self-defeating imperialism by integrating postmodernism and feminism in aggrandizing acts of negation/retrieval/transcendence. This issue is as much political as theoretical: Can critical theory learn from postmodernism and feminism without violating their political "space," hence rebuffing potential allies? I turn to this question in the concluding section of this chapter and return to it throughout this book.

I am very concerned that this book not be read as a male-critical theoretical attempt to subsume feminism and postmodernism. I want to be understood as a person who recognizes the need to *unify* critical theory, feminism, and postmodernism, advancing beyond counterproductive disputation and territoriality. Unfortunately, the likelihood that I may not be read this way only demonstrates the need for a unifying theoretical logic encompassing critical theory, postmodernism, and feminism. In spite of my claim that I respect difference, some theorists may view my argument here as another instance of intellectual imperialism. But this misreading is symptomatic of the times: We *assume* that class, race, and gender are conceptually and empirically separable "realities," to which different theories are appropriate. But difference is not an irreducible "fact." It must be theorized and not assumed. Class, race, and gender are the *same* things—that is, their inferiorization is produced by the same theoretical logic. I realize that I am walking on the wild side when I argue for a unifying theoretical logic! But walk we must, lest we reproduce the fragmentation of the left in these dangerous times.

Ultimately, the possibility of a totality theory turns on the question of whether one *can* tell large empirical stories that have a coherent dramatic tension, narrative, and resolution. I aver that a "science" of society is possible, even if not the positivist science of the Second and Third Internationals. The Marxian possibility of a new science must be articulated by a twenty-first-century critical theory so that (1) we understand the shifting strata of the world system (and the fissures that continually open up to emancipatory agents), and (2) we refuse to cede cognitive and technical functions to a Weberian elite of postmodern technocrats. In renouncing objective knowledge, Derrideans renounce power, hence only reproducing the prevailing power of the social. The risk of science's degeneration into scientism is less immediate than the danger of relinquishing empirical narratives about society that help frame a sober strategic reckoning with "what is to be done." Although, as I just said, I agree with the original Frankfurt theorists that positivism has become the dominant mode of ideology today, the critique of positivism must resist Luddism at every turn. Neither poststructuralism nor postmodernism has a positive epistemological program, a strategy of systematic cognition. They denounce rationality as a ruse of reason and instead revel in the pleasure of the text and celebrate the author's death.

I contend that the word *instead* is misplaced. Science can be playful, passionate, and perspectival—the more so, the more it is done well. Postpositivist philosophers of science have understood this much better than Marx, who unwittingly licensed the Engelsian "dialectic of nature" argument that proved so destructive in Stalinist hands. Early Marx could easily have accommodated a Marcusean-Barthesian notion of playful scientific discourse since he understood how objective and subjective nature blur dialectically to the point of virtual identity. Habermas's (1971) effort to separate the logics of self-reflection and scientific-technical control has set back the Frankfurt effort to develop the possibility of a nonpositivist cognition, a new science, a possibility that could be enhanced significantly in a poststructural climate. After all, Derrida's notion of textual undecidability empowers reading to become a veritable mode of writing, a theme that clearly converges with the Marcusean and early-Marxian notions of knowledge as self-creative praxis.

The antiscience tenor of poststructuralism goes hand in hand with its aversion to totality theory. As I noted earlier, there is some sentiment (e.g., Lyotard 1984) that science leads to political totalitarianism, reflecting the Enlightenment's conflation of knowledge with power: Archimedeanism equals Prometheanism. But I would decouple the dimensions of knowledge and power, giving rise to a more nuanced cognitive map that frames my argument here. There is a strong tendency for epistemological antitotality postures to become antipolitical (except in the case of certain species of radical-feminist theory, which retain a totalizing version of politics). Nevertheless, as radical feminism indicates, there is no necessary connection between these two perspectives. For their part, Marxist critical theory and liberalism share totalizing perspectives on knowledge but differ on political questions, with liberalism defined by its aversion to authoritarian democracy and authoritarian socialism. Epistemology and politics are nonidentical.

THE POLITICS OF TOTALITY

This is not to suggest that political totality is necessarily Stalinist or statist. As this discussion indicates, the politics of totality are dangerous in these times. Any claim of truth risks excluding other truths and hence invites tyranny. Archimedeanism appears to lead inevitably to a Promethean practice of power. This is the sense of Foucault's critique of Marxism, which is central to most postmodernisms. As usual, though, this confuses Marxism as an emancipatory critical theory with the Marxism-Leninism of the Siberian camps, a confusion that is both empirically and theoretically unfounded. As I indicated above, Habermas (1981a, 1987a) has recognized the discourse of postmodernity as a thinly veiled theoretical practice of neoconservatives who, on the one hand, supported Thatcher, Reagan, and Bush while, on the other, endorsing and consuming supposedly postmodern cultural commodities. I (1990) have observed that postmodernism extends Daniel Bell's (1973) end-of-ideology argument, functioning as what Jameson (1984, 1991) calls the cultural logic of late capitalism. This is not to deny that postmodernism has critical potential—a premise of this book. Yet the established postmodernism of the culture industry opposes the Marxist penchant for totality, pretending a prepolitical stancelessness characteristic of this postpolitical age.

Totality issues in tyranny only when (1) science exempts itself from its critique of non-reflexive intellectual systems and (2) power is marshalled to obliterate all otherness. As Adorno (1973a) recognized, the common theme here is *identity and nonidentity*. As he and Horkheimer (1972) argued in *Dialectic of Enlightenment*, science that excludes itself from its critique of myth leads to political hubris, the result of which is fascism. Thought that tries to identify itself with reality aims too high. Concepts are imperfect vehicles of comprehension, as are the language games that they constitute. As Ryan (1982) has noted, here Adorno's and Derrida's critiques of Western philosophy converge, although Derrida does not spell out the implications of deconstruction for political theory. Adorno's depressive *Negative Dialectics* tries unsuccessfully to elaborate a total political theory based on the politics of nonidentity or difference. He retreated from social theory to philosophy and thus failed to theorize new social movements and their transformational potential.

We can move beyond Adorno, while retaining his very important analyses of the logic of domination, including his critique of identity theory. Perhaps more than anyone else, Adorno knew what was wrong with modernity. His deft *Minima Moralia* is an elegant cognitive map of late capitalism. But his *Negative Dialectics*, while a powerful critique of idealism, is scanty social theory. Adorno simply had no conception of what Habermas was later to call new social movements. His reaction to the New Left typified his and Horkheimer's insensitivity to transformational social movements that did not spring full-blown from the brow of *Capital*. This is not to say that Adorno endorsed or articulated orthodox-Marxist scenarios of class struggle. Far from it. But Adorno seemed to require that every transformational actor and movement possess Adorno's own degree of theoretical erudition and cultural elevation.

By now, under the influence of postmodernism and feminist theory, the critique of totality that Adorno initiated has become second nature. It seems that no one on the left endorses modernity and its totalizing logic. This is understandable, given the historical horrors of the politics of totality. And yet Habermas is absolutely correct to insist on a new rationalism that comprehends the sweep of world history and tries to theorize it anew, rejecting both liberalism and orthodox Marxism. Habermas appropriately tries to shift the modernist paradigm of consciousness into the paradigm of communication, thus making way for the possibility of positive political theory. Adorno's disappointment about the failure of class struggle led him to write pessimistic tomes like *Negative Dialectics*, in which he deconstructed the logic of modernity, notably its idealist identity-theory, but did not turn deconstruction in the direction of positive architecture.

It is not easy to politicize deconstruction as a way of developing a rationalist perspective on modernity and postmodernity. The road to this repoliticization should not go through Derrida but through the Frankfurt School (although, as I argue in this book, we can learn the way from Derrida). Even in his disappointment about the project of modernity, including Marxist modernism, Adorno was far more a political theorist than Derrida or Foucault. His disaffection was borne of his modernism, which imagined utopia. Postmodernism prematurely gives up on the promise of the Enlightenment, as Habermas (1987a) has argued. With it, postmodernism abandons the modernist political goals of democracy, including self-determination and workers' control.

The postmodern philosophy of history errs where it suggests that history has already ended, having reached the terminus of modernity. At the same time, it liberates the imagination from the very modernism ontologizing capitalist modernity as historically sufficient. A liberating postmodernism, grounded in the totalizing intention of the Frankfurt School's critical theory, reinvents history as the possibility of a postcapitalist postmodernity that interrupts the continuum of domination. But for postmodernism to project this historical possibility requires it to totalize history, suggesting a possible world-historical vector along which social change can unfold. It is simply inadequate to reject politics because politics for the last two hundred years has been inextricably linked with capitalist and state-socialist modernization.

We are now in an age of decline, which requires us to reimagine history in nonmodernist terms. Neither capitalism nor state socialism successfully provides everybody with a livelihood and social freedom. The aversion to the politics of totality too readily leads to an aversion to all politics, which today only reinforces the political. That is the problem with postmodernism. Critical theory for its part anticipates certain postmodern themes, but without renouncing the political, as Derrida and Foucault do. To be sure, Adorno's (1973a) *Negative Dialectics* is scarcely a manifesto. But I would argue that the time for manifestos has passed; indeed, manifestos reflect a modernist agenda of purposive progressivism that has scorched the earth since World War I. We must be able to articulate a political agenda in ways that avoid the posturing and pretense of modernism, notably the idea that we can remake the world through social engineering. But we must retain the modernist notion that the world can be made different, if only in ways that acknowledge the inchoate limits to transformation constraining all political interventions.

This balance between the modern and postmodern ought to be formulated from within the discourse and theoretical apparatus of modernism (as Huyssen 1986 argues). Otherwise, we eviscerate politics of all transformational possibilities. Too frequently the postmodern agenda is only cultural. Admittedly, politics have been displaced into the cultural arena, as Horkheimer and Adorno (1972) recognized in their culture-industry thesis (and as I demonstrate in my 1990 critique of literary political economy). In this book, as elsewhere (Agger, 1992a), I reformulate critical theory as a version of cultural studies. But culture does not exhaust politics, even though it is increasingly political today. The text is a world, although the world is not all text. In forgetting this, postmodernists inflate cultural style into adequate resistance, when, in fact, style is typically dictated by what Jameson (1984, 1991) calls the cultural logic of late capitalism.

This is a difficult road to walk. On the one hand, political imperatives are now encoded in a diversity of gestures, forms, and language games—discourses—ordinarily seen as beyond the realm of traditional politics. On the other hand, in being so dispersed, they can easily trick us into ignoring political economy, concentrating instead on the political economy of the sign (Baudrillard 1981). Although sign value is important in its own right, we must not lose sight of surplus value, which endures as the fundamental means of exploitation, profit, and domination. Modernism helps bring us back to politics even while seeking power in surprising venues. Modernism refuses to accept the prevailing parliamentarian definition of politics, and yet it keeps the political clearly in view as *a problem to be theorized*—precisely the topic of this book.

For a postmodernist modernism to theorize power requires us to suspend our canonical relationship to Marx. That is, we must treat Marx neither as lodestone nor as animus. To be sure, he composed an important version of critical theory that locates the possibilities of historical imagination in the dialectical contradictions of the present. But, as Horkheimer and Adorno (1972; see Agger 1983) indicate in *Dialectic of Enlightenment*, Marxism is best treated as a version of critical theory and not the other way around. Both the canonization and demonization of Marx disserve the emancipatory project today. Although *Capital* is an important civilizational text, its critique of the logic of capital does not preclude other versions of critique, notably feminist. Saying this risks post-Marxism, one of the most sophisticated versions of neoconservatism (see Laclau and Mouffe 1985; Block 1990; Dandaneau 1992). I do not so much want to get beyond Marx as to insert Marx's oeuvre into the deconstructive ebb and flow of hermeneutic work, a project that cannot rest.

Certain Marxists in their positivism maintain that one can read texts, including Marx's, definitively. This makes possible the establishment of a "Marx" who exhausts the need for revisions, clarifications, extrapolations. Too much of Marxism, whether it calls itself orthodox or something else, embodies this version of literary epistemology. For its part, too much of post-Marxism disqualifies Marx's corpus as antediluvian. By privileging Marx in one direction or another, we lose sight of the possibility that Marx wrote an important, even exemplary, version of critical theory that can guide us, but not overdetermine us, in our theoretical and political work today. Orthodox Marxists and orthodox post-Marxists, especially postmodernists, make it nearly impossible to read Marx deconstructively, democratically. They forget that Marx's own historicism would have disqualified such ontological postures toward his texts.

If Marx is simply a corrigible literary voice, the politics of totality become much simpler. To learn from Marx one need not hold onto his particular version of world-historical change, recognizing that both the *Manifesto* and *Capital* do not adequately capture the complexities of the world today. By the same token, these books have much of value to say about the illogic of capital, which continues to haunt late capitalism in the midst of our second great depression. I choose to subsume Marx's analysis of the logic of capital under a more general critique of the logic of domination, following and extending the lead of the Frankfurt School. This allows me to hold on to totality, hence the possibility of thoroughgoing social change, while producing a new cognitive map appropriate to the 1990s and beyond.

This attitude toward Marx has defined the project of critical theory since the 1920s (see, e.g., Marcuse 1968). The original members of the Frankfurt Institute for Social Research embraced Marx's utopian prophecy while revising his empirical theory of political, economic, and cultural crisis. This revisionism was dismissed as Hegelian idealism by some (e.g., see Colletti 1973). Others (e.g., see Slater 1977) rejected it as apolitical. The Frankfurt reading of Marx makes itself available to be revised, given their apostate view of Marx's oeuvre as necessarily corrigible. The Frankfurt theorists' flexibility in dealing with Marx enabled them to rethink the modalities of capitalism in empirically and politically relevant ways, producing a theoretical logic that has proven remarkably prescient.

Inasmuch as the Frankfurt theorists opposed Stalinism, they were careful to stress the importance of the "non-identical," as Adorno (1973a) called it. They demonstrate that one can produce a total social theory while avoiding fascist and state-socialist outcomes. To be sure, there has been precious little to vindicate their political optimism! However, I believe that this unprecedented era of perestroika and postmodernity, indicating the dual failures of state-socialism and capitalism, makes possible, indeed requires, all sorts of political, economic, and cultural innovations. A feminist postmodern critical theory is ideally suited to addressing these new possibilities, given its stress on liberating the imagination, body, sexuality, domestic labor, and popular culture. In particular, the original Frankfurt theorists, through their linkage of Freud and Marxism, provide an excellent example of what I have called an interstitial critical theory capable of mediating between the levels of what Habermas has termed system and lifeworld, thus accelerating nontraditional resistances and transformational activities.

Ultimately, answering the question of the politics of totality is a matter of resolving *whose* notion of totality is at stake. It is a prior matter to *identify* the conceptions of totality—of what is and what ought to be—embedded in every social and cultural theory. Some theories are more explicit than others about these matters. I would argue emphatically that every version of the social world, regardless of its avowed investment in totality or antitotality, harbors a conception of the whole social universe. Positivism secretly recommends a world precisely where it suppresses its authorship and perspectivity. Liberalism decides for and against competing versions of the world even where it celebrates the plurality of versions and appears not to adjudicate their differences. Postmodernism does not avoid a philosophy of history even where it announces that modernism has failed because the belief in progress has run amok.

Thus, the posture of antitotality is just that—a practiced deception. Value-freedom in science was revealed to be a ruse by postpositivist philosophers of science dating from Heisenberg and Einstein. For his part, Derrida unpacks the perspectivity of all language games, making it rather ironic that postmodernists who write in his name disavow totality. I maintain that conceptions of totality are unavoidably present in every theoretical, scientific, and cultural version of the world, even if, as Derrida indicates, these totalizing conceptions are susceptible to their own self-deconstruction given the aporetic nature of language. That is, Derrida shows that theories purporting to explain "everything" always fail, just as he demonstrates convincingly that theories which purport to explain and advocate less than everything necessarily trade on conceptions of "everything." Ontology—theory of being—inhabits science, theory, language, and culture, making its presence felt most powerfully where these gestures appear free of ontological constructions.

A deconstructive critique of ideology interrogates all theoretical and cultural practices for their noisy or silent partisanship. Simply because postmodernism eschews a millennial view of history does not mean that it avoids a conception of the future for which it quietly agitates. As Horkheimer and Adorno (1972) argued in *Dialectic of Enlightenment*, theories that appear to avoid advocacy advocate all the more convincingly. Their version of Marx's ideology critique excavated ontology out of societal representations and cultural expressions in order to bring their hidden perspectives into the clear light of day. Critical theory as I conceive it deconstructs the discourses of the social for the ideological entreaties dispersed into the sense and sentience of everyday life. These entreaties—consume, conform, capitulate—are all the more enticing for their dispersed nature: They are difficult to detect and thus resist, *to read as texts*. Critical theory functions in everyday life as the activity of critique, sensitizing us to the ways in which what Foucault calls discourse/practices cast a certain politically immobilizing spell over us and pointing beyond the present toward a future in which discourse deconstructs itself. This self-deconstructing discourse not only acknowledges its perspectival authoriality but celebrates it as an occasion of genuine civic discourse, ever the Greek aim of the polity but now extended to include women, people of color, members of non-Occidental cultures.

The politics of totality must be transacted on the ground of everyday life. People need to theorize their own relationship to the global body politic, one of the essential aims of feminism and of Marcuse's (1969) critical theory.

As such, the politics of totality are very much a personal politics, too. The personal and public realms are connected interstitially via the practices addressed by feminism, postmodernism, and critical theory, involving sexuality and household labor, conceptions of the future, and popular culture, respectively. As I said earlier, politics is found everywhere but in the traditional political arena, including the orthodox-Marxist venue of political economies of class. This is *not* to suggest that Marxism has been surpassed but only to suggest that the logic of capital is a local instance of a logic of domination that hierarchizes people according to their putative value, notably including their contribution of what Marx called labor power and also including their contributions of domestic labor. But it should be patently obvious to the left that traditional Marxism does not break cleanly enough with earlier capitalist-modernist theories of the political and social to be adequate in the stage of postmodernity. Left theory needs to retheorize the political, notably through a feminist postmodern critical theory that relates the personal and public in imaginative ways.

THEORIZING POSTMODERNITY

In order to map postmodernity chronologically, one must identify the moment at which modernist millenarianism gave way to a more skeptical, less eschatological philosophy of history. Perhaps postmodernity began with the Tet offensive in 1968, when the imperial American army, and thus capitalist modernism as a whole, was put on the defensive by a pajama-clad army in Vietnam. Perhaps postmodernity began when gas rationing affected American drivers in the early 1970s. Or perhaps it dawned when Nixon resigned the presidency. This exercise in periodization is an important component of a critical sociology of popular culture. It helps us come to grips with the age of decline (see Agger 1991) as it affects people's orientation to politics and the public sphere. Postmodernism is the cultural logic of late capitalism, as Jameson argues. It both reflects and articulates the eclipse of the belief in progress, just as perestroika reflects and articulates the demise of state socialism as a utopian political system.

Together, postmodernism and perestroika are the most important political and philosophical developments of our time. They shatter the modernist faith in progress, which has been inextricably linked to the development of capitalism. I (1990) have argued that one can preserve the possibility of social progress in modernist fashion while decoupling capitalism from modernism and modernity. This has been Habermas's (1984, 1987b) project, which he has tried to accomplish within the framework of what he calls the paradigm of communication. Although I find Habermas's provocative communication-theoretic reformulation of critical theory to be limited, his effort to decouple capitalism and modernism and thus to fulfill the original aims of the Enlightenment—a regime of reason—needs to be extended by a third-generation critical theory as I understand it.

Since Max Horkheimer (1973) wrote "The Authoritarian State," Franz Neumann (1942) wrote *Behemoth*, and Marcuse (1958) wrote *Soviet Marxism*, Western Marxists have understood Soviet-style state socialism to be a travesty of early Marx's ideals of workers' control and the disalienation of labor. It is no surprise to Frankfurt-oriented thinkers that the Soviet Union came tumbling down. Neither is it a surprise that the logic of global capital has become so irrational (e.g., uneven economic development, the underclass, homelessness, the permanent war economy) that people in the West have lost the faith in progress that has always accompanied Western rationalism. I do not agree with theorists (e.g., Poster 1989, 1990) who argue that postmodernity is somehow "beyond" or after capitalism. With Jameson (1991) and Kellner (1989a), I believe that capitalism has evolved into a disspirited, disappointed, and disruptive postmodern mode in which many of the traditional assumptions about the inexorability of progress have been suspended or abandoned altogether. Following Scheler, Denzin (1991) argues that postmodernity produces resentment as a modal emotional orientation on the part of people who are disaffected. Having been led to believe that the future will provide a cornucopia of consumer goods and spiritual fulfillment, people respond to deflated expectations not by rethinking the social system but with embitterment and hostility—what Scheler (1961) perceptively called *ressentiment*.

Depending on one's theoretical perspective, perestroika and postmodernism can lead to further resentment or they can provide opportunities for dehierarchizing all sorts of societal institutions, making way for democratic social movements that transcend both traditional state socialism and capitalism. Postmodernism functions ideologically where it not only acknowledges the failure of politics but celebrates it. A different, more critical postmodernism, inflected by critical theory and feminism, treats the age of decline as an occasion for the restructuring of all bureaucratic societies, both capitalist and state-socialist. This critical postmodernism functions as a philosophy of history that holds open the possibility of fundamental social change while rejecting the millenarian modernism of the Enlightenment. In this sense, postmodernism can help us develop a new mode of imagination about the opportunities and constraints of postmodernity. Martin Jay (1973), in writing about the Frankfurt School, characterized this orientation to the philosophy of history as "dialectical imagination," to which both critical theory and a left version of postmodernism are signal contributions. In the course of this book, I will further develop the meaning of a postmodern philosophy of history as an alternative to both capitalist modernism, which is increasingly hard-pressed to diagnose our age of decline, and a postmodernism that accepts the supposed end of politics with ironic, world-weary resignation, even celebration.

This postmodern version of critical theory views the crisis of modernity as an opportunity for rethinking modernist assumptions about the nature of progress, notably the conflation of modernity with capitalism and its technological conquest of nature. If modernity is limited to capitalism, then postmodernism becomes a radical posture. If postmodernity is viewed as an eternal present characterized by the end of ideology, then postmodernism is only what Jameson calls the cultural logic of late capitalism. Postmodernism can interrogate modernism and modernity for their fatal aporias, or it can accept them as inevitable stages in the unfolding of inescapable Western reason.

Again, for reasons explicated earlier, I am wary about identifying my version of postmodern critical theory *as* postmodernism. To do so invites misunderstandings about the relationship between postmodernism and critical theory. By now, the identity *postmodernist* has acquired an established cultural and political currency. It means that one is:

1. post-Marxist or non-Marxist;
2. generally sympathetic to feminism but not necessarily a feminist;
3. opposed to quantitative methodologies in the social sciences;
4. inclined to favor New French Theory over German critical theory.
5. suspicious of cultural mandarinism and hence the Frankfurt School's theory of the culture industry.

Postmodernism is neither necessarily opposed to Marxism nor "beyond" it. It needs to be feminist. It is intellectually narrow where it eschews the text of science as if science cannot be reformulated deconstructively, according to certain postmodern principles of discourse. One can use the same critical approaches to address popular and mandarin cultures. Postmodernism in the French tradition of Foucault, Barthes, Derrida, Baudrillard, Lyotard, Kristeva, Irigaray, and Cixous is not necessarily opposed to German critical theory, especially where Adorno, Horkheimer, and Marcuse anticipated many postmodern insights (as Ryan 1982 and Jay 1984a have cogently argued).

Thus, what it means to be postmodern is often decided by a postmodern culture industry that banalizes postmodernism as a superficial irony and opposition to politics. One can establish a different postmodern identity, as I argue we must. That requires a great deal of interpretive and interpolative work expended in attempting to show that postmodernism and critical theory could share a common project once postmodernism is appropriately politicized. The problem with postmodernism is that it too often shuns the political simply because official politics offers no significant alternatives to the status quo. But the interpretive methodologies associated with New French Theory afford us tools with which to theorize politics as it has been displaced into apparently nonpolitical venues, notably into popular culture. It is these tools which enable the development of a nonmandarin approach to cultural studies conceived within the German/Marxist framework of the critique of ideology, retained by the Frankfurt School.

This is not to privilege the Frankfurt School's version of critique as if it does not require revisions in its own right. As I said at the outset, critical theory needs to address postmodernity using theoretical and political insights from postmodernism and feminism. I do not see another way to overcome the Frankfurt mandarinism while retaining the School's framework for analyzing the culture industry. If critical theory functions as a critical cultural studies that can detect politics as it has been increasingly dispersed into everyday life, both as entertainment and in gendered relationships (see Agger 1992a), then one could say that it is postmodern and feminist. I return to the nominalist issue raised above. We must recognize that hierarchies may be inferred in the privileging of certain theories as nouns, while others remain only adjectival. This is unfortunate, if perhaps unavoidable.

For me, critical theory owes more to Marx than to Foucault or even Beauvoir. For this reason, Marx's theoretical logic does more work in my version of critical theory than do postmodernism and feminism, even though postmodernism and feminism are vitally necessary in this stage of postmodernity. After all, Foucault eschewed totality, while Beauvoir never attempted it. In saying this I know that I risk further misunderstanding: I am *not* saying that Marxism takes political precedence over feminism or postmodernism but only that Marxism attempts a more totalizing account of power. Of course, neglecting women, it does not achieve this account. A total version of politics and power is completed, not challenged, by feminism and postmodernism. We need the political more than ever in light of the depoliticization of public life, especially in its affirmatively postmodern version. If we cannot locate politics in the interstitial activities bridging subjectivity and institutions, we will fail to interrogate the present for its dialectical openings to possible social change, ever the *raison d'être* of critical theory. Whether one judges my feminist postmodern critical theory Marxist is beside the point. I argue that Marxism, feminism, and postmodernism are, at a fundamental level, *the same* theoretical logic—an identity probably threatening to the male left, feminists, and postmodernists alike!

Chapter Two

Postmodernism and the End of Politics 1: New French Theory

THE AVERSION TO GRAND NARRATIVES

New French Theory (e.g., Foucault 1977; Lyotard 1984) is characterized by an aversion to "grand narratives," Lyotard's term for eschatological stories promising the total transformation of society (see Dews 1984, 1987). Marxism is foremost among these totalizing perspectives. Indeed, as I discussed in Chapter 1, postmodernism is characterized by a break with Marxism, which, people like Foucault and Lyotard aver, is wrong to presage the redemption of humanity through revolutionary social transformations.

New French Theorists are averse to grand narratives because they believe that these totalizing narratives necessarily encode programs of political oppression, no matter how expediently these programs are couched. For example, Lenin's argument for proletarian dictatorship "from without" in the context of revolutionary Russia was explicated in terms of his vanguardist revisions of traditional Marxist theory. However justified Lenin may have been at the time, his appeal to a Marxist narrative about the direction of history served not only to sanction short-term dictatorship by a vanguard party, the Communist Party of the Soviet Union, but added legitimacy to a mode of political and social theorizing that sacrificed human liberty and lives to prophesied historical unfolding. Postmodernism does not fashion itself as neoconservative, as Habermas (1981a) charges it is, but as neoliberal and pluralist in its respect for the varieties of groups and interests that, postmodernists argue, cannot be theorized globally in terms of a teleological narrative.

The most politically potent version of a Marxist narrative was Marxism-Leninism, or Bolshevism, later to become Stalinism. The more than seventy-year history of the Soviet Union is a testament to the power of mobilizing grand narratives like Lenin's revision of original Marxism. In its name the Communist Party of the Soviet Union authorized severe political repression and forced economic development. Soviet Marxism (see Marcuse 1958) was a total theory of historical unfolding, the "telling" of which took the form of *agitprop* and political education, to which virtually no one was impervious. Only with the wholesale collapse of economic central planning under the weight of its inherent irrationality as well as unaffordable military expenditures coupled with international adventurism did the Soviet Union come unhinged, liberating people from the grand narrative of Marxism-Leninism. Interestingly, the narrative of Leninism came to an end rather suddenly, given its immense historical momentum. As soon as Gorbachev initiated economic and political restructuring, Soviet elites and citizens were willing to invest in a whole new metanarrative of Western capitalism. It is apparent to Western Marxists that this narrative will prove as flawed as the Bolshevik one, although it may take Soviet theorists time to recognize the inherent flaws of the logic of capital spelled out in their own political education. The Soviet people will confront the costs of capitalism as they face massive inflation and unemployment when markets open.

As I explore later in the chapter, postmodernism's aversion to grand narratives is conditioned by the French reaction to Marxism. Debates between Althusser, on the one hand, and Foucault, Derrida, Lyotard, and Baudrillard, on the other, help refract these political differences. Unfortunately, France did not have the same sort of Western-Marxist tradition as Germany, which is why there was no alternative formulation of Marxism to Marxism-Leninism, given virtuoso exposition by Althusser (1970, 1971). In Germany, the work of the Frankfurt School offered a counterpoint to orthodox Marxism, preventing German critical theorists from rejecting Marxism altogether in the fashion of the New French Theorists. Indeed, as I argued in the preceding chapter, Adorno and his colleagues anticipated a number of postmodern themes (e.g., his critique of identity theory), which they smoothly integrated into their own sympathetic reformulation of Marxism. The postmodern turn in French thought took place largely because French Marxism was intellectually dogmatic and politically flawed. Although Merleau-Ponty and Sartre provided alternatives to the French Communist Party line, they did not develop a school or institute, as the German critical theorists did, instead indulging themselves in personal vendettas and career building. *Les Temps Moderne* reflected these conflicts, quickly losing Merleau-Ponty to what Sartreans deemed heterodoxy. Sartre contributed to the cult of his own personality, providing little in the way of constructive theoretical and political continuity. And Merleau-Ponty, dead before his time, failed to leave much imprint on the subsequent debate between French structuralists and poststructuralists.

It is tempting to dismiss the *Tel Quel* group, Derrida, Lacan, Foucault, Baudrillard, and Lyotard as theoretical arrivistes. By the high intellectual standards of the Frankfurt School they most certainly are. Virtually no French intellectual could match Adorno's, Horkheimer's, and Marcuse's erudite grasp of German idealism, Marxism, and cultural theory, enabling them to reformulate Marxist critical theory in the context of emerging monopoly capitalism. Whatever comparative judgments one may make about the French and German postwar intellectual traditions, it is clear that there has been relatively little dialogue between them, save for Habermas's (1987a) *Philosophical Discourse of Modernity*, in which he elaborates a critique of postmodernism.

Whereas the German critical theorists salvaged Marxism through psychoanalysis and cultural theorizing, the New French Theorists abandoned Marxism as a failed intellectual and political project. Although I side with the Frankfurt theorists, who attempted to expand Marxism into a general critique of domination, thus providing necessary theoretical and political flexibility, much can be learned from French postmodernism, as I indicated in the preceding chapter. In particular, postmodernists like Baudrillard offer a useful perspective on the politics of discourse and culture, helping explore new modalities of ideology in late capitalism. They (e.g., Foucault) also energize the postmodernist philosophy of history by emphasizing the possibilities of a new historical and political imagination that can genuinely transcend capitalist modernism while actualizing its commitment to reason. In these senses, French postmodernism clearly converges with certain Frankfurt themes, even extending them profitably.

Making use of postmodern insights into discourse, culture, and the philosophy of history in developing intermediate or interstitial approaches to system/lifeworld relationships will seem illegitimately territorial to those very New French Theorists who disdain Marxist theoretical imperialism. It will be maintained that a postmodern Marxism is too Marxist and not postmodern enough. Perhaps. But it seems patent that New French Theory offers German critical theory valuable perspectives on late, or fast, capitalism that challenge critical theory to extend its second-generation Habermasian formulation still further. In this and the next chapter, I summarize ways in which postmodernism and feminism usefully extend and deepen the agenda of German critical theory, acknowledging that in "using" postmodernism I may well violate certain of its most central tenets, such as its aversion to grand narratives like Marxism.

Postmodernists emphasize that Marxism, along with modernism, is moribund. They point to the erstwhile USSR for "proof" of this, although I would hasten to add that the eclipse of the Soviet Union attests to the failure of the Lenin-Stalin version of state socialism and not the vitiation of all Marxist possibilities. Indeed, the authoritarian state capitalism of the Soviet Union had nothing whatsoever to do with Marx's vision of communism in the 1844 *Economic and Philosophical Manuscripts*, in which he talked about the disalienation of labor in positive, even poetic terms. It is obvious that the Soviet version of Marxism entailed immense human suffering, deprivation, and the denial of liberties. But for the New French Theorists, like American and British neoconservatives, to lay the USSR at the door of Marx is mistaken. Marx no more authored the Soviet Union, even in his occasional notions of a transitional "dictatorship of the proletariat," than he did the People's Republic of China. Fanatical Western anticommunism has conditioned the New French Theorists' interpretation of the eclipse of Marxism, leading to the impasse between Lyotard's aversion to grand narratives like Marxism, on the one hand, and critical theory, on the other.

When Habermas (1981a) calls the postmodernists young conservatives he is trading on this notion that New French Theory has been conditioned by a neoconservative assault on the left, which conflates Marx and illiberal uses of his authority. Habermas has drawn fire from those who view Lyotard, Foucault, Derrida, and Baudrillard as liberals, populists, and/or pluralists (perhaps of the Laclau/Mouffe variety). Clearly, Lyotard is not neoconservative in the same sense as Robert Nozick or George Gilder. That is, judging by his (1984) *Postmodern Condition*, he does not favor the dismantling of welfare-state safety nets or tax cuts for the wealthy in the fashion of Reagan, Bush, and Thatcher. Lyotard is young-conservative, in Habermas's parlance, because he joins in the nearly universal conflation of Marx, Marxism, and the Soviet Union, concluding that what went wrong with the Soviet experiment can be traced to Marx's attempt to write a comprehensive social theory with utopian prescriptions.

This postmodern turn has become so pervasive that neo-Frankfurters like me, Luke (e.g., 1989), and Kellner (e.g., 1989a) have to stage a frontal assault on traditional conservatives and neoconservatives, on the one hand, and a rearguard defensive maneuver against neoliberal postmodernists who reject Marxist narratives, on the other. These battles have been rendered nearly, if not totally, hopeless in light of the spectacular "end of communism," simulated triumphally in media images of the crumbling Berlin Wall en route to the merger of the two Germanys and the hectic dismantling of the USSR. Virtually *everyone*, both neoconservative and neoliberal, believes that Marxism has been surpassed by a combination of its internal failures and the superiority of Western capitalism. Neoliberals, like postmodernists, trace the internal failure of Marxism to Marx's grandiose attempt to tell a totalizing story about world history, whereas neoconservatives take the more traditional view that Marxism failed because it adopted a variety of mistaken economic and social premises about the feasibility of central planning and the elimination of human avarice.

This is precisely the juncture at which postmodernism splits into affirmative and potentially radical formulations, as I (Agger 1990) have suggested elsewhere. An affirmative postmodernism argues that modernity has been completed in late capitalism. A critical or radical postmodernism maintains that modernity awaits completion in a postmodern socialist and feminist future. At issue here, as in the first chapter, is the nature of postmodernity. Marxists of my ilk argue that postmodernity will transcend capitalist modernity, whereas postmodernists like Lyotard argue that, for better or worse, the unfolding of the project of modernity has been completed. This is not to say that what I call an affirmative postmodernism is cheerful about the present social order. Indeed, postmodern cynicism despairs about what it takes to be the ineradicability of social problems. Like Weber, a late modernist who bordered on postmodernism in many of his formulations about the bureaucratic iron cage, postmodernists like Lyotard and Foucault reject the project of modernity, both in capitalist and socialist formulations (although they wrongly conflate democratic socialism with the false socialism of the Soviet command economy and gulag). It is not so much that the New French Theorists endorse late capitalism enthusiastically as that they equally condemn Marxism, which they take to be equivalent to the colossal failure of the Soviet Union.

A critical postmodernism can become a mode of critical theory itself where the postmodern rejection of the capitalist project of modernity differentiates capitalist modernity from a possible socialist and feminist postmodernity. For this to happen, postmodernity would stand not for late capitalism, ontologically frozen, but for a future as yet to be created, requiring the fulfillment of the project of modernity, if that project is taken to mean the realization of reason in the world, as it did for the Greeks, Hegel, and Marx. Postmodernism adds historical imagination to a stagnant Marxism, as well as a crucial stress on discourse and culture that refreshes the Frankfurt School's prescient but overly mandarin culture-industry thesis. Postmodernism opens up the question of postmodernity, refusing to shorten the distance between capitalist modernity and a putative postmodernity. Postmodernity is to be the fulfillment as well as transcendence of modernity.

There are many levels of postmodernism here. The New French Theorists condemn capitalism and communism equally, even though, as I am arguing, they wrongly conflate Soviet Marxism and possible democratic Marxisms. The French theorists do not boisterously endorse capitalism (see, for example, Baudrillard's 1988 *America*). Their failure lies in their misreading of Marxism as an arrogant eschatology. Although there are passages galore in Marx that make this sort of misreading possible, the Frankfurt School has demonstrated convincingly that one can read Marx as making way for postmodernity characterized by difference, discourse, and democracy. This reading of Marx has been missed in France, where German critical theory has gone largely unnoticed. (Lyotard refers to Habermas and Horkheimer in *The Postmodern Condition*, and Baudrillard seems to rely on the work of the Frankfurt School for a good deal of his simulation theory.) The French have read Marx either as a scientific determinist (Althusser) or as an incorrigible modernist. Merleau-Ponty (1964a, 1964b) is a prominent exception: He understood what Derrideans call the undecidability of Marxism; unfortunately, as I just noted, his influence on the French reception of Marx was negligible. In fact, his influence on the

American New Left was probably greater than in France, evidenced by his centrality for the early *Telos* group (e.g., Piccone 1971), which developed a phenomenological Marxism.

Apart from misreading Marxism, the New French Theorists remarkably converge with the Frankfurt School on many issues of substance (see Agger 1991). They share Adorno's stress on nonidentity, if not his continued affiliation to the project of historical materialism. But there is another postmodern cultural discourse and practice that is virtually anti-intellectual, let alone uncommitted to the development of a serious philosophy of history. This is the street- and screen-level postmodernism of David Lynch, "Miami Vice," Bret Easton Ellis. It is the commodified and politically denatured postmodernism of the culture industry. Whereas at least the New French Theorists have a social theory, if one that opposes totality as tyranny, the postmodernism of the culture industry rejects theory altogether. Clearly, there is some connection, albeit a tenuous one, between these two articulations of postmodernism. The New French Theorists do not have a positive political agenda, either. At least they have engaged with the Marx question, which is a nonissue for the commodified postmodernism of the shopping malls and Hollywood.

Must Lyotard's critique of grand narratives lead to the rejection of politics? The disenchanted postmodernism of the French theorists facilitates the degeneration of postmodern theory into a commodity and cultural postmodernism, even if these are not identical movements. Bret Easton Ellis writes novels, not theory. But he is made possible by the antipolitical stance of the theoretical postmoderns, who have legitimized antipolitics in their posture toward Marxism as the prototypical grand narrative of the day. One can see this clearly in the mass-mediation of the so-called end of communism, which sells American capitalism and culture like never before. Although David Lynch does not engage the Marx question, his movie *Blue Velvet* could become a cult classic only in a political culture in which politics is identified with untoward radicalism. Derrida and Foucault in a sense legitimate the replacement of politics with irony, the stance of the disillusioned postmodern citizen after Watergate.

POSTMODERNISM, POST-MARXISM, NEOLIBERALISM

I have already discussed Habermas's equation of postmodernism and neoconservatism, acknowledging that one can trace the connection between neoconservatism and neoliberalism better than he has done. Rorty and Lyotard share theoretical common ground with the public neoconservatives who run Western governments and help shape dominant ideology. Neoliberalism is neoconservative in that it, too, endorses the antipolitical stance made fashionable by postmodernism, which, after all, has a much higher cultural profile (if one conflates "Twin Peaks" with *The Postmodern Condition* as equivalent theoretical statements). Both neoliberalism and neoconservatism reject Marxism, although postmodernism takes this one step further and argues that all grand narratives, including the Enlightenment, must be disqualified. Liberalism criticizes Marxism locally, not in terms of what Marxism shares discursively with other millennial philosophies of history but only in light of Marxism's alleged authoritarianism.

Thus, it is possible to identify a number of neoliberal, postmodern, and post-Marxist theorists who together reject Marxism as grand narrative and/or illiberal political theory. Laclau, Mouffe, Lyotard, Foucault, Baudrillard, Rorty, and Block belong in this category. None of these people are politically obtuse; each has labored hard to stake a distinctive claim to progressive social theory, albeit not the totalizing theory of what they take to be Marxism. This goes far beyond McCarthyism, which generated sympathy for fellow travelers among the liberal intelligentsia who otherwise opposed the Red menace. McCarthyism was exceedingly crude by the standards of neoliberalism, postmodernism, and post-Marxism, all of which offer nuanced, if relentless, critiques of Marxism.

Today McCarthyism takes a de facto form. Leftists are isolated, denied jobs, beaten down in various ways. The Allan Bloom (1987) image of a university world dominated by Marxists and feminists is a caricature. Although certain humanities departments house a number of faculty members and graduate students interested in deconstruction, feminist theory and critical theory, there is nothing approaching hegemony on the part of the academic left. In fact, neoliberalism is the prevailing academic ideology in the United States and United Kingdom, characterized by the valorization of affirmative action, multiculturalism, liberal feminism, and environmentalism. Only a conservative like Bloom could possibly confuse neoliberalism with Marxism! They are not only different; they are opposed. Neoliberalism takes license from its rejection of Marxism's alleged stress on collectivism, statist authority, and economic determinism.

This is especially confusing where neoconservatives have launched a critique of the campus left's emphasis on "political correctness," noted earlier. Like Bloom, D'Souza (1991) argues that the university is controlled by left-wing feminist deconstructors intolerant of opposing viewpoints. Although there is some truth to the notion that academic neoliberalism, as I have characterized it, encourages a particularly narrow worldview, this is not a product of Marxism, which is virtually nonexistent in the halls of academe, except as an antiquarian interest. Marxism is assailed by these doctrinaire academic neoliberals for its dogma, male supremacy, economism. Marxism is old-wave. New-wave are French feminism, Lacan, Laclau and Mouffe, postmodernism, multiculturalism, Africana studies. Male Marxists have to defend themselves against the charge of irrelevance as well as illiberalism by neoliberals who are themselves dogmatic.

This creates a very puzzling picture, especially to outsiders. It is convenient for the new right to conflate all of these "isms" into the generic category of leftism. But that obscures their crucial differences, which largely revolve around the issue of Marxism. Although I am trying to revive Marxist critical theory with insights from postmodernism and feminism, I contend that critical theory without a Marxist underpinning regresses behind Marxism to neoliberalism or old liberalism. Post-Marxism does not replace Marx inasmuch as it drops Marx's critique of the alienation of labor, thus regressing to purely moral and aesthetic critiques of oppression that fail to diagnose the causes of oppression structurally. Ours is a poststructural age, as well as an age of decline. As Best and Kellner (1991) argue, poststructuralism (e.g., Derrida, the *Tel Quel* group) made the larger cultural movement of postmodernism possible, vitiating structuralist understandings of the social world offered by both Levi-Strauss and Althusser. Poststructuralists and postmodernists argue that it is impossible to understand people in terms of their location in enveloping institutions whose operational principles can be identified and then reformulated. Instead, people can be understood only in terms of the shifting polyvocal discourses that resist translation into other dialects. The so-called postmodern self (see Denzin 1991) is in fact no self at all, covered over in the multiple significations and simulations characterizing this allegedly postmodern age.

A structuralist social science is disqualified as illegitimate by poststructuralists. All we can know is discourse, not the "realities" underlying or extending beyond discourse. Poststructuralism and postmodern cultural theory vitiate historical materialism, which, now as before, with Marx, argues that the external world can be known, even if its external institutional features are dialectically connected to our internal characters as sentient subjects. Under the psychoanalytic influence of Lacan, poststructuralism declares the subject dead.

Although the thesis of the death of the subject is certainly important and needs to be investigated further (e.g., see Lasch 1984), much as the Frankfurt theorists suggest in their attempt to blend Freud and Marx, this issue cannot be decided aprioristically or with reference to a poststructural philosophy of knowledge and discourse. The deconstructibility of language does not make knowledge impossible but rather narrativizes and historicizes knowledge, challenging scientists to acknowledge the undecidability of their discursive work and not pretend that science mirrors nature. Simply because positivism incorrectly reconstructed the relationship among the subject, discourse, and the world does not disqualify all versions of science.

I detect a very curious contradiction in the position of poststructuralists and postmodernists on the issue of subjectivity. On the one hand, they regard the subject as a useless, even counterproductive, fiction. On the other hand, they install narrative and ethnographic self-disclosure as valid modes of knowledge, replacing the impersonal empiricism of survey research. The notion of a postmodern subject or self, however ironically it is intended, reflects this contradictory stance toward subjectivity. Poststructuralists and postmodernists reject subjectivity when they are trying to undercut Western rationalism (Derrida calls it logocentrism), but they accept subjectivity when they are trying to undercut empirical social science, especially in its quantitative mode.

For Lyotard to replace the Promethean grand narrative of Marxism with local narratives of postmodern subjects assumes that it is useful to compare science or knowledge to a story. The notion that knowledge is narrative pervades New French Theory and its American applications in anthropology, sociology, and political science (e.g., see Agger 1989c; Brodkey 1987; Brown 1987). But I am not convinced that science is a story in the literary sense. Hence, I am unwilling to accept Lyotard's notion that Marxism, for example, is any kind of narrative, whether grand or small. This is not to say that I accept the positivist model of presuppositionless representation, knowledge simply mirroring a world "out there." I believe that science is thoroughly discursive and rhetorical. That is, science presents a worldview and attempts to persuade others of it. But that is not the same thing as telling a story, which implies a more personal, even inimitable recounting of events.

The postmodern critique of large stories decides in favor of small stories. That is really a political decision in favor of the individual as against the collectivity. To be sure, collectivities—the state, capital, vanguard party, and so on—have behaved perniciously for millennia. They are not to be trusted. To be legitimate, collectivities must protect the lives and liberties of individuals, in whose name social change is to be accomplished. But the postmodern decision to invest the individual with narrative abilities, even while proclaiming the subject (author, reader) dead, is taken on metaphysical and not empirical grounds. It is an open question whether people can tell stories about their lives and the world that bear even a semblance of accuracy, given the stupefying character of dominant ideology and given the world's complexity.

For people to "author" their lives should be the goal of all radical democrats, both Marxist and feminist. I am convinced that people have the potential for authorship, be it literary, scientific, or political. Whether they achieve that potential today is another matter altogether. I suspect that they largely do not, given the colonization of our everyday lives by what Habermas (1984, 1987b) calls the "system." We cannot change this with a stroke of the theoretical pen—for example, abolishing structures and investing individuals with narrative competence. Although I, too, share the view that people should be able to converse competently and imaginatively about their civil lives—discourse—I view this as a practical accomplishment of purposeful human beings and not something that we can simply legislate.

Neoliberalism flavors many postmodern political and social theories today (e.g., see Rosenau 1992). It imbues postmodernism with an apparent alternative to Marxism, especially now that the Soviet bloc has disintegrated. But neoliberalism is no better than traditional liberalism at theorizing the dominance of institutions over people, even if democratic Marxists and feminists share liberal notions about the inviolability of the person and civil liberties. Neoliberalism and postmodernism possess no adequate theory of oppression, exploitation, or domination (see Ackerman 1980; Agger 1991: pp. 151–73). The most they can say is that we must heed the different "voices" of individuals and interest groups—Bakhtin's polyvocality—that resonate throughout a multicultural society. This is where the political agenda of academic neoliberals, including most feminists, surfaces in what is euphemistically called political correctness: They argue that all students, staff, and faculty, like people everywhere, possess an equal claim on truth and should be indulged in whatever theoretical and political postures they may take (short of engaging in racist, sexist, and homophobic antilocution, which is now banned on some American university campuses—as if the liberal state or liberal institutions can actually control what people say).

Academic neoliberalism is an unfortunate legacy of the 1960s, when the democratization of the university was a central aim of the New Left. Although I too support democracy in most institutional settings, there is something absurdist about requiring power equivalency between teachers and students or doctors and patients. Most teachers know more than most students, just as most physicians are better doctors than their patients. Admittedly, there should be constraints on the power and authority of teachers and physicians, to use these examples. Teachers should not assign grades arbitrarily, nor should physicians keep patients ignorant about their health or overcharge them. But I am convinced that the convergence of the New Left's dehierarchizing pedagogical agenda, on the one hand, and the academic politics of postmodernism and neoliberalism, on the other, reflects their notion that, in fact, the "subject" is not dead but capable of engaging in sophisticated narratives about itself and the world that should be heeded.

Neoliberalism and postmodernism help make this claim stick because they refer to an informational society (for a critique, see Luke 1989) in which media and entertainment institutions, and the technologies that support them (e.g., microcomputers), provide people with unprecedented ability to tell sensible stories about the world. But the argument that high informational technologies increase public literacy and hence raise the level of public discourse is as specious as the 1950s prediction that appliances would decrease the domestic labor time of housewives (Cowan 1983). In fact, so-called labor saving devices have increased the amount of housework that people do. And they have not demonstrably raised the quality of housework or cooking. Similarly, the accessibility of microcomputers as well as mass media has not edified public life. If anything, it has further privatized people, who can now work and play in the privacy of their homes, setting foot outside only to drive to shopping malls, fast-food franchises, and video rental outlets.

Informationalism has not set us free. It has further eroded civic life and thus added to the power of economic, political, and cultural elites. Many (e.g., Baudrillard 1983) link informationalism and postmodernism by celebrating the postmodern world as a cornucopia of signifiers and sensations. Even Poster (1990) in his *Mode of Information* suggests that informationalism has replaced or at least supplemented the mode of production as a central source of value in late capitalism, a theme he derives largely from Foucault. Lyotard (1984) in *Postmodern Condition* first linked postmodernism and chaos theory, adding an element of high science fiction to postmodern theory.

Although informational technologies need to be examined in detail for their relevance to questions of freedom and control, it is highly questionable that citizens achieve new liberties in postmodernity simply by virtue of their proximity to informational and entertainment technologies. Much of this discussion was anticipated by McLuhan (1967, 1968, 1989), who also addressed the relationship between informationalism and power. Luke (1989) in his *Screens of Power* continues this discussion, through both the Frankfurt School and Foucault. Although the democratization of informational technology and culture has the potential for shifting power, it is not a panacea, especially where people use their home computers to divert themselves harmlessly from their own alienation.

The postmodern and neoliberal empowering of the subject, even contradictorily in face of predictions about its demise, often pivots on an informationalist optimism. This optimism, now as before, is naive at best. The Frankfurt view is neither that subjectivity is dead nor that the subject can be technologically extended via informationalist prostheses. The degree of subjectivity's eclipse is above all an empirical question: How much do forces of discipline and power imperil political imagination and agency? This is exactly the theme addressed in Marcuse's (1964) *One-Dimensional Man*, which remains a more sophisticated perspective on the relationship among technology, ideology, and subjectivity than more recent statements ranging from Lyotard to Poster. Marcuse, like Horkheimer and Adorno, recognized that subjectivity in late capitalism is whittled down to near-nothingness. Yet, as he says in the 1964 book, there remains "the chance of the alternatives," depending on the degree of critical consciousness and the existence of public discourses through which to organize dissent. The Frankfurt theorists' position on subjectivity was politically but not metaphysically pessimistic: It did not seem likely to them that the subject could "narrate" itself out of its social predicament, given the preponderance of the disciplinary society (see O'Neill 1986). Nevertheless, they did not throw in the towel but instead tried all the more vigorously to theorize possible resistances from the ground of the lifeworld (e.g., Marcuse 1969; Habermas 1984, 1987b)—precisely my project here.

The lifeworld grounding of critical theory must not proceed aprioristically, from informationalist or narrativist assumptions about empowered subjectivity. It must reckon empirically with the discursive and political contexts within which individuals find themselves positioned. Although there is a certain idealist strain running throughout Marxism, retained from the more dialectical Hegel of *Phenomenology of Mind*, this idealism must not be allowed to run wild, transmogrifying into poststructural and postmodern conflations of the world and the text (e.g., Derrida's infamous claim that "the text has no outside"). Although the text encodes certain relations and transactions of power (which can be transformed), power extends beyond, as well as infiltrates, the covers of texts.

There is a tendency for idealism today to be displaced into discourse theory, which disavows material practice altogether. Although one can develop a political economy of literary activities (e.g., Agger 1990; Luke 1989; Schiller 1989), it is inappropriate to reduce textuality to sheer *écriture*, the Barthesian word for a primal literariness or protean presence before the page. Although images such as *écriture*, like Habermas's own ideal speech situation, can usefully orient socialists and feminists concerned to revivify notions of the Greek polis and New England town meeting in a communicative age, they must not be allowed to become more than metaphors; they are merely guideposts en route to the development of a civic culture. I am concerned that postmodernists replace Marx's understanding of work as the modal activity of the species with an image of the universal writer—although, as Habermas (1971) indicates in *Knowledge and Human Interests*, Marx's category of work tended to conflate technological activities with self-reflection and communication, hence robbing his own critical theory of epistemological standing.

Discourse theory embodies images of a talkative society in which everybody can make their voices heard. Like John Stuart Mill's notion of the free marketplace of ideas, the idea of unproblematic public speech distorts the power relations involved in all social texts today. It is simply not true that all "subjects" can tell adequate "stories" about their lives. Even if they could, most of those stories would not see the light of day inasmuch as publishing is controlled by dominant interests and access denied to those without sufficient credentials and cultural capital (see Bourdieu 1984). Although the open marketplace of ideas, like Habermas's notion of the ideal speech situation, is an attractive regulative idea—something for which we should strive, realizing that it is probably unattainable in its pure form—the tendency of discourse theorists to imbue the subjects they portray with sufficient efficacy to control their own lives today is problematic. My point here is that this ontological assumption of subjective efficacy is obscured in discourse theory's exuberance to get on with its readings of the many narratives proliferating in popular culture and everyday life.

DERRIDA, FOUCAULT, BAUDRILLARD, AND THE FRANKFURT SCHOOL

So far, I have argued that the basic difference between New French Theory and the critical theory of the Frankfurt School is that the French theorists abandon the political project of thoroughgoing societal reconstruction, proclaiming politics a useless passion. The Frankfurt theorists initiated a line of thought which suggested that politics is not obsolete but merely displaced into venues traditionally viewed as nonpolitical by both orthodox Marxists and liberal parliamentarians. Indeed, the most political venues are those which appear least ostensibly political—sexuality, the household, popular culture. It is in these venues that a feminist postmodern version of critical theory needs to seek vital significances and opportunities for transformation. I further argue that a Frankfurt-inspired critical theory can only politicize everyday life by using theoretical and political resources from postmodernism and feminist theory—the very postmodernism and feminism typically opposed to the Marxist project, whether for its infatuation with millennial grand narratives (postmodernism) or for its male supremacy (feminism).

There is a transparent irony in a critical theorist borrowing from the very traditions to which critical theory stands in counterpoint. Indeed, postmodernism and feminist theory would scarcely exist if a dogmatic Marxism had not in a sense made them necessary. But we can negotiate this irony if we acknowledge certain parallels between critical theory, on the one side, and postmodernism and feminist theory, on the other. If pursued to their logical conclusion, these parallels suggest common orientations to domination and liberation among these three perspectives that need to be identified and then articulated synthetically. In the case of postmodernism, a number of New French Theorists, especially Foucault and Baudrillard, have written books that remarkably resemble some of the work in the Frankfurt tradition. These overlaps suggest that theoretical synthesis is possible once we overcome the apparent incommensurability of the language games of New French Theory and German critical theory, an exercise to which this book is a contribution.

Foucault's writings on discipline (1977) and sexuality (1978) clearly converge with some of the Frankfurt writings on social control and popular culture (e.g., Horkheimer and Adorno 1972; Marcuse 1964). Foucault argues that a disciplinary society is grounded in powerful discourses like criminology and heterosexuality that both create an intellectual/political superstructure, to use a traditional Marxist language, and practices that conform to assumptions embedded in specialist discourse. For example, criminologists reproduce criminality by generating an apparently scientific discourse about the criminal and criminal behavior. Disciplinary discourses (e.g., economics: see McCloskey 1985; sociology: see Agger 1989c) suggest certain worldviews that subtly reproduce the practices they describe as normative. Marcuse makes much the same point in *One-Dimensional Man*, in which he argues that by closing the universe of public discourse to utopian formulations of qualitatively different social arrangements, elites in late capitalism reproduce their own control.

Foucault and the Frankfurt theorists agree that discourses encode certain fundamental assumptions about the nature of society. The disciplinary society exacts discipline by turning discipline into a text. The French theorists add a crucial discourse-theoretic dimension to the Frankfurt School's critical theory where they enable the Frankfurt theorists to understand one-dimensionality as a practice as well as a product, tracing it to everyday life, in which people read and enact the scripts of the quotidian. Marcuse lacked this grounding in discourse theory, as did his Frankfurt colleagues. For his part, Habermas, who has offered such a powerful reformulation of first-generation critical theory, attempted to integrate critical theory and communication theory in a way that is particularly hostile to French postmodern discourse theory (see Habermas 1987a), instead relying more heavily on speech-act theory.

Habermas focuses largely on oral communication, not textuality. Derrida contends that writing has been subordinated to the immediacy and metaphysical presence of speech in Western philosophy. Although I am not convinced that this critique of the hierarchy of speech over text is necessary for a postmodern feminist critical theory, it is clear that the postmodern focus on textuality helps theorize public discourse, including entertainment and advertising, in politically advantageous ways. The fact that textuality is increasingly dispersed into the sense and sentience of everyday life makes it devilishly difficult to identify, let alone read, the texts commanding our experience. Since books have been largely eclipsed as relevant social texts, we must learn to read art, television, advertising, clothing, the body, and cities as the most salient texts of the time. These dispersed, disguised texts argue for a certain mode of social being, even though they do not appear to be didactic or discursive.

Although Horkheimer and Adorno well understood the disciplining impact of popular culture, Foucault, Baudrillard, and Derrida could have helped them read the culture deconstructively, hence suggesting new modes of the popular. British cultural studies has taken a similar approach to popular culture, plumbing it for relevant repressions and resistances. There is little sentiment in the Frankfurt work (with the prominent exception of Marcuse in his 1969 *Essay on Liberation*) that popular culture could be reconstructed, especially from below. It is a particular signature of the Frankfurt theorists, especially Horkheimer and Adorno, to portray a one-dimensional everyday life, including entertainment, as irremediably hegemonized. Adorno was a mandarin modernist, which is why he embraced some of modernism's most esoteric cultural expressions, such as the oeuvre of Schoenberg, as modes of protest (see Adorno's 1973b *Philosophy of Modern Music*). Adorno and Horkheimer were particularly hostile to the excesses of the New Left and counterculture, leaving them with no constituency during the 1960s, no personal or collective subjects of the kind identified by Marcuse in *An Essay on Liberation* (only to be abandoned by him in his 1972 *Counterrevolution and Revolt*).

The Frankfurt theorists were more mandarin and modernist than the New French Theorists, who, almost without exception, participated in and theorized the 1968 May Movement, thus establishing for themselves a sympathetic engagement with the New Left and student movement. Clearly, one of the differences between modernism and postmodernism involves differing perspectives on the politics of culture and theory. Althusser (e.g., 1971) for his part spent a great deal of time theorizing culture ("ideological state apparatuses") and theory ("theoretical practice"). Although he is neither a critical theorist nor postmodernist, advancing a more orthodox interpretation of Marxism, his reading of Marx is very much inflected with the problems of modernity and postmodernity taken up by New French Theory during the 1960s. Indeed, in certain respects Althusser is closer to the Frankfurt School (e.g., in his treatment of ideology) than is commonly accepted.

The Frankfurt School's mandarinism frequently obscured their attempt to identify new social, political, and cultural movements that could replace or supplement the blue-collar male proletariat. Although it was apparent to the Frankfurt theorists that late capitalism had to be theorized anew, a project to which they devoted their attention in a host of venues ranging from the theory of the state to their cultural sociology and criticism, their insensitivity to the popular bordered on disdain. This prevented them from engaging with what others call the postmodern condition in a way that could have integrated the French perspective on culture and discourse with their own theory of the culture industry. Sadly, Frankfurt cultural theory was not informed by developments in French semiotics and discourse analysis that have virtually revolutionized literary theory, especially in cultural studies, a movement ironically begun by early Western Marxists like Lukacs and the original Frankfurt School theorists.

I devoted my (1992a) *Cultural Studies as Critical Theory* to the development of a cultural studies heavily influenced, but not constrained, by the mandarin cultural theory of the Frankfurt School. Postmodern theory has been much easier to adapt to the project of cultural studies, although, unlike German critical theory, it lacks a crucial foundation in Marxism and thus it tends to miss the ideologizing, hegemonizing functions of popular culture. A feminist postmodern critical theory can do valuable deconstructive work—consciousness-raising, in a different parlance—by addressing the various discourse/practices of the culture industry. As I indicate in my (1992a) aforementioned book, these deconstructive readings of the popular must suggest new formulations of everyday life as well as societal institutions. Cultural studies as I conceptualize it is both a reading and a writing—a new version of what is possible. To be effective politically, this critique of cultural practices must be conducted in a sufficiently quotidian language that critique becomes part of the culture itself, hence transforming it. Unfortunately, the high-modernist predilections of Adorno and Horkheimer (less so, Marcuse) stood in the way of public accessibility, creating a critical theory of public life that does not go public, thus losing a good deal of its political impact.

MODERNISM, POSTMODERNISM, AND CULTURAL STUDIES

The postmodern turn in recent social and cultural theory is partly a response to the mandarinism of modernism, both aesthetic and critical. Adorno is the quintessential example of the mandarin cultural critic who indicted certain types of modernism from within the emancipatory framework of modernism itself (see, for example, his 1973b *Philosophy of Modern Music*). However valuable this work was, it led him to ignore the popular, although he and Horkheimer theorized the culture industry in ways that made the latter-day project of a Marxist cultural studies possible. In a sense, the Frankfurt theorists theorized the popular but assiduously avoided analyzing it, perhaps fearing contamination by its banal tendencies. Although the modernist project of Marxism is committed to enlightenment, reason, and justice conceptualized as unfolding diachronically, postmodernism (e.g., see Huyssen 1986) challenges the mandarinism of Marxist modernism in very useful ways. Postmodern cultural studies has helped us focus on the particular venues and discourses of the popular, like television (see Luke 1989; Fiske 1987; Miller 1988), movies (Denzin 1991), and fashion (Faurschou 1987). The agenda of postmodern cultural studies, including its feminist variant, applies the Frankfurt School's culture-industry thesis in the context of everyday entertainments, discourses, and practices that deserve careful deconstructive scrutiny.

Although postmodern cultural studies lacks the transformational intent of German critical theory, it makes a critical cultural studies possible by actually engaging with the particular texts and discourses composing the quotidian in late capitalism. Postmodernism finds modernist mandarinism too confining, although it abandons the transformational agenda of modernist theory. This is not to argue for simple synthesis but rather to extend the Frankfurt School's modernism sympathetically. Postmodern discourse theory, beginning with Derrida, crucially liberates a neo-Frankfurt cultural studies from the high abstractions of Adorno's (1973b, 1984) aesthetic theory, which became a model of critical theory's cultural studies (e.g., see Marcuse's 1978 *Aesthetic Dimension*, which largely repeats Adorno's 1984 *Aesthetic Theory* in a more accessible format).

Later in this book I explore the agenda of a critical cultural studies more fully, having worked through the common theoretical logic of critical theory, postmodernism, and feminist theory. Suffice it to say here that *theory's attitude to the popular* is a defining issue separating many modernists and postmodernists. This cuts across the other important issue of *the transformational stance of theory* to produce a two-dimensional cognitive map on which one can locate both critical theory and postmodernism. The more politically radical, critical theory disdains mass culture even though it theorizes the popular as a necessary factor in capitalist hegemony. Lacking a Marxist political intent, postmodernism gains access to the texts of popular culture by refusing to confine a culture-critical agenda to canonical texts and oeuvres. Critical theory politicizes but does not closely examine the popular as a relevant—perhaps the most relevant—venue of power and discipline today. The integration of critical theory and postmodernism in terms of a unified agenda of cultural studies retains critical theory's transformational intent while grounding a critical cultural studies firmly in everyday life.

The Frankfurt School's aesthetic theory does not break out of concert halls and galleries into the movie houses and living rooms of citizen-postmoderns. Although Adorno's discussions of Schoenberg, Beckett, and Kafka are intriguing in their own right, showing the ways in which an allusive dissonance discloses important theoretical insights about the world today, Frankfurt theory also needs to deconstruct popular texts. Adorno himself (e.g., 1945, 1954, 1974b) applied his cultural theory in readings of radio, television, and newspaper astrology columns, providing a more catholic and concrete version of his own aesthetic-theoretic preoccupations (see Zaret 1992). During his World War II exodus in the United States, Adorno learned the methods of empirical social science, which he applied both in his cultural theory and his (Adorno et al. 1950) studies of prejudice and authoritarianism. There are clearly two Adornos here, the mandarin aesthetic theorist and the close reader of popular mass media.

Postmodernism's engagement with the popular converges with this "second" Adorno—he who was interested in mass culture as a factor in the calculus of domination—and with Marcuse (who, in *Essay on Liberation* and *Counterrevolution and Revolt*, addressed the counterculture and student movement as important oppositional forces). This is not to suggest that their political investments are identical but only to note that both of them theorize the popular as an important political venue. This occasional fascination with the popular notwithstanding, the bulk of the Frankfurt School's aesthetic and cultural theory lacked a grounding in everyday life that could have enabled the Frankfurt theorists to fulfill the critical promise of their own culture-industry argument.

The problem with the culture-industry argument in this sense is that it tends to concentrate exclusively on the institutional production of mass culture, ignoring issues of reception. This imbalance is somewhat redressed by those aspects of postmodern reception theory (e.g., Iser 1978) that make reception and consumption equally important topics. Although the Frankfurt theorists (e.g., Marcuse in *One-Dimensional Man*) addressed the cultural imposition of domination via the lifeworld, extending Marx's original analysis of false consciousness, they tended to ignore the ways in which *discourses* of domination are also literary *practices* and hence can be changed. Their top-down perspective on culture is corrected by the ground-up perspectives of postmodernism, Birmingham cultural studies, and feminist cultural studies, especially feminist film theory. These bottom-up perspectives, as I am calling them, emphasize the role of cultural readers (who can become cultural writers). For example, it is not enough to suggest that advertising stupefies. One has to trace carefully the processes by which particular advertisements and advertising campaigns powerfully simulate a falsely ontological reality, hence discouraging new formulations and figurations of the world. Postmodern discourse theory translates particular social practices into the discourses formulating them, thus suggesting their reformulation. This deconstructive work loosens the hold of various discourse/practices like advertising, entertainment, journalism, social science, and religion, revealing them to be corrigible artifices that conceal a certain worldview.

As such, postmodern cultural studies supplements the more institutional perspective of the Frankfurt School. What I (1990) have termed *literary political economy* relates institutions of textuality like commercial publishing and academia to the various literary practices accompanying them, from writing mass-market trade fiction to scripting technical academic journal articles. It is not enough to notice that mass culture and the university are dominated by hegemonic ideologies of conformity. It is equally important to understand how these ideologies are turned into texts and then into lives. In this sense, the discourse-theoretic agenda of postmodern cultural studies adds a great deal to the cultural political economy of the Frankfurt School, both showing the ways in which we reproduce domination discursively and suggesting new formulations and institutions of textuality, hence new lifeworlds.

There is no necessary contradiction between German and French versions of cultural studies in this sense. Indeed, they are complementary once we reformulate postmodernism as a critical and transformational project. The methodological postmodernism of literary departments proliferates close readings of texts and discourses from popular fiction to movies and television, grounding these readings in no overarching social theory and thus sacrificing the transformational potential of these readings to sheer technical virtuosity. Literary political economy explains why people in the academic world have a serious stake in their critical methodologies: Tenure is earned and careers advanced through arcane publications intended for small circles of colleagues.

Although I am not arguing against "scholarship"—careful cultivation of important texts and discourses—I am suggesting that the nature of scholarship is very much at issue today. Postmodernism helps reformulate the academic life by interrogating disciplinary boundaries and by drawing attention to academic writing as a social practice (see Brodkey 1987; Agger 1989b). Academic writing is very much a political factor, contributing to the overall decline of discourse by virtue of its studied obscurantism. The democratization of academic discourse contributes to the democratization of our political culture and enhances dehierarchization in many institutional and everyday spheres of life. This raises questions not only about careerist scholarly writing but about the accessibility of Frankfurt theory.

Indeed, modernism tries to gain distance from the din of the quotidian so that it can criticize it, ever the posture of Adorno and his colleagues. Although Marcuse's writing evidenced abundant literary felicity as well as sensitivity to the American "ear," he was virtually alone among the Frankfurt theorists in his literary populism. Ironically, the academization of critical theory further depletes it of oppositional energy, as Russell Jacoby (1987) argues in his important *Last Intellectuals*.

The problem of critical theory's inaccessibility is in large measure the problem of modernism itself, to which postmodernism might be a useful response. This is not to say that Derrida is a paragon of clarity; far from it! But the postmodern agenda calls into question the relationship of writers to publics just as it reformulates the relationship of people to the popular. A postmodern agenda might include the effort to turn readers into writers, enabling them not only to crack the difficult codes of mandarin culture and high science but encouraging them to become producers of culture and science themselves. Gramsci is a pivotal figure here, perhaps connecting German critical theory and New French Theory from the vantage of his own Italian imprisonment. He well understood the ways in which dominant ideology is not simply imposed from above, through certain crucial high texts, but is constituted and reconstituted through people's participation in the popular. This does not subsume Gramsci under postmodernism, an academicizing exercise in its own right, but suggests certain crucial parallels between his conception of literary publics and postmodern agendas of literary empowering.

I am not arguing that everyone must "write down." All such metaphors of hierarchy need to be deconstructed. Rather, we could formulate the discursive agenda of postmodern critical theory as the effort to democratize access to elite discourses of culture, science, and power heretofore deemed off limits to the general public. One can crack the code of calculus just as one can learn to appreciate opera. People can read science and James Joyce. These are essential items of a postmodern political agenda that opposes the traditional hierarchization of writers over readers. Not all postmodernists endorse this agenda. Nor do they model dialogical writing by inviting readers into the sense and sentience of their texts, which remain impenetrable except to interpretive veterans. The Barthesian text vitiates Barthes's stress on the importance of textual play, even though there is a great deal to recommend a Barthesian agenda in this sense.

Interestingly, German critical theory, especially in the work of Marcuse, suggests the democratization of science and technology (see Marcuse 1969). Habermas (1971) opposes this as romanticism, although his own later notion of ideal speech appears to reverse his earlier disclaimer. Indeed, Marx in the 1844 manuscripts seemed to argue for the disalienation and democratization of science and technology, even if he later moved toward a more specialist and positivist conception of his own intellectual activity. Marcuse in *Essay on Liberation* argues for a "new science and technology," noted earlier, that express the erotic "life instincts," a theme he had already introduced in his 1955 *Eros and Civilization*, a central document of the Frankfurt School's blending of Freud and Marx. Although Marcuse never spelled out his vision of new science and technology in terms of literary and institutional practices, it is reasonable to infer that the democratization of expertise and communicative opportunities was central to his vision.

The introduction of discourse theory into the overall project of critical theory does not necessarily politicize it. Indeed, postmodern discourse theory turns away from politics where it becomes a celebration of the popular, as in the writing of Tama Janowitz or the chatter of Arsenio Hall. *Spy* magazine adds nothing to the radical critique of civilization. Kroker and Cook's (1986) *Postmodern Scene*, much like the recent Baudrillard (e.g., 1985 *Just Gaming*), turns the postmodern cultural landscape into a delicacy to be devoured by the Epicurean critic, who adorns himself or herself in trendy (black?) attire and becomes a cultural performer. Kroker's foray into music and performance art epitomizes this attempt to turn postmodern theory into a cultural practice itself. Although, as Adorno indicated, art can theorize, drawing attention allusively to the disharmonies of late capitalism, one must insist on the nonidentity of performance and theory so as not to reduce theory's vital distance from the quotidian.

Adorno's mandarin version of critical theory remained so aloof from everyday life that he could not imagine and help to bring about a new lifeworld in which hierarchies of domination are ameliorated or altogether eliminated. Postmodern theory, by contrast, intends its own text as a version of performance itself, confusing discourse theory with public discourse. Both miss the mark: Neither Adorno nor Derrida avoids his academization and hence political neutralization. The difference is that Adorno wanted to contribute politically, whereas Derrida, like other New French Theorists, viewed his own theoretical activities as post- or antipolitical. Michael Ryan (1982) in *Marxism and Deconstruction* addresses the parallels between Adorno and Derrida, closing the apparent distance between them by putting a certain political spin on Derrida, much as I am doing in this book. Whether this is the "real" Derrida is a question that would not be asked by a Derridean!

Whereas modernists like Adorno avoid the quotidian for fear of compromising their theoretical integrity and autonomy, postmodernists like Foucault and Barthes embrace everyday life undialectically, identifying their own challenging texts with public discourse. Although a central agenda of early Marx, Marcuse, and Habermas is the democratization of expertise and expert discourse, this must be accomplished structurally, transforming institutions of textuality so that people's communicative competence and access to public discourse are improved. One cannot simply proclaim the pleasure of the text (Barthes) and automatically transform the popular-culture industry and academic publishing. Although there are important parallels between the Barthesian notion of the pleasure of the text and Habermas's concept of ideal speech, Habermas, like his earlier Frankfurt colleagues, recognizes that ideal speech does not spring full-blown from the theorist's imagination but must emerge dialectically in the interplay between critical theory and practice.

Although *dialectical* is a vastly abused and overused term, it helps us understand one of the central differences between German and French theory. Like the French, the German critical theorists recognized that theory is a version of political practice in its own right. Hence, by proclaiming certain utopian ideals like new science (Marcuse) and ideal speech (Habermas), theory helps bring them about. All discourse is political, although not all politics involve discourse. There is a certain inevitable difference between theory's own performance and the new world to which it would contribute. This difference could be characterized as the dialectical difference/distance between theory and practice. Regrettably, most versions of postmodernism are undialectical in this sense, failing to prefigure a new society in their own discursive practices. Derrida and his French colleagues do not sufficiently differentiate theoretical performance from other discursive performances. Accordingly, they lose the political edge that theory requires in order to call attention to the need for various transformational practices, including, but not limited to, theorizing itself.

By themselves, theoretical performances do relatively little to change social and economic institutions. All performances are theoretical in that they convey a certain view of the world to which others are asked to assent. But confined to the academy, theory has little public purchase no matter how much it may preach accessibility. This is certainly not to suggest that theorists should use shorter words and less twisted sentences! That might even make it easier to integrate and thus defuse critical insights. But theory needs to attend to its own location amidst the institutions of textuality that are complexly connected to other social and economic institutions through patterns of what Althusser aptly calls overdetermination. By pretending that theory can proclaim a regime of pleasurable textuality, we lose sight of the fact that theoretical performance is contextualized and constrained by its institutional housing in the university. Bourdieu (1988) in *Homo Academicus* makes this point well.

A feminist postmodern critical theory resists the reduction of theory to sheer method or exegesis. Numerous dissertations (which become university-press books) expound new interpretations of canonical figures. Theory is important lest we lose our ability to reason, hence our minds. But theory, albeit a performance in its own right, transacts very little in the way of power. I would argue that theory can do some of its best work by reformulating academic disciplines deconstructively, interrogating the political, economic, and cultural roles of the so-called multiversity in the era of human capital.

POSTMODERNISM AND THE "END OF IDEOLOGY"

Critical theory aspires to be a political intervention, recognizing that power is now transacted in venues simply unimagined by Marx, let alone by liberal political theory. Postmodernism and feminism help critical theory locate the political in everyday discourse/practices heretofore ignored by political theory, notably the discourses of culture and sexuality. But postmodernism tends to dehistoricize these discourse/practices, rejecting all philosophies of history as Promethean grand narratives. Hence Foucault can oppose Marxism even though his analyses of the micropolitics of the disciplinary society parallel and strengthen the Frankfurt analysis of domination. To understand fully New French Theory's aversion to Marxism, which Lyotard inflates into a rejection of all philosophies of history (neglecting the fact that antipolitics is perhaps the most political posture of all), one has to appreciate the emergence of French postmodernism as a reaction to the Stalinism of the French Communist Party, particularly in its formulation by Althusserians. French structuralism spawned French poststructuralism, which developed into a broader agenda of postmodernism, combining Derrida's particular critique of knowledge and language with Foucault's discourse theory of discipline.

All of this took place in the 1960s and 1970s. For its part, German critical theory had rejected Soviet authoritarianism some thirty years earlier and thus adopted a more nuanced perspective on the possibility of a neo-Marxist philosophy of history. Orthodox Marxist (e.g., Slater 1977) arguments that the Frankfurt theorists were somehow post- or anti-Marxist notwithstanding, the Frankfurters, like Lukacs, Korsch, and Gramsci before them, carefully positioned themselves with respect to Marx in order to develop Marxism in historically appropriate ways. The Germans were much more successful than the French in simultaneously retaining and revising Marxism. In defining its own identity as post-Marxist, postmodernism regresses behind Marxism.

The French (e.g., the French Communist Party) conflated Marx and Stalin, whereas the Germans differentiated them (e.g., see Marcuse's 1958 *Soviet Marxism*). This differentiation allowed the Frankfurt theorists to denounce Stalinism *in the name of Marxism*, which added important spin to their argument that capitalism's conquest of fascism only streamlined by integrating aspects of fascist totalitarianism. As indicated earlier, postures of post-Marxism typically conceal neoconservatism, as Habermas (1981a, 1987a) has argued with respect to postmodernism (but see Laclau and Mouffe 1985). It is unclear—indeed, it is unimportant—whether postmodernists who distance themselves from Marx's modernism actually adopt a neoconservative political outlook, as Habermas seems to imply, or simply acquiesce to neoconservatism by participating in the denunciation of Marxism's relevance.

The celebration of the "end of Communism" (and, by implication, Marxism) becomes what Hegel (1966, p. 70) in the preface to the *Phenomenology of Mind* called a "bacchanalian whirl in which no member is not drunken." Postmodernists lead the way by declaring Marxism a thing of the past, a trend that began with the May Movement. The problem, now as before, is that the New French Theorists confused Marx, Marxism, and the politics of the French CP. This forced New French Theory into a posture of post-Marxism that, in fact, a good deal of its own work belies (e.g., Foucault and Baudrillard). My view is that one can salvage postmodernism by amplifying its most Marxist and feminist insights, hence strengthening critical theory in heterodox ways.

This issue intriguingly doubles back on itself where the French break with Marxism made possible a host of new theoretical engagements and interrogations closed off to modernists, including most Marxists. Postmodernism is extraordinarily useful where it attends to developments in discourse and domination either ignored or inadequately understood by German critical theory. The break with Marxism at once liberated New French Theory from economism and forced it into the fold of post-Marxism, which is theoretically bankrupt. The politics of post-Marxism are perfectly acceptable *if* Marxism is taken to mean Soviet Marxism. But in rejecting all possible Marxisms, postmodernists lose the power of their own deft interventions in interpretive and cultural theory made possible by a break with modernism.

This is truly oxymoronic: New French Theorists appreciated, indeed participated in, the French New Left and student movement, which creatively reformulated traditional Marxist political categories. At the same time, they surpassed Marxism theoretically. Political gain—genuine heterodoxy—was set against theoretical loss—the eclipse of Marxism and hence the strengthening of incipient neoconservatism. Baudrillard (1981) captures this tension well where he tried to rethink Marxism creatively, only to arrive at the impasse of simulation theory (*Simulations*, 1983), a rather unsophisticated blending of Vance Packard with the Frankfurt theory of the culture industry via semiotics.

Postmodern gain is negated by postmodern loss. Whereas the Frankfurt theorists in their high modernism could not engage with the student movement or feminism, the New French Theorists marched through Paris with both students and Maoists. But New French Theorists in rethinking postmodern capitalism did not comprehend their own iconoclasm as a progressive, modernist moment that could be theorized in neo-Marxist terms, much as Habermas has tried to do. This is not to say that Habermas sufficiently appreciates discourse theory, an issue I touched on earlier. Habermas could learn more from postmodernism than he has, although I fully agree with him that it is important to defend the unfulfilled project of modernity with tenacity. Indeed, he defends modernity—reason, justice, truth—against the very postmodernists who would seem to share his predilection for new social movements (again, see Laclau and Mouffe 1985).

Habermas's (1981b) new social movements theory is borne of the same modernism that animated the 1844 manuscripts as well as *Capital*. Of course, orthodox Marxists (think of Althusser!) would cringe at the notion that Habermas owes anything of substance to Marx, who, they argue, Habermas betrays at every turn. (These same people, e.g., Slater 1977, have already denounced Horkheimer, Adorno, and Marcuse for their apostasies.) But Habermas importantly demonstrates that one can theorize postproletarian social movements from within the totalizing framework of modernism, thus resisting the growing temptation to throw out the Marxist baby with the modernist bath water. This is why Habermas is such an important figure for critical theory today: He reformulates Marxism in contemporary terms without giving up Marx's totalizing political agenda.

Habermas's reformulation of historical materialism as communication theory is so important both because he repoliticizes critical theory within the framework of emancipatory modernism and because he resists the depoliticizing tendencies of French postmodernism. Although Habermas (e.g., 1984, 1987b) does not pay enough attention to postmodern cultural theory or feminism (which is largely why I am writing this book), he convincingly defends the project of modernity, and hence of politics, against the pessimism of Horkheimer and Adorno's (1972) *Dialectic of Enlightenment*. He argues that the first-generation Frankfurt theorists could not escape the German idealist and Marxist "paradigm of consciousness" and thus they could not develop new strategies of subjectivity and intersubjectivity (e.g., "ideal speech") in an era characterized by what Adorno (1973a) called total administration. Although different readings of Adorno are possible (see Agger 1992b), I think Habermas is correct to suggest that Horkheimer and Adorno's political quiescence in the 1960s and 1970s was largely due to their analytical framework, which prevented them from identifying and enhancing new social movements characterized by attempts to democratize the lifeworld.

The original Frankfurt critique of domination exaggerated the eclipse of consciousness (e.g., see Horkheimer's 1974 *Eclipse of Reason*). Habermas argues that there is something inherent in speech (the New French Theorists would say discourse) that militates against total domination. Marcuse (1955) in his Freudian Marxism might have said that there is an internal "second dimension" of desire (Eros) somehow impervious to colonization and manipulation. Like left feminists (e.g., Fraser 1989), phenomenological Marxists (Paci 1972; Piccone 1971; O'Neill 1972; Merleau-Ponty 1964a, 1964b; Agger 1992b) argue that there is a necessary lifeworld basis of radicalism. Habermas extends these traditions of lifeworld radicalism in a modernist direction, in this way retaining a neo-Marxist political agenda that builds on his own (1975) structural analysis of late capitalism in

Legitimation Crisis. In this way, Habermas preserves the political engagement of the original Frankfurt School.

Habermas's oeuvre also defends a modernist progressivism against New French Theorists who declare politics meaningless. Interestingly, Adorno in his political pessimism converges with postmodernists who dispense with politics on ontological grounds, such as their critique of totality theory. The postmodern critique of politics resembles the sociologist Daniel Bell's (1960, 1973, 1976) concept of the "end of ideology," reformulating it in terms of Lyotard's critique of grand narratives. Bell suggests that in advanced capitalism political conflict and contestation disappear, and with them ideology, because technology satisfies all human needs. Even Lyotard (1984) in *The Postmodern Condition* shares Bell's neoliberal optimism, although Lyotard formulates his version of science and technology rather differently.

A trenchant critic of Marxism and German critical theory, Bell situates what he calls ideology historically. Following Weber and then Mannheim (1936), Bell views Marxism itself as ideology, necessarily distorting and simplifying social reality for agitational purposes. As bad science, Marxist rhetoric occludes truth and hence diminishes reason. This is very similar to Lyotard's critique of totalizing philosophies of history in *The Postmodern Condition*, which I discussed earlier. To evaluate Marxism with respect to positivist criteria of validity already decides against it. Marx implies, and the Frankfurt theorists as well as postmodernists, phenomenologists, and many feminists state, that there are no "facts" pregiven to the representational eye of science. Thus, one cannot simply conclude that Marxism is "wrong" in its analysis of society, in particular of the logic of capital. Rather, empirical phenomena must be constructed through theoretical frameworks that, ideally, are explicated by the scientist or theorist. Thus, "bias" is not only unavoidable; when acknowledged as such, it usefully draws attention to science's inherent corrigibility, hence inviting dialogical rejoinders (precisely Habermas's notion of ideal speech).

Bell's reading of Marxism as ideological, to be surpassed in a postideological era, was dominant in cold-war social science and still prevails in mainstream U.S. sociology. Lyotard's dismissal of leftist grand narratives is equally central in the postmodern era. Both contend that Marx's flawed science led to pernicious political practices, notably the Soviet Union. Now, with the collapse of the Soviet Union, neoconservatives join young-conservative postmodernists in celebrating not only the end of communism but the vitiation of Marxism as a science and philosophy of history. (James Coleman, the recent president of the American Sociological Association, added to this celebration in a description of the 1992 ASA annual meetings' theme: "Sociology . . . has been implicated in a major failure of social reconstruction, that is, Lenin's attempt to apply Marx's theories in the Soviet Union, and subsequent attempts in Eastern Europe. However sobering this fact, it is clear that the rationalization of society will continue...") Marcuse (1958) already clearly explained that the USSR was not a Marxist brainchild but rather an outcome of Bolshevist command socialism in an agrarian society. Marxism-Leninism, an ideology of political mobilization and social control in the Soviet workers' state since Zinoviev, is Marxist only in name. Neither Bell nor Lyotard takes early Marx seriously, nor the numerous Western-Marxist readings of later Marx which suggest that Marx was Hegelian and dialectical and not a sheer economic reductionist and positivist.

Habermas refurbishes the edifice of historical materialism as a compelling version of empirical social science. This seeks both to enhance the credibility of Marxism in the academy and to repoliticize the project of modernity at a time when the left is on the retreat and the new and old rights celebrate the collapse of communism. Beyond the proclaimed end of ideology lies a new version of critical theory, informed but not hindered by postmodernism. Suitably politicized, whether through Habermas or other versions of neo-Marxism, postmodernism offers critical theory valuable insights into the nature of discipline and discourse in late capitalism. As I discuss in the following chapter, feminist theory also adds powerful momentum to the revivification of critical theory, even though, like postmodernism, it too readily embraces the thesis of the end of (male) politics.

Chapter Three

Postmodernism and the End of Politics 2: Feminist Theory

LACANIAN FEMINISM

Jacques Lacan (1977, 1982) has been an important figure in the development of what is often called French feminism (see Fraser and Bartky 1992), including theorists like Helene Cixous (1986, 1988), Luce Irigaray (1985) and Julia Kristeva (1980). Although I do not explicate Lacan here, his work is a useful point of departure for discussion of the relationship between postmodernism and feminism. Jaggar (1983) and Donovan (1985) offer overviews of the varieties of feminist theory current today. Here I am primarily interested in postmodern feminism (e.g., see Flax 1990), especially as this species of feminism blends with postmodernism and at once enriches critical theory and blocks its political agenda.

Like postmodern theory discussed in the preceding chapter, French postmodern feminism contributes to the discourse of the end of politics. Like Lyotard, Lacanian feminists reject male Marxist grand narratives both because they are aggrandizing narratives and because Marxism ignores women and male supremacy as important theoretical and political topics in their own right. Just as the postmodern critique of Marxism helps rebuild Marxist critical theory, so the feminist critique of Marxism adds important depth to critical theory's analysis of the politics of everyday life. Although I risk a certain territoriality by discussing feminism and postmodernism with reference to what they add to critical theory, thus potentially effacing their own distinctive identities, I am convinced that infusing critical theory with postmodernism and feminism creates a new theoretical synthesis that genuinely integrates and does not subordinate these perspectives.

Lacanian feminism is distinguished by a neobiologism that flies in the face of all political and social theory, not just the Marxist kinds. This is not to say that all versions of psychoanalysis are antipolitical. The Frankfurt theorists (e.g., Marcuse 1955) amply demonstrate the possibilities of Freudian Marxism, unpacking the depth-psychological effects and causes of domination in useful ways. Indeed, as I argue throughout this book, the feminist stress on the politics of the personal strengthens critical theory's focus on the relationship between what Habermas calls lifeworld and system. But Lacanian feminism does not lend itself to the Freud/Marx integration. The French feminists have adapted Lacan to support a nearly biologistic defense of the ontological, emotional, political, and literary distinctiveness of women, contributing to what most taxonomists of feminism, like Jaggar and Donovan, call radical feminism.

Lacan grounds radical feminism where he can be heard to suggest basic depth-psychological differences between men's and women's modes of imagination. This is rather complicated terrain because it requires a discussion of the relationship among Lacan, Freud, and French structuralism and poststructuralism (to which Lacan makes a notable contribution). By now, Lacanian notions about the relationship between consciousness and language are quite common in poststructural theory, especially in its French feminist variant. In effect, Lacan retains a significant part of the Freudian apparatus, adding to it a linguistic twist. He differentiates between the ways in which men and women think and speak, arguing that men inhabit the realm of the Symbolic (including discursive language) and women inhabit the realm of the Imaginary (see Moi, 1985: pp. 99–101). Extending Freud in a poststructural way, Lacan argues that the unconscious is structured like a language, thus deploying a poststructural version of discourse theory in the analysis of psychodynamic processes.

Lacan's modification of psychoanalysis is an interesting but tangential issue for my purposes here. A great deal has been written about feminist uses of psychoanalysis (e.g., Mitchell 1974; Benjamin 1988). I am interested in the ways in which a Lacanian feminism adds momentum to the project of a postmodern feminism, which in important respects parallels the male postmodernist project in its antipolitical stance. Having said this, I will argue that feminist theory is crucial for a contemporary version of critical theory in its stress on a realm of human activity—allegedly nonproductive activity—heretofore deemed irrelevant by most male political theorists.

There are many versions of feminist theory, some of which contradict each other on issues that I deem most relevant. In the first part of this chapter, I examine the more biologistic assumptions of Lacanian-influenced French feminism. These assumptions hamper the merger of feminism and critical theory for many of the same reasons that it is difficult to merge postmodernism and critical theory. Lacanian French feminism shares New French Theory's aversion to politics, opposing German critical theory in this regard. It is necessary to deal with postmodern feminism before I propose an integration of feminism and critical theory inasmuch as postmodern feminism has gathered momentum and advocates in this postmodern era. Although not everyone who professes postmodern-feminist perspectives is explicitly devoted to Lacan, many of Lacan's differentiations between the psyches, temperaments, and worlds of men and women surface repeatedly in radical, cultural, and postmodern feminisms. We are rapidly approaching a time when the neobiologism of French feminism may replace both liberal-feminist and socialist-feminist perspectives on the emancipation of women, especially as the right's attack on the women's movement gathers force.

The right's assault on women's reproductive rights and other gains made by women in regard to protection against sex discrimination and sexual harassment forces the women's movement further to the fringe in the sense that it isolates feminists in radical-feminist, cultural-feminist, postmodern-feminist, and/or separatist postures. The attack on the women's movement belongs to the overall attack on the organized and theoretical lefts, serving to drive a wedge between radical and more moderate proponents of these new social movements and societal critiques. I am not saying that Lacanian French feminism represents the furthest "left" feminism. On the contrary, in its neobiologistic separation of women's and men's psyches and spheres it remarkably resembles the very male-supremacist biology to which it positions itself in counterpoint. It is important to contextualize postmodern feminism as an inadequate response to the regressive sex-political tendencies of our time, including attacks on abortion clinics and a growing imperviousness to the sexual harassment of women in the workplace. Indeed, it is a response that mimics theoretically the very regression, notably neobiologism, that feminist theory ought to oppose.

French feminists eschew male left theory and socialist feminism on the grounds that Marxism and Marxist feminism androgynize social, cultural, and psychoanalytic theory. Kristeva, Cixous and Irigaray, following Lacan, embrace the so-called female imaginary as a distinctive preserve of women who create culture and social institutions that reflect the uniqueness of women's imagination and expression. The Lacanian notion that women have special access to the realm of nonlinearity is celebrated by French feminists, who view men as occupants of a technical, purposively rational domain in which they define themselves with respect to their power positions vis-à-vis other men (see Moi 1985). Politics is defined and dismissed as male territory, and women are portrayed as denizens of the postpolitical or prepolitical. The French feminists (e.g., see Cixous 1988; Finke 1992) suggest that women write and create culture differently from men, avoiding the linearity and scientific mien of men in favor of "round writing" (reflecting, perhaps, the roundness of women's bodies).

Although French feminists certainly reject Freud's hierarchization of men over women, they endorse a neobiologism whereby men and women are essentially defined by their access to certain expressive systems animated by their different unconscious structures. If Lacan is right that the unconscious is structured like a language, then men and women "speak" their unconsciouses differently, reflecting their basic male/female differentiation. French feminists and postmodern feminists regard this differentiation as extraordinarily liberating for women inasmuch as they no longer have to participate in the male world. Instead, they can poetize and perform beyond the male territorial imperative and power trips that characterize the "male world" today. Lacanian feminists view men as deprived of access to the nonlinear imaginary (much the same argument made by non-Lacanian feminists like Mary Daly 1978).

The problem with this argument is that it abandons the realm of politics and power to men. Instead, feminists are to control culture, protecting women's culture against the technophallic imperatives of men's manipulations of nature and of each other. Feminism becomes a defensive maneuver at a time when many of the gains of the women's movement are being rolled back. Indeed, a new generation of "postfeminist" younger women in their teens and twenties treat the feminist generation of their older sisters and mothers as somewhat archaic, fighting battles that they perceive already to have been won. Women on college campuses divide into younger "postfeminists" who major in management and join sororities and older women who congregate in women's studies programs and cultivate feminist theory. These two cultures are divided generationally above all.

The neobiologism of postmodern feminism converges with a variety of other trends in sociobiology that emphasize the claims of nature (heredity) over nurture (environment). This new biologism appeals to neoconservatives, who want to relegate women to nurturant, domestic roles (just as they relegate blacks to sports). It also appeals to feminists who reject male politics as well as the politics of the earlier women's movement (largely because women are now losing in this political arena). At a time when *feminism* is a suspicious term, postmodern feminists use Lacan to legitimate their withdrawal from "male" politics and social theorizing into the cultural expressions and spirituality of a neobiologistic feminism. It is symptomatic that feminist spiritualism has become an increasingly respectable part of the cultural-feminist and radical-feminist agendas, further evidencing this retreat from political battles that are being lost.

Feminist neobiologism, dividing men and women in terms of their different heredities, emotional dispositions, and expressive and technical capabilities, has a counterpart in the German critical theorists' own retreat from organized politics. For example, Adorno's (1973a) growing pessimism occasioned an aesthetic theory (Adorno 1973b, 1984) that took refuge in the disharmonies of cultural oeuvres all the way from Schoenberg to Beckett and Kafka. By no stretch of the imagination is Adorno's post–World War II political disengagement somehow more defensible than the disengagement of Lacanian feminists, even though Adorno is modernist and the French feminists postmodernist. There is even a certain parallel in their postures of literary allusion: Each writes densely in order not to be co-opted.

Feminist Theory   61

In borrowing Lacan's notion that women have special access to the realm of the imaginary, French feminism lays claim to a valuable aspect of difference from men. Indeed, postmodern feminism (see Weedon 1987) has become a version of what is called *difference theory* (e.g., see Young 1990), emphasizing the basic differences between women and men's modes of thought, emotion, and language. If Derrida can be said to have any political theory, it is a neoliberal pluralism that valorizes the irreducible differences between people and groups as the basis of a moral philosophy of mutual respect and toleration. In the American academic setting, this has become the basis of multiculturalism, an intellectual and political agenda heavily influenced by postmodernism and French feminism. Multiculturalism becomes a pedagogical agenda where the canonical curriculum of great Western books and ideas is "deconstructed," replaced with a curriculum comprising courses resonating with the polyvocal "voices" of minorities, women, and other oppressed groups.

This multicultural pedagogical agenda is often centered in women's studies and African-American studies programs in which difference theory reigns uncontested (e.g., see hooks 1984; Collins 1991). It is argued, through Lacan, Derrida, and the French feminists as well as traditional liberalism and neoliberalism, that these plural social, cultural, racial, and gender groups have distinctive political identities and their own expressive languages or "voices" that are incommensurable with those of other groups (Andersen and Collins 1992). Thus, their "stories" are to be told and heard in the courses addressing each of these groups. There is a strong predilection for postmodern approaches to ethnography (e.g., Marcus and Fischer 1986) and an aversion to quantitative methodologies in the social sciences (e.g., Harding 1986; Keller 1985).

The neoliberalism of French feminist difference theory both fuels and reflects growing academic neoliberalism at large. At first blush this neoliberalism, reflected in the pedagogical agenda of multiculturalism, seems to contrast with the neoconservatism of the overall political culture. (Michael Dukakis's presidential campaign against George Bush was stymied in part because Bush successfully branded Dukakis as a "liberal.") But the neobiologistic roots of Lacanian feminism, which plays an influential role in difference theory as well as in its multicultural academic agenda, are confusingly entangled with the roots of neoconservatism, which is increasingly manifested in a virulent racism, sexism, and homophobia.

In saying this I am not suggesting that postmodern feminist difference theorists agree with the likes of David Duke and Pat Buchanan that we should reverse gains made by the women's and civil rights movements, all the way from *Roe v. Wade* to Title VII. No feminist goes that far! Yet it is increasingly clear that difference theory is embraced not only by French feminists like Irigaray, Cixous, and Kristeva and by radical feminists like Daly (1978) but also by postfeminists who agree that feminism has entered its second stage (Friedan 1981) and should soften its rhetorical postures toward men, family, and children. Erstwhile vigorous feminists like Gloria Steinem (1986) and Jane Fonda have settled down to rather sedate lives with men, thus serving as role models for younger "postfeminist" women unreceptive to the galvanizing 1960s politics of the personal, whether liberal, radical, or socialist feminist.

Put on the defensive by the evangelical right, notably in the vicious attacks on women who visit abortion clinics and on the doctors who staff these clinics, feminists retreat—into marriage, family, careers. Some do this by eschewing feminism; others do it by embracing a postmodern feminism that celebrates women's fundamental differences from men, a move begun by Carol Gilligan (1982) in her work on how women and men engage in different sorts of moral reasoning. To note that women think and behave differently from men (e.g., Chodorow 1978) is only to note the obvious. What matters is how these differences are explained. To explain them in terms of differential socialization and access to power is a perfectly legitimate feminist strategy. But difference theorists like the French feminists explain these differences bio(onto)logically, biologistically, especially with the help of Lacan's theory of the female imaginary.

The defense of women's and men's separate spheres is extraordinarily conservative where women are relegated *by feminists* to the realms of domesticity and poetic imagination. This is not to advocate a liberal feminism that leaves the patriarchal family unquestioned (except to advocate more "sharing" of roles in the household). Instead, it simply urges greater labor force participation and equality for women. Interestingly, the neoliberalism of difference theory and the liberalism of first-stage feminism (e.g., Friedan 1963) are remarkably similar in that they do not interrogate the relegation of women to the sphere of femininity, whether this includes heterosexual marriage and childrearing, for liberal feminists, or the realm of the female imaginary, for neoliberal feminist difference theorists.

The depoliticization of contemporary feminism matches the depoliticization of other perennial emancipatory theories. Marxism is smoothly integrated into the bourgeois academy either as a topic of scholastic interest, producing endless dissertations and monographs on what Marx "really" said, or as a contribution to mainstream social science, especially the quantitative variety (see Wright 1985, 1987; Agger 1992b: pp. 40–55). An academic feminist neoliberalism thrives across the humanities and social sciences, valorizing women's "voices" and proliferating courses and conferences at which themes of gender are considered. Many female graduate students and faculty members identify themselves as feminist theorists, adding momentum to the neoliberal feminization of the university world. Although it is good for Marxism and feminism to be given serious hearings in the university, their academization has occurred at the price of their political engagement, as Jacoby (1987) argues in *The Last Intellectuals*. Indeed, theory itself has become a significant part of the academic culture industry, losing touch with the social problems that originally moved Marx to develop his critique of the logic of capital.

The neoconservative critique of leftist political correctness (e.g., Bloom 1987; D'Souza 1991) is partly a critique of a neoliberal feminism that admonishes those who criticize academic women. Although I too teach and write feminist theory, I was once accused of saying in class that neither women nor people of color could do high-quality theorizing. The issue here is not simply the absurdity of the attribution, which was made by a female senior faculty member, but the effort of a full professor to ensure my compliance with the neoliberal party line of difference theory—multiculturalism.

In my own university, I find as little genuine appreciation of difference among the campus liberal-left as among diehard conservatives, who have blown the hegemony of political correctness way out of proportion. Rather, the effort of zealous difference theorists to restructure the undergraduate curriculum has met with opposition from traditional liberals and conservatives who reject the thoroughgoing deconstruction of the liberal arts. Although multiculturalism, postmodernism, deconstruction, and feminism have made headway in a number of humanities disciplines, they are far from canonical. Increasingly sharp clashes between neoliberals and neoconservatives are staged on the battleground of undergraduate curriculum. So far, there has been more heat than light.

I have resisted the temptation to take sides in this conflict between neoconservatives and neoliberals. For someone with my political orientation, the neoconservative agenda is repugnant on its face, adding momentum to the racism, sexism, and homophobia of society at large. But the neoliberal fetish of multiculturalism, deriving from difference theories (which, in the case of postmodern feminism, owes a great deal to Lacan), capitulates to the countercanonical cant of various gender and minority fractions, each of which has its own "voice," untranslatable into the voices and versions of others.

This reflects the way in which neoliberalism segues into neoauthoritarianism when certain neoliberal grounding assumptions are interrogated by people to the left of liberalism. The Frankfurt theorists have been arguing since the 1930s that liberalism and fascism are two sides of the same coin, the former leading to the latter under conditions of deprivation and shattered expectations. There is no reason whatsoever to assume that the deepening crises of American capital and culture will lead to democratic social movements; these crises could just as well lead to authoritarianism, as attacks on gays, minorities, and women mount.

Feminists are luckier than Marxists in the sense that they do not live and write under the heavy aegis of a canonical oeuvre. *Capital* has a very different status for Marxists than does *The Second Sex* for feminists (see Moi 1990). This is in part because feminism began as a political movement that was not guided or fostered by theory. Feminist theory took shape in the academy over the last decade. Only in the last five years has feminist theory become a minor academic cottage industry, representing the evolution of feminists' self-understanding into systematic form. In some ways, then, feminists have been lucky not to have to account for revisionism with reference to a given canon of work. Feminist theory has genuinely emerged from the ground of practice.

This is not to deny that Marxists have failed to learn from history but only to indicate that they labor under the legacy of definitive texts with reference to which revisionism is deemed apostate. This has stifled innovation and encouraged political intolerance. But Marxist theoreticity has given Marxists the advantage over feminists of a totalizing perspective on the social world. Certain feminist theorists in their self-theorization are beginning to catch up to Marxists in achieving theoreticity and systematicity. And yet there is something about the particularism of the women's movement that has made it very difficult indeed for feminist theory to achieve the totalizing ambition of Marxism.

Many feminists would respond that Marxism fails to achieve totality because most Marxists, like Marx, ignore male supremacy as a distinctive factor in domination. I would argue that Marx's and Marxists' failure to theorize male supremacy disqualifies their particular versions of totality theory but does not change the fact that Marxism, unlike postmodernism and postmodern feminism, *intends* to be a totalizing social theory. Lacanian feminism eschews totalization on grounds of a neobiological differentiation between men's and women's orientations to language and discourse. Although Marx and Engels did not adequately understand the relationship between the logic of capital and the domination of production over reproduction (one manifestation of which is male supremacy as well as class struggle), they avoided difference theory by treating men's and women's life activities as undifferentiable with respect to certain underlying bio(onto)logical issues of sexuality. The fact that for most of human history relations between men and women have been hierarchized does not mean that these relations must be explained in terms of men's and women's supposedly different natures or aptitudes.

Postmodern feminists deny the possibility of totalizing theories both because they are postmodernists (who reject grand narratives or total explanations) and because they are feminists (who reject the typical encroachments of "male" theory). I maintain that one can create total social theory that does not hierarchize men over women conceptually or politically. In this sense, I am neither postmodern nor a difference theorist, even though I think we can learn a great deal from postmodern and feminist critiques of mainstream male knowledge and practice, including those of Marxism. But I insist that this learning can only take place within the framework of total social theory. Whether we name this theory Marxism, critical theory, or feminism is *not* the most crucial question, although, as I discussed in my opening chapter, what Jameson calls the naming of theory raises important questions of hierarchy and dominance.

Perhaps my most radical contention here, to be more fully developed later in this book, is that what it means to be feminist and postmodern is unresolved. For me, feminism and Marxism are not only linked; they are *the same* once we reinterpret them in terms of an underlying theoretical logic, which is their critique of the productivist domination of reproduction. This is not to say that the women's movement is the same as class struggle, or that they should be merged to the point of identity. History makes that impossible. I am saying that it is vitally important to formulate Marxism, feminism, and postmodernism as articulations of an overarching critique of domination or critical theory. The payoff of this integration is the explanation of a host of interrelated phenomena in terms of a singular theoretical logic, hence affording new social movements a common self-understanding and, just possibly, common political strategies.

These claims about the possibility of theoretical and political integration are very threatening to feminists, who have always been embattled with respect to male leftists (see Evans's 1979 account of the splitting of the American women's movement from the male-dominated New Left). But the fact that Marx and many Marxists are sexist and even encode their sexism in their social theories (e.g., dismissing domestic labor as nonproductive in Marx's strict sense) does not diminish the possibility that Marxism and feminism can be written as the same text of critique and liberation once we trace their apparently different theoretical logics to common roots in the critique of civilization. For feminism to "become" Marxist critical theory means simultaneously that Marxist critical theory "becomes" feminist. This is very much a two-way process, which would have significant impact on the ways that men compose critical theory and formulate oppositional strategies. I am not overlooking the fact that the Frankfurt theorists idealized the patriarchal family (e.g., see Lasch 1977) by way of their dubious defense of male authority.

For the left to avoid internecine quarrels requires an intellectual open-mindedness and generosity of spirit nearly universally lacking in our society. People on the left are no less "damaged," in Adorno's (1974a) terms, than anyone else. This is why a defensive territoriality frequently gets the better of left women and men, who cannot seem to collaborate politically. This is not to "blame" women for resenting male territoriality; feminism addresses the ways in which politics become personalized, fatefully enmeshing all of us in the daily scripts and rituals of domination. But we must nevertheless interrogate what it means to be feminist and Marxist lest our texts and tenets do our thinking for us.

In opening up the question of feminism, I expand the possibilities presently available to feminist theory. In particular, I challenge the neobiologism of Lacanian French feminism, which not only ontologizes but celebrates the notion of separate spheres. Sexual differentiation does not have to lead to political differentiation, any more on the left than elsewhere. To identify men as the enemy is already to decide in favor of a certain theory of male supremacy that is fatally flawed by its inability to theorize the complex relationships among gender, daily life, economics, and politics. I identify "the enemy" differently: We must oppose all hierarchies of valued over devalued activity, from paid work over housework to capital over labor and mandarin culture over popular culture. A feminist postmodern critical theory interrogates these *hierarchizations of value,* deconstructing the various discourses and practices through which these hierarchies are ontologized and hence reproduced.

DIFFERENCE THEORY, THE CELEBRATION OF THE FEMININE, AND THE END OF POLITICS

The neobiologism of Lacanian feminism, like other radical-feminist perspectives, reduces politics to male posturing. Politics is displaced by culture—women's fiction, poetry, journalism, and film as well as cultural and literary criticism. The bio(onto)logizing differentiation of men and women inevitably leads to antipolitical strategies based on feminist acceptance of the separation of spheres. In particular, postmodern feminists locate politics, and thus the possibility of social change, in the "male" domain of symbolic expression, technology, and warfare, assigning to women the emotive and expressive. Radical-feminist separatisms abandon the realm of politics and power to men, ironically reproducing male supremacy by leaving it unchallenged. This is equally true of postmodern feminisms, which endorse difference-theoretic conceptions of the essential separability of male and female regions of experience and practice (see Fuss 1989).

Although many American and British feminists are neither knowledgeable about nor partisans of French feminism, postmodern feminist assumptions have permeated feminist consciousness in the United States and United Kingdom, sharpening the split between traditional liberal feminists and cultural/radical feminists, including but not limited to lesbian separatists. This has fired the neoconservative attack on the women's movement as an increasingly zany, zealous movement of maladjusted man-haters, an issue I touched on above. Of course, this neoconservative caricature grossly exaggerates the domination of the women's movement by extremists of one kind or another. American and British women who work outside the home have metabolized the feminist critique of male supremacy as a part of their second nature: "Everywoman" viscerally opposes sex discrimination, sexual harassment, and violence against women.

A certain undercurrent of postmodern difference theory can be increasingly detected among academic feminists. This has begun to spill over into the culture at large, partly by virtue of the fact that significant numbers of women have been enrolling in women's studies classes for over a decade and partly because feminist cultural producers and critics subscribe to difference-theoretic constructions of gender. All of this coalesces into the notion that women have a distinctive voice and experience fundamentally different from those of men. Feminism becomes less a political movement than a cultural practice devoted to the amplification of this voice in popular culture and journalism. (Increasingly, this voice is differentiated into African-American feminism, white feminism, various Hispanic feminisms, all in the name of "difference.")

To be sure, very few of these manifestations of difference theory adopt the explicit identity of postmodernism, Lacan, or French feminism. Nevertheless, they reflect difference-theoretic understandings of social, political, racial, and cultural spheres that can be traced back to Lacanian feminism. For example, the notion that certain movies are "women's movies" or "for women" because they amplify a distinctively female perspective is grounded in difference theory. I am not denying that authorial, directorial, and editorial perspectives are necessarily inflected with gendered, as well as racial and class, interests, leading some women to make and watch movies differently from some men. But it is quite another thing to argue that culture-for-women is somehow a feminist project in the sense that women's culture reflects a distinctively female sensibility, especially where the notion of culture-for-women tends to displace or deflect the political projects of the women's movement.

These are not disjunctive alternatives. Feminist filmmakers can well participate in the move to protect women's reproductive rights. But *the celebration of the feminine and feminist* as a valid cultural project represents a certain postmodern-feminist agenda, even if it does not theorize itself with reference to postmodern French feminism (or even if it does not theorize itself at all). Although certain social movements involve the quest for valid personal and group identities, I would observe that there has been considerable backsliding from a political to a purely cultural and personal feminism. This has happened partly because the conservative assault on feminist gains has been so ferocious, forcing feminists out of politics and into culture. It has happened also because difference theory has made insidious headway into feminist theory and consciousness, leading women to celebrate the feminine as a political project in its own right.

This has always been the curricular agenda of women's studies programs (see Lather 1991). These intellectual activities afford younger women a sense of their own importance and efficacy, continuing the empowering agenda of the original American women's movement (e.g., see Friedan 1963). There can be no denying the political and existential impacts of this aspect of feminist consciousness-raising. But postmodern feminism extends the original radical-feminist agenda, which not only valorizes women's importance but emphasizes their uniqueness, subtly elevating the feminine over the feminist. It is in this sense that feminist difference theory, largely developed out of Lacan, eschews politics, which is regarded as a male domain. That is, women are to be defined in terms of their aversion to the male-political.

Feminist difference theory, like radical feminism before it but with this Lacanian underpinning, depoliticizes the very consciousness-raising that was supposed to represent the core of a feminist political agenda. Instead, women are to engage in cultural creation not in order to heighten their political awareness about the perils of patriarchy but to identify, express, and affiliate themselves, demonstrating in this respect that the postmodern-feminist project celebrates a feminist self that contradicts postmodernism's own aversion to the concept of subjectivity, an issue to which I turn in the following section. As I discuss in the final section of this chapter, women are conceived as texts needing to be written by themselves. Although I agree that women are important authors of both books and lives, I prefer to argue that the text is a woman, thus underlining what women and textuality have in common as degraded subjects and practices today.

Postmodern feminism does not raise consciousness but rather expresses and externalizes it, in art as well as in the "round writing" made possible by French feminist concepts of a feminine literary practice. Here, difference theory emphasizes and celebrates the differences between arguably "male" and "female" culture creation. This raises an important question about empirical reality versus ontology: Do women and men engage in different types of cultural creation and expression because they are bio(onto)logically and/or socio(onto)logically different (see Agger 1989c), or because they are forced into two separate cultural spheres? Could both be true at once, making it difficult to adjudicate the issue of the bio(onto)logical nature of Lacanian and radical feminisms?

It is impossible to decide this issue empirically. After all, Derridean readings of science (e.g., Agger 1989b) suggest that "facts" are a text, too, presented rhetorically in order to make a certain argument about the nature of the world. The openness of history makes social change a permanent possibility. The "fact" that women write children's books and men do science does not make this an iron law. Indeed, social texts representing this "fact" as inevitable and universal help reproduce the present, ironically bringing about the social condition described as immutable by science. Derrideans understand that *there are no such things as facts*, no social nature. Instead, data are frozen pieces of history that can be thawed through deconstructive critique, precisely the effort of a radical cultural studies directed at science itself. Thus, no text, whether empiricist or Lacanian, can decide the issue of women's and men's expressive natures inasmuch as culture and cognition belong to the realm of history, not nature. To celebrate women's difference may only reinforce the hierarchization of male knowledge over female knowledge.

In celebrating the feminine, postmodern feminist difference theorists eschew political strategies designed to pierce the boundary between male and female spheres. Once Lacanians and other radical feminists accept the notion of separate spheres, they in effect abandon political efforts both to dedifferentiate and dehierarchize separate spheres. I am not the first to offer this observation; it is a standard criticism of radical feminism offered by left feminists who reject the celebration of the feminine as an ontological or bio(onto)logical strategy. Left feminists like me do not reject the important contribution that the valorization of women's activities makes to feminist consciousness-raising. Indeed, as I explain in the next chapter, the logic of a feminist postmodern critical theory explicitly valorizes activities conducted by women in their allegedly separate sphere, ranging from the creation of art and culture to household labor. The valorization of reproduction is perhaps the single most important project of a feminist postmodern critical theory, stemming from my contention that the domination of production over reproduction is the axial logic of domination in civilization (and hence the conceptual basis of a new version of critical theory).

We must be very careful to disentangle the valorization of women and women's activities, which has clear cultural and political-economic implications, from the bio(onto)logical celebration of separate spheres. After all, most left feminists do not really expect wages for housework; who would pay them? Rather, they want men to share the burden of household labor and caregiving so that we shatter both gender-role differentiation and gender stratification. They also want to dismantle the sexual division of labor in the sphere of market work. Dedifferentiation and destratification ought to be the political agenda of left feminism. Unfortunately, postmodern feminists tend to celebrate women's occupancy of their separate sphere because they reject "male" political practice out of hand.

The politics of difference theory should not be obscured by the fact that postmodern-feminist theorists eschew politics as a male practice. The two academic manifestations of difference theory are *multiculturalism*, discussed earlier, and *feminist theory*, to be discussed at greater length here. I have already debunked the neoliberalism of multiculturalism as yet another version of American interest-group pluralism. Although this neoliberal agenda appears to shun politics in the name of respect for the individual, this agenda is political inasmuch as it ignores social structures overwhelming the individual. The power of these structures (capital, male supremacy, racism etc.) renders the category of subjectivity extremely problematic, a postmodern insight that confusingly contradicts the postmodern celebration of subjective differences.

The explosion of interest in feminist theory manifests difference theory in the academy. Although there is certainly a distinctive corpus of feminist theorizing, "feminist theory" has become a ubiquitous term to describe virtually any self-referential analytical or expressive activity by women. Self-described feminist theorists do not so much plumb a distinctive literature as understand themselves to be *theorizing their identity as women* (see Lorraine 1990). Women's feminine/feminist identity is defined largely in terms of its otherness—its difference—with respect to male identities (see

Butler 1990). Hence, a feminist theorist is a literary woman who discursively or culturally constitutes her identity in terms of its difference from male identities.

This reflexive nature of feminist theorizing makes it extremely difficult for postmodern feminists to create comprehensive social theory. Instead, *this type of feminist theory creates feminist subjectivity*. Although individual feminists build comprehensive social theory (e.g., Fraser 1989), typically around the analysis and critique of male supremacy, postmodern feminist theory as such is intended to eschew empirical explanation, which is restricted to the realm of male scientific activity. Hence, explanatory and critical theories produced by men, for example by Marx, are deemed "male" not only in the sense that they were fashioned by men but also in the sense that they do not create feminist identity. This issue is tricky because in no way am I defending male theorists' frequent blindspots with respect to theorizing household labor, childcare and violence against women, among other things. These things need to be theorized. But their theorization must advance the attempt to understand and oppose the total social system in which these things happen. It is insufficient to view the object of theorizing as the self-construction of the feminist subject, although that can be a legitimate political byproduct of totalizing social theory.

The assertion that feminist theory is defined by its difference from "male" theory suggests that it is impossible for men to write feminist theory, a topic I address further in Chapter 6. It also implies that it is impossible for men to create a feminist identity. Both of these positions are wrong, reflecting postmodern difference theorists' separation of people into naturelike affinity groups rooted in certain overt common interests and/or characteristics. It is not obvious that feminist theory must be done *by* women, or that feminist theory is even uniquely *about* women. What it means to write feminist theory, books, and culture depends entirely on what we mean by *feminist*, an issue that has not been adequately resolved and to which I return later.

Feminist theory locates the oppression of women deep at the root of civilization. I develop an outline of such a theory in the next chapter, where I propose the domination of reproduction as a unifying theme for Marxist critical theory, postmodernism, and feminism. In this sense, feminist theory as a theoretical logic makes perhaps its most fundamental contribution to postmodern feminist critical theory in identifying the domination of reproduction as the distinctive way in which women are oppressed (see O'Brien 1981, 1989). In the next chapter, I amplify the notion of the domination of reproduction by extending feminism into Marxism and postmodernism. This move depends on the politicization of feminist theory, deploying it in venues heretofore unanticipated by many feminists. In terms I develop later in this book, I *transcode* feminism into critical theory and postmodernism, both enriching them and identifying a common theoretical logic among them.

Although feminists who theorize create both themselves as feminists and a feminist culture, theory also explores an object domain external to it. Theory's topic is not theory itself; that is metatheory. Nor is it the feminist subject, although theory can theorize the political formation and deformation of subjectivity as a legitimate topic of analysis. Feminist theorists must theorize the world and not simply themselves; feminist subjectivity is objective, although all objectivity cannot be reduced to issues of subjectivity.

Admittedly, work on the self can well be political, especially inasmuch as the personal is political (see Benhabib 1992). But neither the self nor the transformation of interpersonal relations is the only political agenda, as both the self-help and feminist movements suggest. A feminist critical theory needs to focus on the mediations among subjectivity, intersubjectivity, and institutions. Economic reductionism and postmodern neoliberalism ignore subjectivity and institutions, respectively. Neither adequately addresses the intermediate linkages between the personal and political. In fact, they ignore both the personal and political, which have to be understood in terms of each other. Disavowing politics as male territory does not avoid it: Postmodern neoliberalism reproduces the status quo by celebrating differences within it, failing to dig deeply underneath apparent difference to identify common principles of administration and hierarchy that underlie the production of stratified differences today.

In American political culture the self is elevated above the polity, much as Locke triumphs over Rousseau. The celebration of the feminist self, defined in terms of its difference from the male techno-phallogocentric subject, is no different from the celebration of other modalities of subjectivity—gay, Hispanic, African-American. Although cultural pluralism is to be defended against occidental ethnocentrism, it is hardly a valid utopian construct when it amounts to lip service on the part of the dominant group and does not promote real difference. Difference theory is certainly correct to defend the claims of individuals and groups against the state. But the narrowing of difference theory into a politics of subjectivity tends to ignore the structural and institutional nature of politics today, what Macpherson (1962) calls the politics of possessive individualism. Although the ultimate aim of politics is to liberate subjectivity, this is not to be achieved via a program of self-transformation involving therapies and technologies of adjustment, from twelve-step programs to aerobics.

Feminist consciousness-raising, characteristic of the first stage of the American women's movement in the 1960s and 1970s, began with subjectivity, liberating women from sexist ideologies relegating them to subordinate household and economic roles. But this "c-r" work moved beyond subjectivity, recognizing that the goal of raised consciousness is transformational agency—the formation of consensus and the mobilization of groups. Although first-stage feminists recognized that false consciousness is self-imposed as well as imposed, the self was not the endpoint of social change but only the beginning. Feminist subjectivity struggled to create intersubjectivity, and hence whole social movements. Today, the women's movement, under sway of postmodernism and blocked by a misogynist backlash, reverses this priority, subordinating politics to self-change. A postmodern feminism gives voice to this, although, contradictorily, it also insists that the singular, stable self is a relic of modernity, an issue I take up shortly.

Feminist theorizing not only constructs feminist/feminine identity, in Lacanian counterpart to maleness. It also serves as a bridge between feminists, affiliating them to each other. But this is not the concerted group formation of 1960s feminism, the opening of raised consciousness to activism. Rather, postmodern feminist theorizing is a semiotic medium for constructing one's value as a feminist in quotidian (including academic) exchanges with other women. Symbolic value is attached to the depth and extent of cultivation of one's feminist sensibility, as reflected in the seriousness of one's feminist-theoretical affiliation. The most serious feminists are those most "into" feminist theory (although, again, this is not to deny the possibility that feminist theory can be an exercise in comprehensive social theory, as it is for me here). This is especially true of postmodern feminists, who stress the contribution of feminist theory to the formation of feminist identity. One's theoreticity is represented by the degree to which one's feminist identity is an artifact of studied, self-referential cultivation. These varying degrees of theoreticity position one hierarchically in feminist community and feminist networks, especially in the university.

Among many academic women feminist theory is a highly valued activity, reflecting erudition and gender commitment. Academic feminists traffic in feminist-theoretical ideas, texts, and citations, thus adding value to their stature as feminists. Feminist-theoretical products exist as cultural works demonstrating one's identity and commitment. In this sense, identity is matched by affiliation, which in turn redoubles identity. Feminist affiliation as an academic language game takes place through publication, teaching, and conferencing, the networks traditionally exploited by male academics to further their careers.

Male theorists, even left-wing ones, build careers and charisma deliberately. But to suppose that the feminist cultural and intellectual project is somehow unsullied by these contextual concerns misses important parallels between feminist academic culture and the mainstream male version (sometimes evocatively called "malestream"). Both cultures are often hierarchical, in spite of feminist lip-service, even sincere political commitment, to "feminist process" and democracy. This is not to deny that senior feminists can and should actively mentor junior feminists, a necessary nurturing relationship in any cross-generational endeavor. Indeed, that is the possibility of political education. But feminist theorizing in its supposed elevation serves semiotically to distinguish those who "can" from those who "cannot," creating a lopsided feminist community in which certain sisters are more equal than others.

I have said in this section that feminist theorizing both creates feminist identity and serves as a semiotic medium for creating and distributing feminist cultural capital. Hence, feminist affiliation is hierarchized into senior and junior feminists through the production and reception of feminist theorizing—those who theorize and those for whom theorizing takes place as gender education. To engage in feminist theorizing is largely a didactic activity, although it does not transmit a canon, as orthodox Marxism does, but rather a certain sense of identity—what it means to be feminist.

THE PROBLEM OF THE POSTMODERN FEMINIST SUBJECT

Just here, postmodern feminism contradicts itself. On the one hand, it reduces feminist theorizing to matters of identity and affiliation while, on the other hand, declaring subjective identity to be a modernist relic ("death of the subject") and rejecting political community as a phallogocentric ruse. *There can be no postmodern subject, whether feminist or anything else.* Barthes has already declared the subject dead. Derrida deconstructs the stable, singular subject of traditional Western philosophy. Foucault depositions the subject in order to understand the disciplinary society. Interestingly, those attracted to postmodernism are frequently the same people who endorse various versions of the politics of subjectivity. For example, some American symbolic interactionists have rushed to embrace postmodernism, even though George Herbert Mead's and Herbert Blumer's symbolic-interactionist social psychologies made ample use of the concept of subjectivity, in violation of postmodernism's injunction against subjectivity (e.g., see Denzin 1991; Altheide 1985).

This is not to argue against applications of postmodern themes in empirical social analysis. I strongly endorse those applications inasmuch as they help repoliticize critical theory after Adorno. Foucault's work is relevant to the critical reorientation of criminology. Barthes and Derrida add volumes to cultural sociology. Baudrillard contributes to the sociology of advertising. I, too, plunder postmodern theories and concepts, which I adapt to the agenda of a critical cultural studies. However, the valorization of subjectivity as a central theoretical and political construct, as in feminism, directly contradicts the postmodern thesis of the decline of the subject, making postmodern-feminist borrowings extremely problematic. Postmodernism suggests explicitly that there is no such thing as a postmodern "self," or any other self for that matter. This is the basis of Derrida's whole critique of Western philosophy's logocentrism and metaphysic of presence. Derrida usefully deconstructs the notion of a stable subject capable of making truth claims about an external world in unambiguous language. The self does not so much use language as get used by language, which is seen to position the person in various language games unfolding according to their own rules and internal logics.

As I (1992b) and others (e.g., Luke 1989) have argued, postmodernism adds a great deal to the empirical and theoretical agendas of a critical social science. This book infuses critical theory with postmodern theory and feminism, producing a useful theory of capitalist postmodernity. But there is something contradictory about a postmodern politics of subjectivity, whether feminist or otherwise. In fact, feminists who claim postmodernism do not read deeply enough into the postmodern theoretical text but simply acquire certain trendy rhetorical flourishes that give their work cachet and differentiate it from Marxism. There are numerous postmodern cultural commodities available in the marketplace—television shows, music, haircuts, even theory. In my (1992a) *Cultural Studies as Critical Theory* I distinguish between the theoretical postmodernism of Baudrillard, Derrida, Lyotard, and Foucault, on the one hand, and a commodified postmodernism, on the other. This commodified postmodernism mouths certain words like disintegration, decentering, and deconstruction, adding a certain sign value (Baudrillard!) to its theoretical practice (Althusser!), but failing to generate a program of postmodern selfhood apart from consumerism.

In my aforementioned cultural studies book, I suggest that postmodernism has become a consumer movement, losing the valuable theoreticity that allows it to be integrated with German critical theory. Most devotees of film director David Lynch know nothing of Lyotard. Lynch is considered postmodern because that is one of the newest slogans used by reviewers and cultural taxonomists to describe the offbeat and self-referential. This is not to deny that we can classify architecture and art as genuinely postmodern (e.g., Portoghesi 1983) but to suggest that we must argue these terms, deriving them from a theoretical system. Although certain postmodern feminists (e.g., Flax 1990) have considered their postmodern investments carefully, I would observe that a feminist politics of subjectivity has little to do with the work of Lyotard, Foucault, Derrida, and Baudrillard and perhaps not much to do even with the technical apparatus of Lacan apart from an investment in difference theory.

Feminists often call themselves postmodern in order to differentiate themselves from the projects of male Marxism and German critical theory. As I said above, I believe that feminism can produce a useful program of political subjectivity. But the notion of a distinctively postmodern feminist subject defies postmodern theory's own rejection of any and all subjectivisms as illegitimate. According to postmodern theory, theory cannot instruct people how to live in the sense of telling them how to treat themselves and others. Postmodernism refuses the concept of identity and views political affiliation as a mythic residue of modernist grand narratives. Understandably, feminists do not concede everyday life to male supremacists. Nor should they. But the postmodernization of feminism does not advance the project of a politics of subjectivity even if we ground that political agenda in the development of feminist identity and affiliation. For most feminists, postmodernism functions as a counter to male Marxism, giving feminism a certain leverage in this age of the "end of communism."

The notion of feminist selfhood implies that the feminist subject creates her identity through her own choices. On the basis of this identity, she selects her affiliations, joining feminist community. But postmodernism deemphasizes choice, arguing that the world, notably language, chooses us, not the other way around. Feminists are of course correct to try to hold onto agency, thus breaking out of the grids of patriarchal everyday life. Yet I doubt that this revivification of agency is best achieved through postmodernism. Marxist critical theory is a much better vehicle for the nurturance of feminist agency. Postmodernism best complements feminism where it stresses our embeddedness in language and thus makes way for a cultural studies that, in the case of feminism, becomes feminist film theory, or cinefeminism. For example, Foucault's (1977) analysis of discipline (think of his discussion of Bentham's hypothetical Panopticon) shows the ways in which social control is accomplished through the various quotidian discourse/practices comprising the literary institutions of power and discipline. Foucault is long on the demonstration of social determination and short on the revelation of agency, which is not to deny that he can inform the feminist project, as Fraser (1989) aptly indicates. In fact, Foucault informs feminism (see Sawicki 1991) in his discussion of the institutions of heterosexuality and heterotextuality in *The History of Sexuality* (1978).

Postmodernism, in deconstructing the discourse/practices of the quotidian, debunks them but does not eliminate them in helping author a new everyday life. It has been remarked often that deconstruction's antifoundational relativism negates its political possibilities, although I am arguing here that postmodern discourse theory can valuably flesh out the Frankfurt School's analysis of mass culture. A postmodern feminism better leads to a feminist cultural studies (e.g., see Walters 1992), which demonstrates sexism at many discursive levels of experience, existence, and expression, than to a notion of feminist subjectivity that creates its own identity. After Derrida, there can be little doubt that identity is largely chimerical, just as political affiliation borders on collectivism. This does not mean that feminists must accept Derrida to be feminist but to observe that Derridean discourse theory's valuable contribution to feminist critical theory lies in its emphasis on the encoding, engendering, entrapping power of cultural practices like film (see Mulvey 1988; Lauretis 1984, 1987).

Postmodernism is thought to best Marxism, leading people who flee politics to do this through postmodernism, even if postmodernism does not literally authorize the politics of subjectivity, feminist or otherwise. In my view, this is why radical and cultural feminists gravitate to postmodern Lacanian feminism. In this postpolitical age, the rejection of politics is conflated with the celebrated eclipse of Marxism. And for most feminists, Marxism has always been a "male" discourse. One thing leads to another.

Feminists who reject Marxist politics increasingly do so through postmodernism, which then inflects their own version of the politics of subjectivity and everyday life. This is fatal where they conduct this move to the postpolitical through Lacanian feminism, which introduces all sorts of bio(onto)logical constructs like the supposed difference between the male realm of the symbolic and the female realm of the imaginary.

Although all of these theoretical positionings look extremely byzantine to the uninitiated, there is a certain logic here. To be fair, most male Marxists have been an appropriately tempting target because they stubbornly refuse to theorize male supremacy within, or to extend the logic of, Marx's theory of alienated labor. I (Shelton and Agger 1992) and other left feminists have maintained that Marxism can be reinterpreted in a feminist direction, thus salvaging, indeed enriching, the leftist political program (which, appropriately reconstructed, must include a politics of everyday life). But feminism becomes increasingly radical and cultural, avoiding "male" politics, including the left kind, like the plague. This is as much the fault of orthodox male Marxists as of defensive feminists. By ignoring or denying the importance of the politics of sexuality and gender, Marxists have caused feminists to decamp from the left—precisely what is happening today, as feminism is being inflected by antipolitical postmodern themes.

For many people on the left, including feminists, postmodernism is the route they take to avoid politics in general and Marxism in particular. Ultimately, there is no avoidance of politics, as the Frankfurt School argued. The denial of politics (e.g., positivism) is perhaps the most potent political stance of all. Yet it is increasingly clear that the *Zeitgeist* of the 1980s and 1990s is antipolitical, occasioning projects like feminist postmodernism, no matter how contradictory such projects may be in light of the postmodern denial of the subject. A return to subjectivity is occasioned by the mistrust of politics and politicians, the world-historical enterprise of Marxism notably included.

This is perhaps unavoidable, given the collapse of the Soviet Union and Eastern-bloc state socialism as well as the venality of American politics after Nixon and Reagan. To move "beyond" Marxism-Leninism seems to require a "post" position of one sort of another—postmodernism, poststructuralism, post-Marxism. Postmodernism serves this function best inasmuch as theorists like Lyotard have blamed Marxist grand narratives for the meaninglessness and authoritarianism of politics today. Since its break with the male-dominated American New Left and its earliest grounds in consciousness-raising groups, feminism has always addressed subjectivity, intersubjectivity, identity, and affiliation. Friedan, Greer, and Steinem, liberal feminists all, intended the feminist politics of subjectivity to initiate thoroughgoing social transformations in a way remarkably parallel to the Frankfurt School's own Freudianized-Marxist politics of everyday life (e.g., Marcuse 1969). And because these feminists were liberal and not leftist (few were in the 1960s), the recent collapse of Bolshevist states segues into postmodern theory inasmuch as liberals, like neoconservatives, have always accepted the conflation of Marx, Marxism, and Marxism-Leninism.

Perhaps postmodernism does not require its own rigorous interrogation inasmuch as it samples the theoretical text playfully. Postmodernism leads to its own depoliticization because it presents itself as performance, not as explanatory or critical social theory, an issue I raised in the preceding chapter. Therefore it is not surprising that difference feminists do not treat postmodernism theoretically, canonically, analytically, or critically but instead read and write it with a sense of abandon. Indeed, this playfulness of writing and interpretation is authorized by the New French Theorists themselves. It remains for those of us outside postmodernism (e.g., Kellner 1989a; Aronowitz 1990; Luke 1989, 1992; Agger 1990, 1992b) to politicize postmodernism sympathetically for the purposes of its integration with critical theory. That is to say, postmodernism contains useful insights, even if it defies its own utilitarian exposition by political theorists.

Although it is crucial to deconstruct linear positivist notions of the presuppositionlessly representational text, this does not mean that deconstructively playful texts need to avoid scientific explanation and political criticism. All texts can be read as undecidable. But some texts interrogate the world in a systematic and critical way. The main contribution of postmodern discourse theory to the cultural theory of the Frankfurt School is that it helps unpack cultural discourse/practices as corrigible, perspectival versions. The codes of these texts can be cracked and then reformulated, ever the possibility of social change. As I argued in the last chapter, postmodern discourse theory offers critical theory useful ways of identifying ideological elements in discourse/practices heretofore regarded as epiphenomenal by orthodox Marxists, especially in the realm of popular culture. In particular, postmodern discourse theory helps critical theorists offer nuanced readings of popular culture, hence demonstrating the possibility of the popular's transformation (a possibility largely precluded by Adorno).

THEORIZING FEMINISM: THE TEXT IS A WOMAN

It is certainly possible to repoliticize a postmodern feminism once one identifies its theoretical logic as the critique of the hierarchy of value (men) over valuelessness (women), as I do in the following chapter. It is crucial to decouple feminist theory from feminist politics in the sense that a comprehensive feminist critical theory should be informed by and inform, but not reduced to, the strategic exigencies of the women's movement. This may seem like a strange sentiment for a Marxist. But Western Marxists since Lukacs and the Frankfurt School have been arguing for exactly the same thing in the parallel sense that they decoupled as well as dialectically joined critical theory and working-class politics. Although critical theory addresses the alienation of labor, as Marx did, it develops a much more comprehensive social theory that addresses but is not limited to the tactical exigencies of class struggle. Western Marxism insists on the nonidentity of theory and practice in order to retain theory's autonomy at a time when all thought is rendered affirmative.

Liberal feminist theory has been insufficiently disentangled from the official feminist practice of the mainstream women's movement and from the politics of feminist subjectivity, causing feminist theory to have a purely tactical function. Although little is more important today than protecting the right of women to have legal abortions, feminist theory must transcend single issues, whether pro-choice politics or the feminist self. Similarly, although it is crucial for women to have healthy self-esteem and bond with other women, identity-formation and affiliation are inadequate political goals. Feminist theory, like critical theory and postmodernism, must integrate analytical themes heretofore neglected by it, thus arriving at a comprehensive theoretical logic—the project of this book. Feminists, critical theorists, and postmodernists approach this theoretical unification from different directions, although they can arrive at the same destination, recognizing, with incredulity perhaps, that they were really speaking the same language all along.

The decoupling of feminist theory and practice does not mean that we abandon feminist practice. It means rather that feminist theory needs to achieve distance from as well as dialectical contact with the everyday exigencies of personal and political struggle in order to theorize autonomously above, as well as about, the fray. Feminist theory needs to step back from its role as theoretical practice in order to comprehend and thus practice. This is not to argue for theoretical purity or value-freedom. Rather, I suggest that most species of feminist theory are too bound up with the nurturance of feminist subjectivity and intersubjectivity, thus losing comprehensive perspective.

My critique does not apply to systematic theorists of male supremacy, of whom there are notable ones (e.g., Firestone 1970; Eisenstein 1979; Hartmann 1979; Delphy 1984; Walby 1990). These theorists have contributed very important insights to what I am calling a feminist postmodern critical theory, notably in helping us theorize the relationship between what Marxists call production and reproduction (also see Brodribb 1992, for a trenchant critique of postmodernism). Indeed, the theory of reproduction is a central feature of my formulation of feminist postmodern critical theory, owing much to left-feminist capitalist-patriarchy theory. Nevertheless, left-feminist theory is not dominant in American feminism, even in the academy. Radical and cultural feminisms are being strengthened by Lacanian postmodern feminism, described above in this chapter. Left feminism is increasingly eclipsed by noneconomic feminisms that utterly reject the attempt to connect Marxism and feminism.

Theories of patriarchal capitalism attempt to relate male supremacy to capitalism. Orthodox Marxism resists this integration on the grounds that household labor and childcare do not directly produce surplus value. But, as I noted above, it is possible to extend Marx's analysis of the logic of capital to include unwaged domestic labor, as the early theorists (e.g., Dalla Costa and James 1973) of the Wages for Housework movement tried to do. Indeed, I argue in the next chapter that it is wrong to assume the initial separability of Marxism and feminism, only to connect them later by way of elaborate theoretical maneuvers (er, man-euvers)! One can uncover a common logic in the feminist critique of male supremacy and the Marxist critique of the alienation of labor, a version of which the Frankfurt School called the critique of domination. This logic combines theories heretofore regarded as separate, effacing the Marxism/feminism distinction altogether.

These explanatory and critical theories of capitalist patriarchy are increasingly abandoned by feminist theorists precisely because they consort with Marxism. Indeed, socialist feminists have been relatively unconcerned with issues of feminist identity-formation and affiliation, preferring to concentrate on more structural problems of the gender/class relationship. This is not to say that the theoretical logic of left-feminist capitalist-patriarchy theory precludes a politics of subjectivity. Virtually all feminist theorists agree that the politics of the personal are somehow related to structural issues of politics and culture. The extent to which feminist theorists emphasize the personal is largely a matter of degree. By concentrating on the gender/class relationship, socialist feminists do not preclude the analysis of the feminist politics of subjectivity, especially as those "micro" issues relate to the "macro" issues of feminist political economy.

Left feminists like me argue that the appropriate link between the micro and macro occurs at the level of household labor and childcare (see Shelton and Agger 1992; DeVault 1991), clearly a venue of feminist subjectivity and intersubjectivity. But whereas Lacanian feminists stress issues of feminist identity and cultural affiliation, socialist feminists stress the link between women's unpaid reproduction of the household, men and children and the production of surplus value. The domination of reproduction takes place through the sexual division of labor, which restricts most women to unpaid housework and childcare and underpaid market labor.

Although cultural feminists and capitalist-patriarchy feminists seem to be at odds, one can develop a cultural-feminist analysis of the domination of reproduction that does not require a bio(onto)logical Lacanian underpinning. My version of feminist literary and cultural theory endorses the thesis of the male-supremacist/capitalist/modernist domination of reproduction, a theoretical logic more fully elaborated in the following chapter, where I elaborate my notion that the text is a woman. Just as women are dominated by structures of capitalist patriarchy in the household and labor market, so is textuality dominated by labor and science in the realm of culture (precisely why postmodern feminists must not endorse the French feminist relegation of women to the realm of the imaginary). The text is seen to belong purely to the realm of reproduction (reflection, representation), where in fact the text helps produce material reality by presenting or representing the world unalterably. This is the special project of the positivist social sciences, which deceptively freeze reality, thereby, through the ideologizing postulate of social laws, attempting to bring it about—hence "proving" the posited laws to be true after all. For example, when sociologists proclaim the nuclear family to be an essential feature of modernity (while recognizing that people live productively in many different arrangements of intimacy), they (re)produce a familied world in which women are subordinate to men and capital. I (Agger 1989c) have called this feature of literary reproduction *heterotextuality*, suggesting the way in which social texts like positivist social science normalize and normativize various types of social hierarchy, which I characterize as the domination of production over reproduction in its most generic sense.

Like women, heterotexts do much important, if invisible, work. Culture is not merely epiphenomenal, as mechanical readings of Marx suggest. Horkheimer (1972), in his programmatic statement "Traditional and Critical Theory," suggested that so-called base and superstructure are becoming more tightly interlocked in late capitalism, giving lie to casual dismissals of critical theory as idealist. The text (as a "woman") struggles to liberate itself from heterotextuality, refusing to reproduce its own subordination to a productivist rule of value by representing/reproducing the world as inert, naturelike. This notion of heterotextuality broadens the concept of heterosexuality, which is now understood not narrowly as sexual orientation but rather as an ensemble of familied practices that reproduce hierarchy. Women, like texts, participate in a heterosexist political economy that wants to keep them out of sight, hence perpetuating their subordination to male productivist value. By the same token, as I (1989a) have argued in *Fast Capitalism*, ideologies today are dispersed into a postmodern everyday life, eluding deconstructive triangulation. All of the entreaties for consumption and conformity cluttering our quotidian environment, particularly purveyed through popular culture, zip by unread (and are thereby uncritically enacted).

This critical cultural theorizing locates a feminist politics of subjectivity and culture within an encompassing structural theory of domination, or heterotextuality. Whereas postmodern feminism defines domination in terms of men and maleness, this version of feminism defines domination with respect to the relational dynamics between the realms and practices of production and reproduction, including market labor, housework, and cultural creation and reception. This is precisely how a feminist theoretical logic can attain a universality denied to the antianalytic, antipolitical stances of Lacanian feminists, who would change the world by way of feminist cultural practice and the study groups that nurture feminist identity and affiliation. Although, as I said above, consciousness-raising is necessary in any contemporary political strategy, what it means to have feminist consciousness is very much unresolved, especially given that

Lacanians define feminist being negatively with respect to male being. Lacanian feminists thus acquiesce to the prevailing sexual division of labor, which relegates women to the realm of reproduction, obscuring the fact that *re*production produces.

We ought not to define feminism and feminist existence simply with reference to maleness lest women—*wo*men—become simply men's other. We should define feminism politically and personally in terms of women's structural locations in discourse, everyday life, household, and economy. Instead of defining women in terms of men, we should describe them in terms of reproduction's relation to production, which is not necessarily the same issue. This develops a feminist theoretical logic that can double as comprehensive social theory. Once we assume that feminism is only "about" women, then we deny it all sorts of analytical and political possibilities, especially when it comes to finding common cause with people (called men) who share similar theoretical aims. In this book, I define those common aims in terms of an assault on the domination of production over reproduction, a structural principle of domination that is global in its scope and variety.

A feminist theoretical logic can provide useful insights into the relationship between production and reproduction that help formulate a feminist postmodern critical theory in contemporary terms. This strengthens and preserves feminism. If we conceive every text—every act of reproduction—as a woman, we universalize feminist concerns about the hierarchy of (male) production over (female) reproduction, recognizing that this hierarchization plays out in any number of ways, involving class and race as well as gender. It is crucial to recognize that textuality is a thoroughly productive practice and not simply an act of cultural reproduction or representation. The dichotomies of material/ideal, economics/culture, and man/woman are really hierarchies, as a critical Derridean analysis suggests. It is tempting to accept these dichotomies as both invariant and separable, hence reproducing them. Lacanian feminism does exactly that, restricting feminist theory to the realm of culture and ignoring the fact that culture is a thoroughly material practice, just as economics is thoroughly cultural and personal.

Feminist theory thus addresses all heterotextual hierarchies of production over the "merely" reproductive. It is in this sense that a feminist theoretical logic identifying production's priority over reproduction broadens the Marxist critique of domination into a critical theory of civilization. Without this theoretical logic, albeit extended into domains heretofore regarded as off-limits to feminists (e.g., class, race, the environment), German critical theory remains at the early stage of Horkheimer and Adorno's critique of domination in *Dialectic of Enlightenment*. The problem with their critique is that they do not fully understand the ways in which domination is a "micro" as well as "macro" practice. Their critique of domination does not ground itself in discourse and everyday life, even though Marcuse

(1955) uses Freudian psychoanalysis to explore the internalization of domination. Marcuse deploys the Freudian apparatus to show that everyday life can be "erotized," fundamentally liberated, offering a critical theory of resistance as well as of surplus repression that merges nicely with left-feminist theory.

In the next chapter, I further explore the feminist-inspired theory of the domination of production over reproduction as the central logic of feminist postmodern critical theory. In this chapter, I have tried to make it clear that a Lacanian postmodern feminism avoids power and history, ever the pitfall of positivists and liberals. Postmodern feminism fatally capitulates to the hierarchized dichotomies of civilization in endorsing them as bio(onto)logical sexual differentiations—difference. Its adherents forget Derrida's point that difference often conceals hierarchy, thus producing difference theories that relegate women to their "proper" place in the Lacanian realm of the imaginary.

Feminist theory powerfully adds to critical theory when it is redeveloped as a comprehensive theoretical logic applying to all sorts of hierarchized activities, not only the activities of women. Women are a text on which male-supremacist, productivist civilization imprints supposedly ontological values, inducing women, like culture, to accept their inferiorized lot. This is the role of heterotextuality, which reproduces production's dominion by appearing only to re-present society as nature (e.g., the alleged "laws" of positivist-sexist social science). Like all textuality, women produce when they reproduce (men). For women to recognize this empowers them, like texts, to become strong agents in history—scientists and theorists as well as children's writers.

Chapter Four

Producing Reproduction: The Logic of Feminist Postmodern Critical Theory

RETAINING THE CONCEPT OF STRUCTURAL PRIMACY

The theoretical logic of the feminist postmodern version of critical theory I am proposing turns on the issue of the alleged primacy of production—paid labor. In broadening the Frankfurt School's critique of domination, which was itself a broadening of Marx's analysis of the logic of capital, I seek an axial principle of civilization that has served to oppress people across time, place, culture, class, gender, race, and ethnicity. Identifying such a principle risks oversimplification. But the theoretical payoff is immense in the sense that I can make differences similar, thus suggesting common bases of critique and struggle that unite heretofore differentiated, even divided, groups. It is in this vein that I have challenged the notion, above, that Marxism and feminism are different theoretical systems and address different "subjects"—class and gender, for example, or labor and women. Indeed, the task of this chapter is to show that feminism is Marxism and Marxism feminism, making way for other theoretical mergers.

A unified critical theory needs to address issues of structural primacy, assuming, with Marx, that the world system, to use a Wallersteinian turn of phrase, is indeed arranged around certain fundamental principles of social organization. Modernity has been structured axially so that certain hierarchies are reproduced through bottom-up as well as top-down social behavior. Marx's analysis of ideology, Gramsci's analysis of hegemony, and Lukacs's analysis of reification began to address the way in which hierarchy is self-produced as well as imposed. An interstitial critical theory addresses principles of mediation between what Habermas (1984, 1987b) calls system and lifeworld, thus articulating strategies of organization and resistance to these mediating principles of domination. It is simply wrong to suppose, with Althusser, that certain "structures in dominance" are somehow independent of "subjects," as in his history-without-a-subject argument. It is equally wrong to suppose, with French feminism and Rorty's pragmatism, that a politics of subjectivity and intersubjectivity can autonomously transform large-scale systems. I believe it is clear that mass social movements must arise from and inform lifeworld struggles if the world order is to be transformed at the levels of both deep structure and surface, a distant prospect at best.

Indeed, the implausibility of concerted global social change occasions Lyotard's (1984) postmodern rejection of Marxist grand narratives as misguided stories of transformation that only make the bad worse. His description of the difficulties often involved in accounts of change is not wrong. I only dispute his notion that the scale and scope of Marxist narratives (big rather than small) are somehow problematic. I would argue not that we should abandon grand narratives but that we should refresh timeworn large stories with new empirical evidence and better theorizing—precisely the project of critical theory since Marx. Once we abandon classical Marxism as an exhaustive narrative, we are free to improvise theoretically in ways that need not call into question the very notion of totalizing structural primacy (e.g., the logic of capital or male supremacy) but only particular versions of it that may not comport with the world today.

This sort of talk risks positivism. To call for Marxist engagement with empirical data suggests a positivist Marxism. This need not be the case. If we establish dialectical principles of epistemology and playful methodology (see my 1989b *Reading Science*), we can allow empirical evidence to refresh theoretical arguments. Indeed, we must do so, if we are not to be surprised by events. Perestroika in the Soviet Union has made a mockery of economistic Marxism, which had already been abandoned by Western Marxists more than seventy years ago. I am not calling for Marxist journals or books that contain hypermethodological treatments of survey-research data, although there is nothing in principle that should disqualify those presentations on either epistemological or rhetorical grounds. I am calling for rigorous engagements of theory with the world, acknowledging that theory is already in the world and necessarily transforms it.

It is crucial to disentangle positivism as a socio(onto)logical strategy from all possible versions of empirical social science. In *The Discourse of Domination* (Agger 1992b) I argue for a dialectical social science that avoids positivism and yet enriches grand-narrative-like theoretical logics with empirical readings of the social world. Many developments in the postpositivist philosophy of science, from Kuhn to Feyerabend (see Diesing 1991), suggest that data do not "make or break" theoretical models but only confirm what scientists think they always knew—knowledge already framed by dominant paradigms. Of course, paradigms can change, as the shifts from Ptolemy to Copernicus or Newton to Einstein indicate.

A dialectical social science integrates theory and empirical evidence in a nondeterministic way. For example, German critical theory retains Marx's theory of the logic of capital but adds a critique of state intervention and cultural domination to explain that capitalism persists, despite Marx's expectation of its demise, because of certain unforeseen coping mechanisms like the expansive state and popular culture. In turn, these theoretical revisions make way for further revisions. As I have argued in my discussion of feminist theory, the domestic-labor debate within feminism challenges Marxists to expand the concept of value to include domestic labor and other aspects of caregiving as well as work in the informal sector of the economy. Theoretical concepts, like the structures they describe, are elastic, changing in response to historical transformations and in turn allowing those transformations to be interpreted in intelligible ways. Good science allows its theoretical modeling of the world to be *surprised*.

As Kuhn and many others have pointed out, these theoretical revisions do not take place simply through the accumulation of piecemeal empirical evidence. Rather, theories are paradigms or general frameworks within which evidence is given a consistent interpretation. Eventually, scientists confront evidence so troubling that it cannot be conveniently explained within the particular paradigmatic frame of reference but requires wholesale paradigm shifts, as Kuhn called them. Marxism is such a paradigm, not a set of lawful propositions produced by hypothesis testing. As a paradigm, Marxism both responds to circumstances and remakes circumstances through its own theoretical practice, which involves both knowledge and critique. In postmodern terms, paradigmatic science is a story whose plot permits embellishments and segues to suit the audience. Plot changes are to be dictated by the confrontation of history with imagination, not by political orthodoxy.

This account of the philosophy of science challenges Marxist positivism which, like all versions of positivism, treats Marxism as verifiable with respect to the representational analysis of an external world "out there." Marxism is dialectical because, like all social sciences, it participates in the world it theorizes, notably as a political actor. In this vein, Marx in the eleventh thesis on Feuerbach said that the purpose of theory is to produce a new world, not simply passive representational truth. As such, truth is historical in the sense that it works toward a world as yet unrealized. Theorizing, which includes political critique, intends to bring a certain world into being, not an intractable, ontological Being. What existentialists call being-in-the-world, or existence, cannot be separated from history, which is forever indeterminate inasmuch as the future does not disclose itself in the present (thus suggesting parallels between existentialism and Western Marxism, best exploited by Merleau-Ponty and Sartre). For Marxists, truth is possibility, inspiring action.

Although new knowledge does not falsify or disprove a theoretical framework in the sense of disabling it entirely, new knowledge may suggest the need for new frameworks that can account for it. Data are always constructed by the theoretical language game at hand. Accordingly, they can be ignored or interpreted perspectivally. Household labor is a good example. Orthodox Marxists simply deny that household labor is productive labor, with reference to Marx's original notion of value-producing activity in *Capital*. This cannot be proven or disproven with evidence but only challenged from within the framework of a different theoretical system—for instance, feminism. When Marxists confront the problem of household labor, either they dismiss it as a nonproblem or they integrate it by modifying their own theoretical logic.

In this sense, data are dialectical. Not outcomes of an inevitable, eternal social nature, they inherently possess a certain political fluidity inasmuch as they can be transformed, in part by recognizing their intrinsic historicity. In this sense, theory affects practice, even though theory cannot be reduced to practice. Indeed, theory is a special type of practice, one that affords a certain reflexivity or self-understanding. The world instructs theory only if theorists are willing to adapt their own theoretical logics in ways that account for history's indeterminacy, something that orthodox Marxists have been reluctant to do, thereby losing nearly all theoretical and political validity. This is why orthodox Marxism is an embarrassingly easy target for post-Marxists, postmodernists, and feminists, who can readily point to societal changes unforeseen by Marx.

Little is sacred in the era of postmodern capitalism. Although I am a Marxist in the sense that I believe Marx provided the best example of a totalizing critical theory, every proposition of Marx is subject to debate today. Indeed, I conceive of my project here as a broadening of Marxism to address theoretical logics and topics heretofore deemed off-limits to most Marxists. I retain Marx's basic analysis of the self-contradictory logic of capital, the epicenter of his theoretical system, but I reformulate that notion of structural primacy as the principle of reproduction's domination by production (which augments the Frankfurt School's critique of domination, itself an elaboration of Marx's analysis of the logic of capital).

Marx was fundamentally correct to recognize capitalism as a totalizing social system that inexorably colonizes the whole world system, hence creating the conditions of its own demise. That is what is meant by the *logic* of capital—a self-propelling structural mechanism that expands ever outward and inward. I do not think that Marx understood the full implications of his theory of structural primacy, particularly ignoring the extent to which culture and the human sensibility and body could be colonized by system-serving imperatives. In Frankfurt School terms, Marx lacked a theory of the culture industry and of surplus repression. In this book, I synthesize theoretical developments after Marx, including German critical theory, New French Theory, and feminist theory, in order to revise and revive Marx's theoretical logic, which remains the original exemplar of comprehensive social theory that seeks to join theory and practice. I retain Marx's idea that there is an underlying structural logic to postmodern capitalism that can be expressed theoretically to explain all domination.

In this age of difference, such contentions are subject to ready ridicule. Even to call oneself Marxist, or to admire Marx's theoretical systematicity, is suspect. Critics point to the collapse of communism as proof that Marxist prophecy has failed, disqualifying all comprehensive critical theory as a result. This is precisely the appeal of postmodernism, which not only declares the death of Marxism but the eclipse of all theoretical systems and political ideologies. These things are so inextricably linked that it is difficult even to have this sort of discussion about Marxist revisionism. Postmoderns simply dismiss this project as irrelevant. Feminists, too, reach for their pens when confronted with supposedly phallogocentric theory ("male Marxism") that wants to integrate—ingest?—feminist insights.

Can we develop a theory that privileges structural primacy, regardless of how we conceptualize that primacy? Does the social world still (or did it ever) integrate around various principles of structural primacy, whether the logic of capital, domination, male supremacy, or, as I argue here, the domination of reproduction? To say that this question is empirical does not mean one can simply gather positive data that resolve the question of structural primacy without reference to paradigmatic argumentation. Who would have guessed that Marx's various writings, from the 1844 manuscripts through the *Manifesto* to *Capital*, would have spawned so much internal debate about the adequacy of concept formation as well as empirical and political applications? The undecidability of (Marxist) language ensures that a heroic exegesis of Marx cannot resolve all of these issues. I maintain that one must evaluate theoretical adequacy with reference to the analytical and political work that theory does and not with reference to sacred texts, however important these texts may be as theoretical exemplars.

The "work that theory does" is not a simple utilitarian criterion according to which any theory will suffice as long as it produces testable hypotheses or revolutions. To say that theory must do work means that it must comport with the contemporary world and not remain blind to lively issues. To return to the domestic-labor example again, it is clear that the relationship between market and household labor is a central structural problem for women, particularly American women under age 55, 75 percent of whom do "double duty" as both income earners and homemakers (see Hochschild 1989; Shelton 1992). Marxists cannot comfortably ignore the relationship between the paid-work force and housework force, denying the productivity of domestic labor on doctrinal grounds.

I am not saying that the precise relationship between market and household labor stares us in the face. This relationship must be theorized. But a comprehensive critical theory should not ignore the domestic-labor question inasmuch as it is a real structural problem in contemporary capitalism. What makes it "real"?—say, "realer" than other social problems like teenage drug use or gang crime? Again, this issue must be resolved with reference to theoretical logics, inviting a certain lamentable, if inescapable, theoretical circularity. The very notion of "domestic labor" is theoretically constructed. Few houseworkers would recognize their activities as domestic labor without already understanding the theoretical meanings of these terms, which are produced through what Althusser calls a theoretical practice.

Therefore, it is to the various theoretical practices of the day that we must turn if we are properly to adjudicate the question about what matters in the way of social problems, which in turn dictate ways in which empirical evidence—history—is allowed to transform (deepen, extend, qualify) extant social theories. There are no easy answers here. One establishes an argument for a particular principle of structural primacy with reference to data, which are themselves already theoretical constructs. Positivists seek to escape this vicious circle by establishing epistemological criteria of presuppositionless representation. But methodology, which is often used to vouchsafe validity, is nothing but a form of rhetoric—a way of making arguments artfully. Methodology solves no intellectual problems. Indeed, it only creates them. This is not to abandon method, including quantitative method, but only to recognize that method is a text like any other, which we can understand only by approaching it simultaneously from within and without, a process that Sartre (1963, 1976) called the progressive-regressive method.

BEYOND POSTSTRUCTURALISM

My argument for structural primacy in social analysis challenges Derridean poststructuralism, which belongs to the overall project of postmodernism. The notion that we have somehow moved beyond structures and can thus dispense with structural analysis is a popular one, especially among postmodern theorists who conflate structuralism with Marxist authoritarianism and determinism. Althusser is a key figure here inasmuch as he is the frequent target of New French Theorists since Derrida. Althusser (1970, 1971; Althusser and Balibar 1970) endorses a structuralist Marxism that is essentially Bolshevist in its political theory and strategy. Although there is a good deal of affinity between certain Althusserian phrasings and the work of the Frankfurt School, for example their analyses of ideology as what Althusser calls a "lived practice," they differ politically in substantial ways. As I remarked earlier, New French Theory arose out of the 1968 May Movement in France, pitting a poststructuralist analysis against Althusserian and other structuralisms.

The issue of structure has a peculiarly Gallic flavor. Debates since Durkheim run the length of recent French thought, including Sartre, Merleau-Ponty, Levi-Strauss, Althusser, Derrida, Foucault, and Lyotard. In effect, these debates have involved issues of agency versus determinism. In

Germany, debates about agency have taken a rather different form inasmuch as German critical theory took its bearings from Marx and thus conducted its disputes about agency and determinism on a more overtly political plane. For the French these issues have been largely philosophical, mythological, and linguistic, reflecting the comparatively weaker position of Marxism as a theoretical practice in France. German critical theorists identified themselves much more clearly as Marxists than did their French counterparts, thus conducting their own debates about structuralism in terms of substantive social and political theory. For the French, these social and political issues were somewhat submerged in disputes about the roles of consciousness and language in social practice.

The influence of French poststructuralism has been significant in North America, where leftist politics and social movements are nearly absent. In the United Kingdom and Germany, philosophical debates about agency and structure have been conducted much closer to political struggle, reflecting important comparative differences among these political cultures. Neo-Marxian arguments for what I have been calling structural primacy have been less convincing in France and the United States, where social and cultural theory is increasingly marked by a poststructural commitment to difference and pluralism. Again, this is not necessarily consistent with Derrida himself inasmuch as strict Derrideanism would appear to disqualify the politics of subjectivity and identity, as I discussed in Chapter 3. Nevertheless, it is apparent that poststructuralism has flourished in political cultures in which a significant left alternative has been absent (or, as in France, where the left alternative was equivalent to the neo-Stalinism of the French Communist Party in the case of Althusser).

The argument for structural primacy turns on one's relationship to the poststructural and postmodern arguments against what Lyotard calls grand narratives. I have already suggested that this relationship should be determined by one's empirical reading of history, although I have also acknowledged that empiricism is necessarily contextualized by pregiven theoretical frameworks within which empirical data are constructed. Thus, to phrase my earlier argument somewhat differently, I cannot just appeal to "facts" that reveal or disclose structure's primacy, for example, in the case of capitalist-patriarchy theory or Marx's analysis of the logic of capital. I must construct these facts by way of theories of structural primacy, which are supported by facts that I enlist in their favor. Nevertheless, having said all of this in a Kuhnian vein, I maintain that the argument for structural primacy hinges on a reading of history animated by certain comprehensive theoretical logics or narratives. Thus, to tell history's story in modernity requires recourse to structural arguments in order to proceed with the story both synchronically and diachronically.

Without structuring narratives, history simply makes no sense. Of course, Nietzschean-influenced postmodernists would discount any meaning in history! I am not saying a priori that meaning exists; we give history meaning by historicizing it: writing it, theorizing it, attempting to change it. By telling history's "story" we suggest both plot and resolution. At the margin, existentialists instruct us that history has neither plot nor resolution. But it is an act of Sartrean (1956) bad faith not to accept the challenge posed by the indeterminacy of the human condition, which, as Heidegger (1962) remarked in *Being and Time,* is characterized by our reckoning with our own mortality. This is not to suggest that poststructuralism is simply nihilism, an argument frequently heard, especially from the right. Relativism and relativity are values in themselves, even if they conceal their value orientations underneath the veneer of cosmic disinterest. As for postmodernists, irony is secret political theory, even if it eschews politics and power, rejecting the polity as a venue of meaning today. Rather, poststructuralism and postmodernism acquiesce to social fate by denying themselves access to the sort of world-historical storytelling engaged in by millenarians like Hegel and Marx. They limit their options to deconstruction, lacking a positive political program.

I will readily concede that all structuring narratives can be deconstructed against themselves, showing their ample limitations—self-contradictions, false closure, omissions, aporias, Prometheanism. But this does not mean that the poststructural aversion to totalizing social theory, with its political agenda, is preferable, especially at a time when the avoidance of politics is perhaps the most potent form of political advocacy, ceding the public arena to elites. The marginal deconstructibility of all grand narratives does not decide in favor of small narratives, which are equally deconstructible. Small politicians can become small tyrants. Multiculturalism, based on difference theory, does not avoid perspectivity, even though it pretends to avoid totalizing political agendas. All perspectives are agendas (totalizations, structurations), no matter how much they may posture as agendaless, representing only the "voices" of those in whose name they speak.

Structuralism has been usefully reformulated by Giddens (1984) in his so-called structuration theory. He well recognizes that one need not choose between agency and determination. In this sense, he finds a course between the more reductionist structuralism of Althusser and the poststructuralism of Derrida. Similarly, and much before him, the Frankfurt theorists, believing that they were following Marx in this, suggested a dialectical social theory that had room for both the micro and macro, agency and institutions. Derrideans are correct to draw attention to the self-limiting tendencies of all narratives, great and small. But an acknowledgment of these limitations does not decide in favor of a narrativelessness or small-narrativeness that paints with finer brush strokes. In the end, all stories misrepresent, even those that pretend to avoid representationality in favor of more deconstructive postures.

The fad of the poststructural goes hand in hand with the postmodern fad of post-Marxism. At a time when all political systems seem suspect (postmodernism), it is equally tempting to suppose that all theoretical systems or narratives are bankrupt (poststructuralism). The aversion to politics is matched by a resistance to theory (see Man 1986) paralleling the differentiation between poststructuralism and postmodernism. Here, as elsewhere, we are severely constrained by the dualisms of bourgeois civilization, forced to choose between structure and agency, even if strict Derrideans disqualify any talk of agency as logocentric. The Frankfurt theorists, Lukacs, Gramsci, Sartre, Merleau-Ponty, certain feminists, and Giddens suggest the possibility of dialectical social theories that refuse the duality of agency and structure, hence avoiding the fashions of poststructuralism and postmodernism. All of the people just listed embrace politics, an alien stance for Derrida, Foucault and Lyotard. For this reason, perhaps, they all seem more characteristic of the 1960s and 1970s, when the young left in universities were plowing through Western Marxism and feminism in order to find concepts with which to explain their own experiences of alienation and utopian imagination.

One almost has the sense that the aversion to structural analysis inversely relates to the structuration of the world system as well as lifeworld. The more structures matter, the less credence they are given by Derrideans. To be sure, one must strictly separate structuralism as a substantive social theory from linguistic, philosophical, and mythological structuralism, the difference between German and French versions of it. Derrida is not necessarily to be slighted for avoiding a substantive theory of the social, even though his oeuvre encodes a secret theory of social texts. Nevertheless, there is a striking parallel between poststructural aversions to both substantive and philosophical varieties of structural analysis. Both varieties of poststructuralism (postmodern post-Marxism and Derrideanism) are formulated in response to all sorts of totalizing philosophical, political, and cultural frameworks since the Enlightenment, including but not limited to Marxism.

I have already discussed the politics of totality in my opening chapter. It is an article of faith among poststructuralists and postmodernists that totality theories are philosophically inadequate and politically wrongheaded. Again, I would suggest that the assault on totality inversely relates to the empirical reality of global totalization, which proceeds under the banner of capitalist modernization. CNN, McDonald's, and Coke headline this totalization, as do all sorts of corporate and political interlocks that increasingly integrate the world. The internationalization of capitalist modernity parallels the homogenization of quotidian experience, ironically read to suggest the end of ideology and great-power conflict. But what Mandel (1975) and Jameson (1991) call multinational or postmodern capitalism should occasion a greater emphasis on totality inasmuch as the cultural and economic logics of capital are, in Habermas's terms, colonizing.

This (totalizing) analysis of the cultural and economic logics of capital is regarded suspiciously by non- and post-Marxists, for whom the world is characterized by difference and heterogeneity. As I suggested earlier, this is not an argument that can be resolved outside of the explanatory frameworks within which evidence is constructed as meaningful. Non-Marxists will not interpret the world according to the logic-of-capital argument, instead explaining global capitalist modernization in terms of healthy postmodernity. This requires us to debate the meaning of terms like *modernity* and *postmodernity*, a taxonomic exercise that is really an exercise in substantive social theory, allowing one to decide the theoretical significance of the opening of a Russian stock market or the franchising of American fast-food outlets in the People's Republic of China.

Poststructuralism positions itself with respect to postmodernity, arguing that in the postmodern era structures of language and society disappear (or never existed)—they decenter, to use the technical language properly. But I maintain that postmodernity is not characterized by the dissolution of structures. Structures of discourse and society endure; they are increasingly dispersed into the quotidian, one of the distinctive characteristics of practice and experience in fast capitalism. The supposed break between modernity and postmodernity is largely illusory (see Huyssen 1986) inasmuch as postmodernity is a higher stage of capitalism and not a qualitative break with structures of domination (at least not yet). There can be a genuine postmodernity (what Marx called the end of prehistory) in which the continuum of capitalist modernity is ruptured. But that is not the sense of the term *postmodern* typically in use (e.g., see Denzin 1991: pp. 26–27).

Domination is *always* structural. We can simply infer structural primacy from the reality of domination. As I have said repeatedly, there is no "simply" about this project because "domination" is a theoretical artifact and not a thing-in-itself available to every representation. Poststructural theories of society (e.g., Brown 1987) ignore domination because they assume wrongly that the world is all text. As a materialist, I contend that there is an outside to texts, as well as certain internal transactions of power within the nucleic societies of texts. Derrideans assume the dominationlessness of texts because they privilege the literary as a site of playfulness and freedom of expression. Think of Barthes's (1975) notion of the pleasure of the text in this regard. Yet a literary-theoretic version of critical social theory identifies the many ways in which texts, notably including the dispersed texts of money, science, edifice, and figure, contribute to domination.

Consider advertising (see Williamson 1978; Wernick 1991). Although postmodern advertising campaigns play on their own artfulness, it is clear that advertising is an artifice of power, reproducing certain lifestyles, hence discipline and surplus value. Although one can read beer campaigns (e.g., "Why Ask Why?") with a postmodern sense of irony, there is much more to the social text of advertising than that, including what the advertising excludes from itself (e.g., labor relations in the beer factory, alcoholism, automobile fatalities). Through television shows like "thirtysomething" as well as through popular marketing and communication majors in universities, advertising has become a fashionable postmodern industry in which yuppies script their own lives playfully, without ostensible commitment. Where long hairs used to frequent Greenwich Village (the 1950s) and campus political demonstrations and rock concerts (the 1960s), today they wear ties and work "on the creative side" in advertising, creating the illusion of their own aesthetic authenticity when in fact they are shills for a cosmopolite version of postmodern life.

This has been said about advertising before (Packard 1957). Advertising in postmodern capitalism is a central source of social control and surplus value as well as a repository of certain postmodern literary urges, almost a new aesthetic venue. A deconstructive reading of advertising shows convincingly that textuality transacts power, especially since texts no longer repose between covers but are now dispersed into public things that defy distancing, mediating readings. It is theoretically important that advertising in the electronic media as well as in periodical magazines rushes by at an extraordinary rate of instantaneity, defying readings that could challenge ads' embedded social ontologies (much the way Marx challenged both religion and bourgeois political economy). There is no countertext to advertising, no slow reading that can challenge it, except in arcane cultural and literary journals (e.g., *camera politica*, *Cultural Critique*). As such, simulations like advertising have an ineluctable power over the lives we live, even if we refuse the commodities they purvey. They stand for *commodity itself*, making it nearly impossible to conceive of, let alone work toward, a decommodified social order in which people do not exchange substantive social freedoms for the ephemera of what Marcuse (1955) called repressive desublimation.

My point here is that poststructuralism profits where it demonstrates the playful literariness and hence openness of the world. Although there is an important emancipatory message in Derrida to the effect that reading writes, hence modeling all sorts of empowering engagements with dominant authors and authorities, poststructuralism fails as social theory where it obscures the boundary between text and world as well as the politics and economics immanent in language games themselves. Discourse theory buttresses critical theory where it shows the ways in which ideology is written, read, and lived. But discourse theory oversimplifies where it substitutes the text for labor and power as paradigmatic metaphors of social activity. In this sense, it occludes the reality of domination, which is only deepened through the social texts of consumption and conformity inundating us from morning to night.

Poststructuralism either avoids politics or suggests interesting new ways to locate politics in the quotidian (e.g., see Luke's 1989 *Screens of Power*). There are many Derridas. Derrida is close to Adorno in his implication of a politics of discourse and textuality, a project that Foucault turns in a more sociological direction. I am less against Derrida than I am against Derrideans, who in his name reduce literary and cultural theory to play and pyrotechnics. Anyone can "read" anything deconstructively; this quickly becomes method, losing sight of truth and power. Jacoby (1987) does not pay enough attention to the academization of the New Left under the guise of literary and cultural theory. Neoconservatives, for their part, ridicule deconstructive "litcrit" (e.g., Newman 1985; D'Souza 1991) as the epitome of faddish academic irrelevance. David Lodge's (e.g., 1984) novels capture this culture best, tweaking it from within. Nevertheless, one can rescue New French Theory from its own fashion, as I do in this book, once one enlists it in the emancipation of imagination as well as in a discourse-theoretic version of the critique of ideology.

PRODUCTION OVER REPRODUCTION

The preceding section was a digression necessary to consider the issue of poststructuralism's resistance to the notion of structural primacy. I suggested that the survival of domination, indeed its textual dispersal in fast, or postmodern, capitalism, suggests the viability of structural analysis. I contend that we need "more" structural analysis (albeit with the aid of a poststructural critical theory that decodes disguised, dispersed scripts of power). Power is concealed in postmodern capitalism, one of Foucault's basic points. It is found everywhere but in the traditional political arena, which is truly a commodified venue of cynicism. We have trouble accepting the notion of structural primacy because many of us are beholden to Orwellian and Stalinist images of structure-as-subject—total surveillance or the Siberian camps.

Marx, in a sense the first Derridean, identified structure in the otherwise invisible logic of capital, reading money deconstructively for what it could tell us about the capitalist world and the human activities of production, consumption, and circulation underpinning it. Structure was not a singular subject for Marx but rather many subjects—capital, labor power, commodity fetishism, money, ideology. He initiated a deconstructive critical theory whose central strategy is the identification of institutions, practices, and discourses sustained by falsely conscious human activity. That is, Marx was interested in the ways in which people sustain a social order inimical to them, partly through ideology and partly through participation in exchange relationships.

He assumed, as we cannot, that texts' power could be undone once read carefully enough. Structural analysis was to lead to, and inform, political practice. Hence, *Capital* was a thoroughly agitational document, as Cleaver (1979) has rightly noted. But this assumes that people read and write books like *Capital*—texts that stand at one remove from the world and consider it critically in terms of what it lacks and what it could be. I think it is extremely dubious that textuality today enjoys a certain critical distance from the world in order to convey the critical deconstruction of ideology and hence mobilize social movements. The autonomy of textuality itself is at stake in fast capitalism, something that Marx neglected, living at a time when books stood apart from the world to which they were critical addresses.

This insight, among others, leads me to reformulate the Frankfurt School's critique of domination, which is itself a reformulation of Marx's critique of the logic of capital, as a critique of the domination of production over reproduction, including both textuality and unpaid domestic labor (hence connecting postmodernism and feminism with Marxist critical theory). At stake in this reformulation of critique are the scope and depth of a comprehensive social theory. Indeed, Marxism has not ranged far enough sufficiently to comprehend the axial structural logic of domination, which I am rephrasing as the hierarchy of all value over nonvalue (or production over reproduction). In this reformulation, I am increasing the adaptability of critical theory in order to address a whole host of hierarchies heretofore either ignored by Marxism or subsumed somewhere underneath the general theoretical logic of the critique of capital. The underlying structural principle of modernist civilization, then, is expressed in a range of hierarchies of production over reproduction, from capital/labor to men/women, white/colored, science/art, material/ideal, West/East, North/South, labor/text, exchange value/use value, and many others. What these hierarchies have in common is the subordination of activities heretofore regarded as nonproductive or reproductive to a productivist rule of value—for example, in a capitalist society exchange value, or in a sexist society men's work.

My version of critical theory, addressing the subordination of the inferiorized realm of reproduction to production, deconstructs the various manifestations of this hierarchy in order to suggest that *reproduction is secret production that production requires for its dominance of reproduction*. Indeed, production requires reproduction in the same way that domination requires positivist science to bring it about and men require women who take care of them and their children. These are instances of heterotexuality, including all of the quotidian scripts and practices that reproduce production's dominion. This is a liberating insight because it shows that "merely" reproductive activities are productive in their own right and should be valorized, claiming their share of social and economic power.

The valorization process takes place through ideology critiques that interrogate the supposedly naturelike character of these productive/reproductive hierarchies. The feminist critique of male supremacy is a classic example of this interrogation, which actually reverses the priority of production over reproduction by showing that reproduction was productive all along and that what passes for male production is actually supported by the secret, silent work of women. Valorization is thus matched by a systematic debunking: Production is shown to live off the sweat of others—Others, in postmodern parlance—thus losing its supposedly natural rights.

I submit that all modernist dominations can be traced to this generic hierarchy of the productive over allegedly unproductive or reproductive, from economics to culture and sexuality. This formulation of domination is superior to Marx's logic of capital, the Frankfurt School's critique of domination, and feminism's critique of male supremacy in the sense that it explains more cases, showing a range of apparently separable moments of domination actually to be instances of the same structural logic. This common theoretical logic can make way for coordinated political and social movements that no longer fly the flags of differentiated interest groups (in the name of postmodern and neoliberal multiculturalism) but now understand their interconnections, indeed their inseparability.

In this way, one can map Marxism onto feminism and postmodernism such that their theoretical logics are reduced to a common theory of hierarchy. Critical theory addresses global hierarchies through this common theoretical logic, refusing to accept the theoretical and political territoriality of social theories and movements uncritically. We can no longer safely assume that the women's movement is, or should be, "about" women and the class struggle "about" male proletarians. Once we establish that reproduction is secret production, we can map one group's apparently differentiable domination onto those of other groups, demonstrating the universality of otherness that unites differentiable groups in common cause once they have understood the unified theoretical logic of their common opponent.

This is above all a political project, grounded in theoretical reformulation of the global logic of domination. We circumvent the positivist problem of somehow proving that different peoples and groups "actually" suffer from the same structural malady, as if evidence could resolve this question representationally, without recourse to theoretical constructs. As I do here, we must argue theoretically that production's dominion over reproduction is a universal logic, defending the efficacy of this formulation in terms of the analytical work that it can do. We must risk pragmatism by assessing theories in terms of their capacity for what Jameson (1991) calls *transcoding*, translating one domination into others with reference to certain common structural principles producing them.

For example, we can demonstrate the utility of my reformulation of critical theory in terms of this transcoding exercise, explaining the sexual division of labor in exactly the same terms we might use to explain the dominion of mandarin over popular culture. Or we might demonstrate that racism operates according to the same logic as heterosexism. This transcoding establishes both theoretical and political commonality, allowing groups to dig beneath their own assumed theory of oppression, which is simply generated by the dominant discourse/practice in question. Hence, liberal feminism is borne of the male-supremacist liberalism that defines political discourse in capitalism. Liberal feminism does little transcoding work because it cannot theorize structural sources of domination any more than male liberalism can. By contrast, socialist feminism challenges both Marxist and feminist assumptions about the relationship between so-called productive and reproductive spheres, defying their more traditional understandings of the relationships between market work and domestic work.

This collapsing of theoretical categories via transcoding risks oversimplification, endorsing what Adorno (1973a) called identity theory (see Piccone 1976). Totalizing theories tend to efface nuances. Since I take such a firm stand against postmodern difference theory, this is a real problem. I hasten to add that I oppose postmodern and neoliberal difference (e.g., multiculturalism) *in the name of* what I contend is real difference, which is only made possible on the basis of universal liberation, as Marx argued in the 1844 manuscripts. I oppose prevailing difference theories because they do not really nurture difference but simply perpetuate theoretical and political differentiations that serve to keep the left divided. (One might hesitate to use the term *the left* in a book about postmodern theory inasmuch as the term suggests a bygone era of leftism. I use the term deliberately, especially as it can be qualified by adjectives like *New*, *feminist*, and *postmodern*.)

The differentiations among interest groups, characteristic of pluralism, oppose the theoretical project of transcoding in the name of postmodern antitotality perspectives. Jameson (1991) staunchly resists this aspect of postmodernism, insisting on the utility of totalizing social theories, which he formulates by way of certain useful postmodern categories. Jameson's visibility in the theory community is somewhat surprising given his commitment to Marxist grand narratives. Perhaps the theoretical reading public is not sophisticated enough to recognize what is going on in books like *The Political Unconscious* (1981) and *Postmodernism, or, the Cultural Logic of Late Capitalism* (1991). Jameson is not subverting Marxism through postmodernism but simply periodizing capitalism in terms of various postmodern cultural and theoretical gestures that have gained recent ascendance as false alternatives to Marxist critical theory. Jameson fights the end of politics through an interpretation of postmodernism articulated in Marxist categories, an exercise he advances with the aid of Ernest Mandel's theoretical apparatus.

Jameson has failed to develop a version of critical theory that can do ample transcoding work. His book *Postmodernism* (1991) remains a postmodern pastiche, a rhetorical style that he otherwise eschews as characteristic of postmodern cultural expression. Like Adorno's (1973a) *Negative Dialectics*, which in some respects his book resembles, *Postmodernism* lacks systematicity if not heft and scope. I suspect that Jameson appeals to literary and cultural theorists because they are largely unfamiliar with German critical theory, including Habermas, and thus they do not notice the relative absence of structure in Jameson. Jameson is not mainly a social theorist but a very sophisticated literary and cultural critic who phrases his criticism through social-theoretical categories that greatly enrich his criticism. Jameson's oeuvre, including works like his early (1971) *Marxism and Form*, has theoretical vitality and a sharp political edge because he is on the outer fringes of literary theory, proximate to critical social theory. He reads the same people I do. But he is stopped short of a fully theoretical practice, whether called transcoding or cognitive mapping, because he does not aim for the explanatory sweep of Marx or Habermas. Like Eagleton, he impresses students of literary and cultural theory because he is more "social" than Fish (1980, 1989) or even Lentricchia (1980).

The motif of production-over-reproduction, with which I replace older theoretical motifs like the logic of capital, reification, domination, and male supremacy, should not be deployed to resolve all empirical and political problems. It cannot explain "everything," even though it helps explain a great deal more than traditionally differentiated social theories like classical Marxism and feminism. My own version of feminist postmodern critical theory must assiduously resist its own tendency to become a recipe repeated whenever thought cannot do its own work. Theories merely stimulate creative applications. They run the desperate risk of abuse in the hands of political people who seek to harness theory to practice, a joining almost always threatening to theory's—thought's—vital autonomy and thus to autonomy in general. I would like to see it impossible for anyone to become a card-carrying critical theorist, much as it was impossible for students of Adorno to become practicing Adornoians, given his own antipathy to system as well as to his own cult of personality.

I would also like to believe it possible for one to combine Adorno's aphoristic acuity and reflexive, self-deconstructing style with the structuring mien of a Habermas. That is my aim, although it requires more than a short book to demonstrate its possibility. It may be that no single volume can contain that much energy and systematicity, given the nature of literary economies today. Rather, one has to evaluate the complete oeuvres of theoretical writers, which cannot be fully or fairly appraised until they have gathered sufficient momentum to be recognizable as distinctive bodies of thought, constantly evolving and changing.

ESSAYING CRITICAL THEORY

I did not intend to produce such an oeuvre when I began to write *Socio(onto)logy: A Disciplinary Reading* (1989c) in 1985. I was in the midst of engaging recent Continental developments in the theory of interpretation, from poststructuralism and postmodernism to French feminism, in order to extend the Frankfurt School's analysis of the culture industry by way of European discourse theories. I realized that these largely French developments had a great deal to offer German critical theory. At the time, I did not foresee an oeuvre in the making but only a single book on the textuality of discipline (hence, a book on my own discipline, sociology). As I moved from project to project, however, I began to conceive of each new project in terms of the others already done and those that lay ahead, recognizing the emerging identity of an oeuvre constituting a comprehensive and yet reflexive critical theory. This book is a reckoning with the results of my unfolding projects, a stock-taking that is relatively tightly structured into components, or units, which I integrate. This volume aims more at Habermasian structure and closure than at Adornoian or Jamesonian allusion, although both are necessary, if not in single volumes than across the grain of an entire oeuvre.

For Anglo-American audiences, this whole issue of the logic of theoretical presentation inevitably becomes mired in the spurious issue of "clarity." Critics of Adorno and of books like my *Socio(onto)logy* complain that they are difficult, even obscurantist. Unself-conscious of their own cultural conditioning in a positivist environment, these critics are deaf to the dialectical, deconstructive nature of writing, which is necessarily fraught with what Derrideans call undecidability. There are different legitimate logics of presentation. Some are more systematic and taxonomic than others. Compare Habermas's architectonic *Theory of Communicative Action* with Adorno's devilish aphorisms in *Minima Moralia* or Irigaray's lyrical and indefinite *This Sex Which Is Not One*. I would like to believe that an oeuvre can contain both allusive, enigmatic phrasings, attesting to the muddiness and ambiguity of things, and a more discursive style that approaches theoretical artifice the way engineers approach building bridges.

These are not incidental issues, for they speak to the matter of totality, a leitmotif in this book. The more a comprehensive theory can double back on itself and open itself up for self-interrogation, the more convincing its approach to comprehensiveness will be, acknowledging that no story is complete or without blindspots. Habermas is a fabulous systemizer and a terrible storyteller. Indeed, one has the impression that Habermas avoids the rhetorical flourishes of Adorno and Horkheimer precisely in order to legitimate critical theory in the university. Although this is an admirable aim, it has the consequence of expunging the authorial aura from Habermas's text, as well as agency and irony.

In other words, one can write totalizing social theory without forgetting that theory is simply one text among many that do not bear a representational relationship to the world. Too many theorists allow concepts to do their work for them, reifying them to the point of absurdity (much as their hated quantitative enemies fetishize methodology). Neither theoretical constructs nor methodological techniques win arguments; they are merely forms of rhetoric, ways of talking about the world. Sometimes they are convincing; sometimes they fall flat. In any case, theory can be composed in a voice that acknowledges its own undecidability, hence acknowledging its finity and fallibility, both intellectual and political.

With few exceptions, the only critical theorists to have found this voice have been essayists, people who eschewed both system and encyclopedic tomes. Adorno "essayed," although he also wrote full-length works, combining these modes better than most. Nevertheless, his full-length works were essentially long exegeses and immanent critiques, not what one might call positive social theory after Habermas's fashion. *Negative Dialectics* and even *Aesthetic Theory* do not compare to Habermas's *Theory of Communicative Action* in terms of their degree of systematicity. Merleau-Ponty essayed, as did Sartre. Walter Benjamin is perhaps the most notorious example of a dialectical ironist who employed the fragment in order to form postmodern pastiches before their time. Buck-Morss's (1989) book on Benjamin's Paris works, *Dialectics of Seeing*, discusses Benjamin's mode of theoretical presentation as constitutive of his overall theoretical logic, if one can call it that. But there is nothing about the irony of essaying that cannot be transferred to the full-length work, thus enabling critical theory to transcend Jamesonian flourishes or Adornoian aphorisms.

This does not require us to confine ourselves to the essay form—thirty or forty pages of relatively unstructured prose about a delimited topic. We can essay the totality where we recognize that our writing is corrigible and indefinite. We should not only acknowledge this corrigibility but celebrate it, precisely what Barthes might have meant by the pleasure of the text. Finally, we need to write as if we were begging responses, treating textuality not as a private expressive moment but as community building, recognizing with Wittgenstein (1953) that texts are veritable forms of life or what Hymes (1974) calls speech communities.

To "essay" is to take a literary posture, a textual attitude. It recognizes, with Derrida, that books write authors as much as authors books. One's topic, format, audience—as well as the very caprice of textuality itself, in its serendipitous nature—determine "what" one says, as well as how. Although authors strongly intervene in the sense and sentience of texts, as do readers (who are authors in their own right), we need to abandon the model of a lonely auteur plucking words out of the sky according to some deliberate literary plan designed to produce a certain meaning and hence reader response. For my own part, although I sit down with an outline and proceed from sentence to sentence, paragraph to paragraph, I am continually surprised by the direction of meaning taken by my writing. This is not to endorse aimlessness, especially where a comprehensive critical theory must be analytically rigorous, but simply to recognize that the text quickly takes on a life of its own, something that must be contained lest it overrun its banks and flood out of its confines or covers.

The rhetoric of critical theory is important intellectually and politically. My production-over-reproduction motif totalizes, as do all universal theoretical logics. But I must develop the utility of this framework in the contingent contexts of usage inevitably confronting any social analyst. That is, totality is not attained simply by substituting one theoretical logic for another—for example, production-over-reproduction for Marx's logic of capital. One can approach totality only by essaying theory—literally, attempting it. These attempts are framed by the times, topics, and problems confronting the social analyst—violence against women, oil spills, imperialist wars. Theory is not only a system but discourse, a mode of approach and intervention. It is a way of being in the world. I develop this point further in my concluding chapter, where I extend my argument that critical theory is an interstitial activity arising from the lifeworld and aiming to transform institutions.

As I suggested earlier in my discussion of the political pitfalls of totality, the great challenge for critical theory is to combine Archimedeanism—objective truth claims—with a sense of fallibility. Derrida provides this fallibility brilliantly in his notion of literary undecidability, which can be transcoded into notions of theoretical and political polyvocality. Objectivity needs to be tempered by a sense of historicity, perspectivity, mortality, and contingency. As I understand it, this was precisely Merleau-Ponty's (1964a, 1964b; see O'Neill 1970) argument for an existential version of Marxism. He recognized that no political order can eliminate the delicate tension between particular human beings and general humanity. He said that no revolution is worth even one life, although he meant one life expended needlessly, not lives lost in defending life itself. Merleau-Ponty overcomes Marxist hubris by showing that politics cannot solve the riddle of existence, which remains tragic. Derrida overcomes Marxist hubris by showing that all texts unravel deconstructively when read against their grain.

In this sense, critical theory needs to be essayed, written out of the particular contexts of existence that require political solutions, and not deduced dogmatically from first principles. Although theory needs to address the world structurally, in terms of its patterned interrelationships, it must not lose sight of the fact that systems are only as good as the work they do, or better said, that they are only as good as the lives they lead. One can live *Capital* just as one can live *One-Dimensional Man* if one reads them as versions of a new political order to which they are themselves contributions. Derrida shows both that writing matters and that matter is a kind of writing, a circumstantial textuality. In this sense, books would become lives where people treat them as practices to which, and beyond which, they can contribute their own versions. Gramsci's notion that the revolution must overthrow *Capital* is very important here. He suggests that readers must become writers, hence authors of their own fate. Like Derrida, he suggests a relationship to textuality that I am here calling essay.

This returns me to my notion of an oeuvre as an expanding, self-correcting body of work. It is both a body and a life, the way people record their own circuitous but structured attempt to live the books they take seriously. It is easy to see how religious people do this. The "born again" return to the books of faith that they recognize must be rewritten in the conduct of their own lives. Although born-again Christianity is riddled with deceptions and dogma, it nevertheless provides an example of how a book (in this case a "good" one) extends into an oeuvre, a life lived according to its precepts, which must be formulated in particular quotidian contexts. This is not to say that I am composing born-again critical theory. Religion belongs to the realm of mythology, no matter how deconstructive its relationship to its own text may be. But, as Horkheimer and Adorno argued in *Dialectic of Enlightenment*, science is not far removed from myth where it fails to understand its own corrigibility. By comparison to positivist versions of science, certain versions of religion are downright emancipatory (Latin American liberation theology, for instance).

Science is all the more mythic the less it admits this about itself. Theories that pretend to have no chinks in their armor—blindspots, tensions, lapses, inconsistencies, even contradictions—explain very little. Theoretical logic gets in the way of persuasive social analysis, which rarely conforms to the simplifications of our theoretical constructs. This is hardly an argument against theory. How else are we to understand the world, whose appearances are increasingly illusions, simulations? When I say that critical theory must be essayed I am only saying that critical theory must embody deconstructive principles of corrigibility, contextuality, and correction that invite dialogue as a way of building community. Theory cannot be architectonic, nor can it solve all problems. This is precisely where the Prometheanism of the Enlightenment went wrong, producing all manner of calamities in its name.

Habermas demonstrates the tension between ideal speech and a system so airtight, so removed from the lifeworlds it venerates, that it undermines ideal speech at every turn. Habermas appears deaf to the tenor of his theorizing. Although I have noted that he rightly wanted to legitimize critical theory in the university, this does not mean that he had to out-Parsons Parsons in composing a theoretical system utterly beyond experience. The great truth of phenomenology is that theoretical constructs can be traced back to their pretheoretical constitution in everyday life, thus demonstrating their political vitality and relevance. Piccone (1971) and Paci (1972) stake out a phenomenological Marxism that tests theoretical concepts against their lifeworld relevancies, as does O'Neill (1972) in another context. I am particularly indebted to O'Neill's formulation of theory's umbilical relationship to the body politic in *Sociology as a Skin Trade* (1972) and *Making Sense Together* (1974), two important statements of phenomenological and ethnomethodological Marxism. O'Neill goes on to invest the concept of essay with a certain theoretical status in his study of Montaigne, who developed the essay form as a legitimate mode of philosophical presentation. O'Neill's *Essaying Montaigne* (1982) instructs my exercise in theoretical self-reflection, albeit without my grounding in European discourse theory.

Habermas takes up the challenge set by Marx to reformulate the whole edifice of historical materialism. Yet Habermas squeezes all life out of his system. This is not the usual Anglo-American complaint about Teutonizing writers; of course, I would be convicted of the charge of obfuscation, too, as certain American sociological reviewers of my books continue to note! But it is not Habermas's literary style that troubles me; after a few attempts, he can be readily mastered, if not easily imitated. Rather, his vitiation of his own call for ideal speech reflects an insensitivity to the requirements of public discourse and thus casts doubt on his political relevance today.

This is decidedly not to endorse plain language, whatever that means. There is nothing inherently wrong with technical language, especially where it realizes certain literary economies. I do not object to technical usages except where it is supposed that definition and taxonomy solve intellectual problems in their own right. Yet elite discourse must continually attempt to publicize itself in order to build the very body politic it desires. This is not accomplished through wrongheaded translation exercises whereby difficult words are replaced by simpler ones, although sometimes that is necessary. It is achieved through a version of writing that empowers readers to become writers, continually weaving back and forth between technical and public usages in order to elevate citizens to a higher level of competence as well as edification. Habermas needs not only to write for specialists but also to create specialists anew, an aim consistent with his commitment to communicative democracy.

There is no formula for alternating between technical and public usage—call it education. Writers achieve this differently, depending on their contexts of meaning as well as on their literary abilities. One must have the capacity for clarifying complicated concepts without relinquishing a conceptual apparatus altogether. Derrideanism is immensely important in the way it suggests an empowering engagement between readers and texts. Derrida suggests that readers necessarily write where they are confronted with texts' ineluctable undecidability, which they have to resolve through contingent acts of sense making. This is similar to Husserl's notion of intentionality, suggesting that consciousness is a strong, directive capacity and not a blank slate, giving rise to the aforementioned phenomenological Marxism (closely resembling a Derridean Marxism, which in some sense is what I am composing here).

In my *Reading Science* (1989b) I suggested that the text of science could be essayed, hence democratized. One can retain methodological technique while narrating method, acknowledging that it is simply one way among many of making an argument. In that book, I also argued that theoretical writing had become similar to quantitative methodology in its compulsive reliance on a mystifying, self-elevating technical apparatus. Suffering from science envy, theorists work overtime to lard their work with parenthetical citation sausages that disrupt reading and authorize the argument being advanced. Although theorists should be able to cite others' work and to deploy technical language, just as people should be able to use quantitative methods and their ensemble of figural strategies, I contend that theory, like science, should be essayed—that is, composed with an ear open to its own undecidability and inimitability. As such, then, theorists would attempt to empower readers with a certain literary competence just as they scrupulously edit out compulsive usages of obscurantist technical language. As an essayed text, theory might aspire to publicity, but an erudite, edified publicity in which citizens can engage with complex arguments and not consume civic discourse reduced to the level of sitcoms and tabloid newspapers.

This is a delicate balance indeed. My oeuvre in its early stages argued for, but did not sufficiently attain, this balance, instead erring on the side of complexity and allusion. In part this was a purposeful way to deal with the banalization of theoretical language at the hands of Anglo-American empiricists, for whom theory has become largely an exercise in hypothesis testing. In part this was a way to resist the co-optation of renegade discourses like Marxism and feminism. In my more recent work, like *Reading Science* and *The Decline of Discourse*, I have shifted the balance toward a more public vernacular, albeit, as I just said, not a vernacular that makes many concessions to the quotidian. I firmly believe that any reasonably well-educated person can read Bloom's (1987) *Closing of the American Mind*, Jacoby's (1987) *Last Intellectuals*, and my own (1990) *Decline of Discourse*. This book is not an easy read for people unfamiliar with the theoretical sources under discussion. And yet one can move back and forth between my argument here, relying in part on my citations, and secondary sources that explain postmodernism, critical theory, and feminist theory (e.g., Agger 1991: pp. 19–42). It is politically important that theory neither pander nor reduce itself to pedestrian usage. This is the sense of my call for theory as a challenging public essay.

TOTALITY, RELATIONALITY, TRANSFORMATIONALITY

I defend my notion of production over reproduction as the axial logic of civilization in terms of the rhetorical work it can do. That is, it is a flexible and wide-ranging literary strategy allowing one to attack a whole host of problems. In particular, my essay of critical theory embraces *totality*, embodies *relationality*, and suggests *transformationality*. In these senses, it is superior to, while incorporating, other theoretical logics such as the logic of capital (Marx), reification (Lukacs), domination (Marcuse, Adorno, Horkheimer), distorted communication (Habermas), and male supremacy (feminism). Although my notion of the domination of production over reproduction builds on these traditions, it goes beyond them by stressing totality, relationality, and transformationality in ways that the other theories do not. This does not mean that this trinity of terms can solve every problem, nor that this approach can be summarized tersely, in a single formulation or even whole book. Rather, it means that they are valences, themes, tenors, modalities, and moments of my oeuvre, which continues to unfold here. One might call them deep structures of my version of critical theory, although I am also arguing that they have surface importance, too.

The production/reproduction logic is totalizing in the sense that it explains all modernist dominations, from class to gender and race. It is relational in the sense that it well understands, with Hegel and Marx, that domination happens relationally, between people and among groups. Those who dwell within the realm of the merely reproductive, albeit as secret producers, are "other" to those who occupy the realm of production and produce these dualities as ideology in the first place. The production/reproduction logic is also transformational in the sense that it suggests a dynamic process whereby reproducers recognize that they are in fact producers and thus mobilize themselves to wrest both discourse and material power from those who have heretofore arrogated privilege to themselves. In other words, the production/reproduction hierarchy always contains the potential for its deconstruction via coming to consciousness, new public discourse, and organized social movements.

These are advantages of the production-over-reproduction format. This is not to deny that other theories of domination are also totalizing, relational, and transformational but only to suggest that my critique of the hierarchy of value over alleged nonvalue has greater intellectual and political advantage. Again, this raises the issue of whether utility is equivalent to truth, an issue that needs to be addressed forthrightly. Many empirical social scientists attempt to assess explanatory validity in terms of methodological techniques, typically quantitative in nature. Thus, two paradigms, like Marxism and structural functionalism, might be reduced to operational indicators such that the theories can be compared in terms of the amount of what methodologists call "variance" each theory can explain. But this conveniently forgets what I said in the preceding section about the rhetorical, hence undecidable, nature of methodology. Technical pyrotechnics cannot solve intellectual disputes; they merely clarify the grounds on which they take place. No amount of data, nor their statistical manipulation, can objectively demonstrate the superiority of Marxism over feminism or vice versa. Data are simply a text, a canvas on which the researcher imprints her or his meaning, which, as Derrida indicates, is undecidable in terms of other systems of meaning.

Even my notion that the production/reproduction motif does more work than other frameworks for analyzing domination threatens to substitute a productivist vocabulary—*more work*—for a methodological one (" . . . explains more variance . . . "). *More work* is simply shorthand for my own conception of intellectual and political versatility, which of course is framed by what I view as legitimate work. One can explain lots of things using a neoclassical economic framework, or the newfangled rational-choice theory. A critical theorist would view these explanations as illegitimate, or the problems explained as nonproblems. We necessarily frame our notion of validity circularly, in terms of how we construct the social world theoretically. This is not to endorse or accept relativism because, with Jameson, I believe that we can and must transcode theoretical logics into each other, thus enriching our own versions through dialogue.

This notion of dialogue is not premised on Mill's liberal notion of the marketplace of ideas or even on Habermas's notion of the power of the strongest argument but on the premise that public discourse is good insofar as it creates community, which in turn humbles as well as nurtures individuals. Hegel and Marx accepted this Greek notion, albeit in very different ways. This is the problem with Derrida. The undecidability of texts is taken as license for political relativity, which in turn is translated into neoliberal pluralism, precisely the framework of what earlier I called difference theory. But I view undecidability as an occasion for public talk and not the retreat of people and groups into incommensurable subject positions, from which they talk in their own "voices." Alternatively, perspectivity can make way for a politics of public discourse that eschews pluralism without denying the evident plurality of numerous existing language games and subject positions.

It is very difficult to relinquish the positivist notion that public speech will allow us to arrive at a singular stable truth. For the Greeks, politics was good in itself, helping us understand our differences (here, different theoretical logics), learn from each other, and buffer our mortal aloneness. The notion that politics is good (see Arendt 1958) is so far from contemporary experience that one must vigorously defend the idea that public discourse is redemptive. After Watergate, politics is seen by most as venal to the point of postmodern absurdity. Ross Perot was the quintessential postmodern political candidate in this sense. But a postmodern notion of the political need not endorse postpolitical assumptions about the failure of public discourse. Indeed, my oeuvre has tried to demonstrate the possibilities of a postmodern public life that is neither cynical nor corrupt. This postmodern notion of publicity is distinguished by its celebration of dialogue and textuality, precisely what Barthes must have meant by the pleasure of the text.

Again, it is important to disentangle questions of validity from positivist strictures about presuppositionless representation, which require validity to be evaluated without reference to their theoretical frames, indeed, which disqualify the very notion of theoretical framing. It is equally important to avoid the anti-Archimedean relativism of postmodernism. Although I endorse the notion of textual playfulness, this is not a subjective literary attitude as much as a necessary feature of undecidable texts and oeuvres that necessarily elude interpretive representation, precisely the connection between the positivist philosophy of science and the objectivist New Criticism (see Fekete 1978). It is not so much that the author plays as that the text exhibits characteristics that one might describe as playful, polyvocal, pluralizing, and perspectival. In this, the text does not give up validity but requires us to evaluate validity in nonpositivist terms, whether these are summarized in notions such as "the work theories can do" or "the way in which theory changes the world" (viz., the eleventh thesis on Feuerbach). One might describe textual playfulness as the extent to which the text acknowledges that its validity is conditioned by its own theoretical logic as well as by readings, resulting in an intellectual circularity that need not lead to nihilist conclusions. Indeed, critical theory should not be viewed purely as an occasion for literary self-expression but also as a contribution to comprehensive social analysis. In no way are these contradictory or incompatible goals.

Chapter Five

Critical Theory and Everyday Life 1: Against Economism

My preceding chapter suggests a unified theoretical practice combining what pass for the autonomous traditions of German critical theory, feminist theory, and New French Theory, or postmodernism. This chapter is, first, an exercise in transcoding these three logics of domination into a common theoretical logic that stands opposed to Marxian economism. Second, it develops strategies of resistance and reconstruction grounded in this unifying transcoding of a feminist postmodern critical theory.

TRANSCODING THE LOGICS OF DOMINATION

The critique of the domination of production over reproduction, discussed in the preceding chapter, suggests the valorization of reproduction as productive. In the following section of this chapter, I discuss the way in which a transcoded version of postmodernism valorizes and thus liberates the imagination, which is conceived as a literary actor, unleashing it from the quotidian and empowering it to create a nonmodernist philosophy of history and new discursive practices appropriate to it. I then turn to a discussion of how a transcoded feminism valorizes and thus liberates both the body and domestic labor, unleashing it from the male-supremacist sexual division of labor. In the final section, I discuss how a transcoded critical theory valorizes and thus liberates the popular, creating a "high" culture from the ground up, thus enhancing public discourse and community. I discuss the valorization process with respect to these three theoretical transcodings, but I stop short of offering blueprints of new social movements conducted in their name. Although that work is crucial, it requires thorough treatments by students of political sociology. For the most part, though, even the most sophisticated new social movement theorists and analysts (including those deriving from Habermas) do not have an adequate theoretical understanding of how these social movements depend on what I am calling the valorization of reproduction as their guiding theoretical and political logic.

These three theoretical transcodings produce a unified version of critical theory that aspires to global explanation. Nevertheless, although they can be transcoded or translated into an overarching theoretical logic, I am treating them here as if they are more or less distinctive traditions, with rather different topical perspectives. My argument is that an effective transcoding of postmodernism, feminism, and German critical theory will produce a common theoretical logic, which can be applied in the three realms addressed by these three perspectives—the imagination or philosophy of history (postmodernism), the body and domestic labor (feminism), and popular culture (the Frankfurt School). Although I argue for theoretical unification, having established their common theoretical logic, I would deploy these similarly transcoded theoretical perspectives in different venues, recognizing that some theoretical division of labor is useful in fast capitalism. That is, the transcoding of postmodernism, feminism, and German critical theory suggests that they have different emphases but *not* different theoretical logics. By arguing the commonality of their theoretical logics, I suggest their political complementarity, hence ending the territoriality dividing their proponents.

In the next chapter, I address the issue of whether men can be feminists and write feminist theory. I insist that they can be feminists and write feminist theory once feminism has been transcoded into a theory addressing all hierarchies of production over reproduction. I have already challenged the notion that feminism is distinctively by or about women, although on the surface women are the obvious subjects and objects of feminism since they are primary reproducers in all modernist social systems. I need to spend time on the question of men and feminism because the influence of postmodern feminism has been sufficiently strong to raise questions about whether men can hear or use the so-called woman's voice. Just as I have already argued that the text is a woman—a metaphorical and material reproducer—so will I contend that certain men are women, risking the simplifications accompanying this identification.

My transcodings of these three logics of domination link up with everyday life by opposing an economism that has little patience for the politics of everyday life, having restricted itself to purely structural analysis. Postmodernism, feminism, and critical theory all trace domination downward to everyday life and delineate strategies of critique and resistance grounded in the lifeworld. This focus on everyday life is crucial for critical theory, although critical theory should not fetishize the politics of subjectivity but must instead link everyday life and political economy through an intermediate mode of theorizing.

A unified theoretical logic appears oxymoronic by suggesting both that domination pervades everyday life (e.g., Marcuse's 1964 *One-Dimensional Man*) *and* that there are ample, if sometimes disguised, emancipatory opportunities available. I see no contradiction whatsoever between a structural theory of hegemony and a populist theory of counterhegemony, a balance attempted, if not completely attained, by the proponents of the Birmingham School's cultural studies (e.g., see Hall 1980a, 1980b, 1988; Willis 1977, 1978). The problem with economism—for example, Althusser's notion of history without a subject—is that it reproduces the very condition of powerlessness that it bemoans. It does this through positivist literary strategies that turn history into a text of necessity representing iron laws, albeit socialist and not capitalist. Marxian economism fails to hasten the social change that its own normative critique of capitalism implies. Determinism does not extricate us from the social text of ontology, whether religion or revolution, but in fact makes that text more impregnable.

Derrida suggests that every reading strongly rewrites texts. It is easy to put a left-wing spin on Derrida's claim in this regard: People are empowered, and empower themselves, to rescript the social texts of acquiescence and adjustment enmeshing all of us in a seemingly intractable everyday life. These social texts include traditional ideologies like religion and economic theory and contemporary discourses like education, science, architecture, television, movies, and newspapers. I have argued in *Fast Capitalism* that it is difficult to identify these social texts because they have been dispersed into the sentient environment, zipping by us and thus insinuating themselves into our interior and exterior worlds. It is one of the missions of the critique of ideology, enriched by postmodern discourse theory, to identify and then deconstruct these enmeshing social texts, both disqualifying the frozen worlds they recommend—the quotidian as we know it—and writing new ones.

In this sense, the critique of ideology pursues a deconstructive strategy of consciousness-raising, urging readers to become writers and hence public citizens. Inasmuch as Derrida notes that readers are *already* writers (but frequently do not know it), this sort of literary empowering is not as unlikely as it sounds. It moves the critical theory of the Frankfurt School a significant step beyond Adorno's pessimism, expressed amply in *Negative Dialectics* and *Minima Moralia*. Adorno and his Frankfurt colleagues did not sufficiently understand ideology as a discursive practice and hence they did not approach ideology critique as a deconstructive activity. For this reason, they arrived at the same fatalistic impasse as the economistic Marxists they rightly criticized. The Frankfurt School's critique of domination suggested no exits apart from the aphoristic, allusive activity of aesthetic resistance. But, as I have noted elsewhere, Schoenberg is hardly a vital source of counterhegemonic energy or insight today, if he ever was.

The Frankfurt theorists were pessimistic about the possibilities of social change not for metaphysical reasons but on empirical grounds. The "one-dimensional" society (Marcuse 1964) appeared impenetrable by critique or action. As prescient as the Frankfurt theorists were about the administered society that was to emerge after World War II, when liberalism mixed with fascism, they lacked a sufficient understanding of the negativity produced by a social order rooted in deep structural contradictions. The postulate of capitalism's eternal resilience and co-opting powers is not supportable, given the rampant anomie, alienation, and anxiety today. It would not take much for these aspects of discontent to boil over into bottom-up transformational activities, given a certain level of public understanding about the structural causes of their malaise. Unfortunately, the decline of discourse (see Agger 1990) causes the rate of public intelligence to decline still further (see Jacoby 1976), hence reproducing domination.

Critical theory requires postmodernism to liberate the imagination about historical possibilities and then to formulate discourse/practices that break through the oppressive quotidian. This is not to say that most New French Theorists have very vivid political imaginations or agendas. Most of them take their political bearings from the rejection of Marxism, which, as I have argued above, only repeats the neoconservative proclamation of the end of ideology (see Bell 1960). Domination is not seamless, especially where it can be decoded as a set of everyday discursive practices. Once we transcode postmodernism into a version of critical theory—that is, once we give it a certain transformational political agenda—we can enrich the critique of domination with discourse-theoretic resources that highlight the existing negativity, and hence potential for social change, in late capitalism.

In some ways, Foucault understood this better than Adorno, who abandoned the possibility of radical social change in light of his acute understanding of how capitalism both colonizes the lifeworld, in Habermas's terms, and co-opts dissent and critique. I do not dispute Adorno's analysis on the evidence. I simply suggest that his reading of oppositional and transformational possibilities was overly monochromatic because he lacked sufficient appreciation of the literary character of ideology and domination today, which makes rebellious readings and writings possible. Foucault's reading of social texts, exemplified in works like *Discipline and Punish*, adds a utopian dimension to Adorno's work via discourse theory, thus giving critical theory significant political momentum at a time when the ideological critique of texts appears to have lost its bearing in fast capitalism.

Slater's (1977) rejection of Frankfurt theory as accommodationist is misdirected. Economism is accommodationism—secret scientism—which cancels both agency and imagination. The Frankfurt theorists always conceived of themselves as Marxists, albeit Marxists who opposed economism, which, they argued, subverted the revolutionary opportunities amply available during the Second and Third Internationals. Jacoby's (1981) *Dialectic of Defeat* nicely traces the origins of Western Marxism in the political disappointment of turn-of-the-century European Marxists like Lukacs and the Frankfurt School theorists. Adorno did not blithely choose to subdue his political optimism because he liked to travel first-class, listen to opera, and smoke expensive cigars and hence secretly supported the social order that made this possible. Rather, he felt that the effort to change the world miscarried, as he wrote in *Negative Dialectics*, hence requiring Marxists like him to return to the theoretical drawing board. My only quarrel with Adorno's critical theory is that Adorno, lacking a Derridean discursive foundation, missed resistance amply present in late capitalism, notably in the lifeworld. In Gramsci's terms, Adorno understood hegemony but not counterhegemony, co-optation but not critique.

All of the Western Marxists (see Jay 1984b; Agger 1979) recognized that economism obscures the ground of institutional transformation in everyday life. The Western Marxists maintained that critical theory needs a ground in everyday life in order to make credible the possibility of resistance and reconstruction. Whether or not they explicitly deployed a phenomenological language (as Paci 1972 and Piccone 1971 did), they recognized the importance of everyday life both to explain the surprising survival of capitalism via introjected domination (Marcuse's "surplus repression") and to plot its demise. Horkheimer and Adorno's own culture-industry thesis rested squarely on an appreciation of how domination was reinforced by cultural products and practices that seriously foreshorten people's political imagination and lull them into a narcotic consumerist stupor, a line of argument extended by Marcuse (1964) in *One-Dimensional Man*.

Everyday life was a necessary construct for critical theorists, whether they used it explicitly or trafficked in synonyms, because it allowed them to capture the important political plasticity of subjectivity and thus both to oppose economism's fatalism and help explain how subjectivity has been harnessed to the preservation of late capitalism, hence vitiating Marx's nineteenth-century prophesy of its demise. Marcuse, Habermas, Sartre, Merleau-Ponty, Paci, and Piccone used concepts of subjectivity and everyday life to indicate the indomitability of desire as well as the plasticity of human needs that prolong the system—for example, Marcuse's (1964) famous notion of false needs, which has drawn so much critical fire for its apparent Archimedeanism. Marcuse in particular adapted a psychoanalytic notion of ineradicable subjectivity as a basis of his emancipatory hopes, a line of argument begun in (1955) *Eros and Civilization*, which in (1969) *An Essay on Liberation* he tied to the New Left notion of a human being with nonalienated needs who begins to live social change in the immediate present, refusing to postpone liberation.

Unfortunately, Adorno's (1967, 1968) much gloomier Freud did little to shed light on the indomitability of quotidian desire. Adorno did not appreciate the new social movements of the 1960s, which he rejected as irrationalist threats to high-European mandarin-modernist values. Unlike Marcuse, he and Horkheimer thought that the counterculture was *against* culture, hence dangerously regressive. He exaggerated his critique largely because he felt that reason had been betrayed by the civilization erected in its name. There are real differences in the ways that the Frankfurt theorists deployed the concepts of subjectivity and everyday life in order to explain the new depths of domination in a malleable subjectivity *and* to suggest lifeworld-grounded strategies of opposition. Adorno is at one extreme, rejecting the possibility of ground-up social change, Marcuse at the other, celebrating the New Left as the harbinger of a reconstructed lifeworld and democratic social movements (even though by 1978, the year of publication of Marcuse's *Aesthetic Dimension*, he had largely come around to Adorno's monochromatic view of domination).

All of the Western Marxists, including Lukacs and the Frankfurt theorists, opposed the economistic notion of history without a subject. Subjectivity is a crucial political factor in late capitalism, the new battleground of class, gender, and race struggles. This is exactly the same point made by feminists, who regard the personal as political. Interestingly, feminists have better connected the politics of everyday life with social and political movements in the public sphere (e.g., abortion rights) than have critical theorists, who appeared to give up on mass political movements as a means of transformation. Habermas (e.g., his 1975 *Legitimation Crisis*) is a notable exception, especially where he has argued that economic conflicts in late capitalism are increasingly displaced into the political sphere. Habermas has extended this line of argument in his theory of new social movements, which, on the surface at least, appears to link up with feminist theories in a host of compatible ways (in spite of Fraser's well-taken 1989 critique). Habermas, in *The Theory of Communicative Action* (1984, 1987b), explicitly returns to the language of phenomenology in his system/lifeworld motif, giving added impetus to a lifeworld-grounded version of critical theory.

Economism fails, therefore, on two scores. First, it neglects the role of subjective and intersubjective agency in social change, preferring to model change on the alleged laws of the physical sciences. Second, it does not understand domination in contemporary terms, clinging to an outmoded version of Marxism that does not theorize the new depths to which domination has sunk in late capitalism (e.g., as addressed by Marcuse's 1955 concept of surplus repression). Economism is the basis of what many call orthodox Marxism, a version of Marxism that repeats literal Marx, thus failing to adapt him to contemporary circumstances. The best antidote to economism is an appreciation of the cultural and gendered politics of everyday life, precisely the contributions of Western Marxists and feminists, respectively. But, as I said with respect to Adorno, a lifeworld-grounded critical theory need not be cheerfully optimistic about bottom-up social change, especially since it appreciates the plasticity and thus heteronomy of subjectivity in late capitalism (as Lasch argues in his 1984 *Minimal Self* and as Jacoby argues in his 1975 *Social Amnesia*).

The issue of whether a lifeworld-grounded critical theory should emphasize domination or the indomitability of the subject ought to be resolved entirely on empirical grounds (if not with reference to positivist notions and standards of evidence). During the 1960s, Marcuse had some reason to believe that lifeworld-grounded social change was occurring in the United States. College students successfully stopped the war in Vietnam and brought about the resignation of President Johnson. The civil rights movement won important gains for African-Americans, as the women's movement did for women. The counterculture developed a cultural politics that offered striking alternatives to bourgeois modernism, even if the counterculture was quickly commodified and metabolized by the culture industry, as Marcuse pointed out in his 1972 *Counterrevolution and Revolt*. (Read Marcuse's exuberant *Essay on Liberation* just before viewing Oliver Stone's movie *The Doors* for a striking juxtaposition of positive and negative appreciations of the social movements and cultural politics of the 1960s, both having some validity. Perhaps the best account is Gitlin's 1987 *The Sixties: Years of Hope, Days of Rage*, written from the perspective of an erstwhile New Leftist and now proponent of cultural studies.)

Ultimately, a transcoded critical theory needs to emphasize both lifeworld-grounded domination and bottom-up insurgency. It is important that these inflections not be arrived at a priori but rather through careful empirical analysis. It is difficult to escape the impression that Adorno's critique of metaphysics was metaphysical in its own right, lacking the empirical nuance necessary to achieve theoretical apperception according to which we can view people as at once heteronomous and autonomous. Although Adorno's biting critique of affirmative culture is compelling, critical theory must get beyond its Adornoian phase and phrasings. Unfortunately, although Habermas is to be praised for his thoroughgoing reconstruction of historical materialism as communication theory as well as for his lifeworld grounding of critical theory, he regresses behind the original Frankfurt emancipatory agenda in crucial ways and also lacks a sufficient grounding in discourse theory to make good sense of the circuitries and structures of what he calls communication. I conceive of my project here as a feminization and narrativization of Habermas's otherwise imaginative reformulation of historical materialism.

In the next three sections of this chapter, I outline the substantive contributions of transcoded postmodernism, feminism, and Frankfurt theory to a singular version of critical theory. This singular version will be catholic enough to retain nuances of difference as well as an intellectual division of labor. I realize that transcoding feminism, postmodernism, and critical theory simplifies. I am convinced, however, that these three theories are transcodable because they all address the hierarchy of value over the allegedly valueless. Nevertheless, in transcoding these theories I want to retain certain discursive differences among them in order to preserve important aspects of their identities. Whereas in the preceding chapter I outlined the general theoretical logic of a postmodern feminist critical theory, here I want to differentiate the respective contributions of postmodernism, feminism, and German critical theory to a singular theoretical logic. It is possible to read these three theories as *both* different *and* the same, thus preserving their vital autonomy as well as emphasizing their common project.

POSTMODERNISM AND THE DISCOURSE OF IMAGINATION

As I discussed in Chapter 2, New French Theory offers critical theory a discourse-theoretic basis for ideology critique, reading what Baudrillard (1983) calls simulations as disempowering social texts. As such, New French Theory offers critical theory a discourse of imagination that liberates political and social theorizing from the stranglehold of capitalist modernity. This depends entirely on the transcoding of postmodernism into a critical social theory that does not celebrate the present but instead challenges it as insufficient—what Marx originally called prehistory. Postmodernity needs to be conceived as a qualitative break with capitalist modernity, the articulation of which is the responsibility of theorists who not only criticize present societal scenarios but also create new ones.

This may appear oxymoronic at first glance: a postmodernism that endorses political vision and utopian speculation? More cynical postmodernisms reject politics as a legitimate venue of meaning, refuting the venality of politicians with a certain cosmopolitan irony (see Agger 1992b). This is the commodified postmodernism of popular culture, fashion, architecture, and post-Marxist social theorizing. Above, I identified a renegade postmodernism, as Huyssen (1986) has done, which rejects modernity as a capitalist project, instead arguing for an authentic actualization of the Enlightenment through a postmodern break with modernity and modernist social theory. This version reads Marx as postmodern in his deconstructive accounts of money and power in *Capital* and in his antimodernist utopianizing in the *Economic and Philosophical Manuscripts*.

In this regard, there are important postmodern themes evident in Frankfurt theory. Marcuse's (1964) *One-Dimensional Man* calls for critical and utopian thinking in order to overcome stultifying one-dimensionality. In *Reason and Revolution* (1960) he calls this negative thinking, which embodies both critique and rearticulation. More than the other Frankfurt theorists, Marcuse gave eloquent voice to the utopian agenda of critical theory, which in his view needed to amplify the otherness of a radically different society, to be achieved through negative critique and positive reason. A postmodern Marcusean version of critical theory (see Agger 1992b) can better articulate the ways in which a socialist-feminist postmodernity will differ both institutionally and phenomenologically from the capitalist-modernist society of the spectacle (see Debord 1970).

Above all, postmodernism helps liberate the critical imagination, which gains voice in a new postmodern public discourse of the kind I discussed above. At its best, postmodernism interrogates the smooth continuum of capitalist-modernist "progress," endorsed even by Marx in his socialist progressivism. In debunking the myth of progress, postmodernism suggests more valid concepts, discourses, and practices of progress, qualitatively shifting the terms of discussion from "more" technology and capital to new conceptions of the good life, notably involving a reformulation of discourse and practice within the public sphere.

In this regard postmodernism provides feasible notions of publicity and public life (also see Sennett 1977; Wolfe 1977, 1981, 1989) with which to inform a bottom-up perspective on social change. The Athenian polis and New England town meeting alike can be buttressed by a postmodern notion of the undecidability of all discourse, giving philosophical and literary foundation to the notion that the Good is talk and all talk is good. Of course, this is a thoroughly Greek notion. Habermas notices that a Marxist conception of the Good should involve communicative principles of what he calls ideal speech, thus (e.g., see his 1971 *Knowledge and Human Interests*) protecting Marxism against its own reduction to natural science, which Habermas argues convincingly is vital in order to preserve the possibility of leftist agency.

Postmodernism formulates this concept of the Good discursively, improving on Habermas's own metaphors of communication (e.g., what he calls ideal speech), which are drawn variously from John Stuart Mill and speech-act theory. I agree with Habermas that Marxism needs a concept of publicity with which to orient praxis today as well as to protect critical theory against its own degeneration into social physics. Literary and discursive notions of the undecidability and playfulness of texts do this theoretical work better than Habermas's rather disembodied notions of communicative practice. Perhaps this observation reflects little more than my sympathy for New French Theory, which Habermas (e.g., 1987a) dismisses as young- or neoconservative. But it seems to me that Derridean and Barthesian notions of literary praxis can usefully inform critical-theoretical notions of public praxis once we generalize the postmodern model of the reading and writing of literary texts to the reading and writing of all social texts, from culture and politics to architecture.

Part of the apparent difficulty in politicizing literary theory is that the deconstructive agenda is readily methodologized in the disciplinary contexts of literary departments. There is nothing about deconstruction that requires it to avoid political work, especially if textuality and ideology are increasingly dispersed into the sentient environment of fast capitalism. Postmodern theory can help detect texts—hence, arguments—wherever they are to be found, especially at a time when, as I have argued in *Fast Capitalism*, books do not exist. That is, the traditional distance between reasoned texts and reasonable interpretation cannot be assumed inasmuch as the boundary between text and world fades in mass-mediated postmodern capitalism.

One can easily debunk the postmodern agenda as apolitical, as I have done in Chapter 2 (also see Best and Kellner 1991). Of course, the right indicts postmodernism's leftish political penchant, evidencing their defensiveness when confronted by the demythologizing stance of Derrideanism. Deconstruction is increasingly blamed (D'Souza is notable here) for the alleged agenda of political correctness in American universities, discussed earlier in this book. No matter that empirical work in the sociology of higher education (see Lewis and Altbach 1992) has revealed the political-correctness movement to be largely an invention of the paranoid right, documenting few instances of the left's political encroachment on intellectual autonomy. Bloom (1987) blames deconstructors as well as erstwhile New Leftists supposedly inspired by Nietzsche and Heidegger for the political corruption of the university, railing especially against the moral relativism supposedly implied by Derrideans.

There are no "great" or timeless books that require great or timeless exegeses. Books have as many writers as readers. The neoconservative assault on deconstruction's political absolutism misrepresents the Derridean text to the point of absurdity. Derrida makes all orthodoxies impossible, recognizing that no exegesis fails to change the original text's direction of meaning. This is not to argue for the abandonment of all values but only to suggest that one should be suspicious of political and moral absolutes. The deconstructive critique of orthodoxy is extremely useful at a time when cant gathers momentum and true believers flourish everywhere. If anything, I think that deconstructors need to take a more tenacious political stance, albeit recognizing that no text can settle arguments absolutely, given its undecidability.

Deconstruction becomes critical social and political theory when transcoded into a critique of the hierarchy of modernity over premodernity and postmodernity, according to the framework which I established in the preceding chapter. Postmodernism can redeem the open possibilities of the future in much the way that French existential Marxists like Merleau-Ponty, Sartre, and Beauvoir did. As Merleau-Ponty (1964a: pp. 81) suggested, "the date of the revolution [is] written on no wall nor in any metaphysical heaven." Sartre suggested that politics is a project to be chosen deliberately as a way of dealing with the meaninglessness of things. Following from but going beyond Nietzsche, this leftist version of existentialism surpassed nihilism by accepting the moral imperative to eradicate oppression in all its forms. At the same time, these left existentialists debunked all orthodoxies, especially that of modernist Marxism, by suggesting that the future cannot be preordained politically. The problem with capitalist modernism, according to both Foucault and Merleau-Ponty, is that its teleological optimism precludes the autonomous agency necessary to bring about a better world. In Sartrean terms, economism is bad faith.

There are important parallels between this postwar existential Marxism (see Poster 1975) and postmodernism. Both opposed leftist eschatology, just as both accepted the desperate risk and abundant challenge of liberation. Merleau-Ponty's stylish essays suggest some of the playfulness of Derrida and Barthes, even though he was more self-consciously political than the later postmodernists. Merleau-Ponty and Sartre need less transcoding to become critical theorists; indeed, Merleau-Ponty was the first person to use the term *Western Marxism* in order to describe his political project.

All of these theorists, from Merleau-Ponty and Sartre to Derrida and Foucault, derive from Nietzsche's and Heidegger's critique of the Enlightenment as mythological, which fueled their critique of modernity. The closer these particular theorists have been to Marxism, the less of the modernist project they jettisoned, notably the commitment to reason, justice, equality, and truth. It is clear that this critique of the Enlightenment is closely paralleled in Horkheimer and Adorno's (1972) *Dialectic of Enlightenment*, which is hardly a political tract in the ordinary sense. I maintain that one can develop a Marxist appreciation of Nietzsche, a stance that positions itself between the Enlightenment's catastrophic hubris and the antipolitical relativism of Heideggerians, which segued into postmodernism. I do not think that this project of a Nietzschean Marxism requires yet more Nietzsche monographs but a serious rethinking of how one can combine the critiques of positivist mythology and ideology with a positive political program, which rests here on what might be called the discourse of imagination. I find both New and "old" French Theory much more energizing in this philosophical-political project than I do Habermas's rather unreconstructed commitment to modernity and modernism in *The Theory of Communicative Action*. Habermas simply is not ambivalent enough in his defense of rationality, which rests on the transformation of the paradigm of consciousness into the paradigm of communication. Numerous critics have argued correctly that Habermas's faith in ideal speech and undistorted communication raises the old problems of the transparency of meaning and language that were first addressed by Nietzsche.

Nietzsche is no solution, only an opening to a politicized postmodernism, which parallels both the Parisian left-existentialists and the Frankfurt School. Nietzsche humbles Marxist Prometheanism but does not necessarily require the abandonment of political and social progressivism—what Habermas calls new social movements. A transcoded postmodernism liberates political imagination from capitalist modernism and helps ground emancipatory practice firmly in the lifeworld, recognizing that the Enlightenment's social physics must be challenged at the level of subjective and intersubjective agency. People must learn (teach themselves!) how to talk about and thus participate in the creation of a new polity in which democratic public discourse helps dehegemonize hierarchies of all sorts. In particular, there needs to be a lifeworld-grounded political discourse that avoids eschatology and hence mechanism and, at the same time, reinvents the vocabulary of social change in ways not beholden to modernist images of "more" technology, power, domination of nature.

It is enormously difficult today to imagine that Nietzsche's dystopian critique of civilization could be transcoded into a positive critical theory. As the most fundamental critic of the Enlightenment, Nietzsche remains an important figure, much as Marx remains the most important critic of Western metaphysics. We must retain Nietzsche's radical transvaluation of all values while preserving Marx's sense of autonomous political agency and his vision of total social change. Of course, Nietzsche probably would have disdained Marx, even made him the object of book-length condemnation, much as he ridiculed Socrates in *The Birth of Tragedy*. It is futile to read Marxism into him in the sense that we treat texts like *Beyond Good and Evil* and *Thus Spake Zarathustra* as revolutionary calls to arms. Everything Nietzsche stood for indicated an aversion to politics as the epitome of colossally misguided hubris.

Nevertheless, there is a radical and postmodern Nietzsche (see Deleuze and Guattari 1977). New French Theory has made good use of Nietzsche, who also inspired Adorno. Nietzsche is important here because he demonstrates the possibility of a radical critique of the Enlightenment so fundamental as to show us a route beyond capitalist modernity and its stunning philosophical intention to conquer uncertainty and master external otherness. But Nietzsche did not simply abandon science and enlightenment as objective possibilities. Nietzsche authored the notion of a playful science, which inspired Marcuse in *Eros and Civilization* (1955) and later in *An Essay on Liberation* (1969). This rhetorical and cognitive playfulness closely resembles many of Derrida's strictures about undecidability, difference, and differal in language, again suggesting a certain constructive parallel between critical theory and postmodernism.

Nietzsche meets Marx on the ground of the discourse of imagination. Nietzsche shows that there is no way out of, or beyond, discourse, no Archimedean posture from which to transvalue all values, which are, in Derrida's terms, inherently undecidable. There is only a relentless interrogation, a perpetual negativity, which scrutinizes all claims for their embedded ontological assumptions, starting dialogues and hence building community around the search for the Good. Marx adds to Nietzsche's deconstruction of Archimedean values the notion that one can imagine and work toward decent social, political, and economic arrangements even as one accepts the corrigibility of all emancipatory theories and social movements. Although Marx was far too close to Enlightenment hubris for a Nietzschean's taste, Marx's dialectical utopianism and Nietzsche's civilizational ironism are compatible, especially when they are transcoded into a positive as well as negative critical theory.

Adorno (1973a) wrote *Negative Dialectics* because he thought that Marxism had gone too far down the road toward an Archimedean and hence authoritarian concept of social change. In Adorno's terms, Marxism had become an identity theory, accepting the Promethean notion of a conquering subjectivity characteristic of the Enlightenment and leading to all manner of barbarism in the meantime. Adorno identified the conquest of otherness by an arrogant collective or personal subject as the centerpiece of his critique of civilization. It is impossible to imagine Adorno's studies of authoritarianism (e.g., see Adorno et al. 1950) without a Nietzschean influence, which gave Adorno's theoretical as well as empirical pursuits a tragic foreboding and circumspection. Nevertheless, *Negative Dialectics* has lost some of its context in postmodern capitalism, when a totalizing critical theory needs to be revived especially now that communism has collapsed. Who among us prophesies an international socialist revolution? Such talk is laughed out of court by world-weary postmodernists, who could use a dose of Marx to supplement their inveterate Nietzscheanism and Derrideanism. This is precisely why postmodernism needs to be transcoded into critical theory, albeit without losing Nietzsche's critique of Enlightenment hubris, which is so vital in order to humble every effort at radical social reconstruction.

FEMINISM AND THE VALORIZATION OF REPRODUCTION

As I argued in the preceding chapter, my transcoding of critical theory into a generic critique of the hierarchy of production over reproduction borrows unashamedly from the language of feminist theory, which has long attempted to politicize and economize the sphere of reproduction as a site of value in patriarchal capitalism. *Reproduction produces*. The chores millennially assigned women in the prevailing sexual division of labor, from compulsory heterosexuality, housework, and childcare to poorly paid pink-collar labor, all belong to the sphere of what is taken to be reproduction by both bourgeois economists and Marxists, all of whom devalue the work that women do in order to reduce or altogether deny their wages.

In my concluding chapter I will suggest new ways to think about the transcoding of feminism and Marxism that salve territorial anxieties about theoretical and political encroachment. I pose and answer the question about whether men legitimately can write feminist theory (see Connell 1987; Agger 1989a). Here, I want to suggest the particular substantive contribution that a transcoded feminism can make to general critical theory in terms of its liberation of the theory and practice of reproduction. In all sorts of crucial ways, feminist theory draws attention to the millennial hierarchies of value over the devalued reflected in my overall theoretical logic, hence going far beyond the politics of gender as ordinarily construed by liberal feminists. By understanding the generic logic of the domination by men of women, and hence reproduction by production, we can understand the domination of labor by capital, colored by white, South by North, East by West, nature by society, popular culture by mandarin culture. I maintain that capitalism is an instance of production's epochal domination of reproduction, thus suggesting that feminism was Marxist long before Marx! Indeed, Marx's critique of the logic of capital is only a relatively recent example of how a transcoded critical theory grounded in the production/reproduction motif has done good intellectual and political work.

A transcoded feminism must include but not limit itself to the politics of gender and sexuality. Although a theory of gender domination is crucial to understanding the particular episodes of male supremacy that wreak havoc with women's lives today, it needs to show that it can do extra work in realms ordinarily understood to be outside of or beyond gender politics, like all of the other venues I just mentioned. Feminism must be transcoded into a generic theory and critique of reproduction, hence liberating concepts and practices of reproduction to become productive in their own right. A good example of this, discussed above, is how the socialist-feminist theory of domestic labor shows convincingly that domestic labor does in fact make a substantial, if somewhat indirect, contribution to the production of surplus value, hence requiring Marxists to take account of the housework force as a central factor in radical politics. By valorizing reproduction as secret production, feminism demonstrates that the hierarchy on which male-supremacist civilization rests requires the false premise that men's activities are more valuable than women's activities, a notion theorized by Parsons (1951; Parsons and Bales 1955) in his distinction between male instrumental and female expressive work.

Heterotextuality is the name I have given (see above; and Agger 1989a) to the way in which people discursively reproduce the supposed hierarchy of production over reproduction. Heterotexts ranging from sociological theory to popular culture give literary form to the premise that women's work is necessarily less worthy than that of men, or, generically, that reproduction in its very name is less important than production. Feminism disrupts the discourse and practice of heterotextuality by insisting on the value of activities heretofore relegated to the realm of reproduction, hence both raising consciousness and organizing collective behavior around the theme of valorization.

Heterotexts like the magazine *Cosmopolitan*, *Guess* jeans, and the movie *Fatal Attraction* reproduce the hierarchy of production over reproduction in exactly the way that women are supposed to reproduce the hierarchy of men over women. Women reproduce their bondage to men by reproducing compulsory heterosexuality and the normative male-dominated family, thus positioning themselves subordinately in the sexual division of labor both in domestic and market spheres. There are many heterotexts in fast capitalism—all the discourses, scripts, and mass-mediated spectacles announcing the allegedly ontological hierarchy of value over alleged valuelessness, here men's value over women's value (see Hennessy 1993).

A feminist critical theory valorizes activities subordinated by the discourses and practices of heterotextuality, arguing for their importance. This can begin with a critique of compulsory heterosexuality, which is a major goal of radical feminists who argue that the coupling of women to men almost automatically leads to their subordination in every sphere of their existence. In valorizing the possibility of women-with-women relationships, feminist critique pierces the heterosexual heart of male supremacy, and hence all domination, by understanding sexual orientation as a thoroughly political issue. Although recent researchers trace sexual orientation to biological causes, this does not mean that lesbianism cannot also be viewed as a political practice, especially through the lenses of feminist theory.

The critique of compulsory heterosexuality is extraordinarily relevant for a feminist critical theory since it goes to the core of heterotextuality—the way in which the reproduction of reproduction's subordination to production takes place from the ground up, through the everyday texts that have become our lives. The most intimate and important aspect of what feminists call the personal—sexual orientation—is political in the sense that it helps define the power balance in relationships. A well-regarded study (Blumstein and Schwartz 1983) shows that, unlike straight and gay dyads, lesbian dyads are typically structured in egalitarian ways, especially in decoupling earning power from relational power. In restructuring their personal lives, lesbians begin to restructure power in society at large as well as draw attention to the politics of everyday life, which is now revealed to be very much a contested terrain. Lesbian communities across the United States are distinctive in their commitment to democratic personal and public arrangements, which makes them fundamentally different from couples composed of a man and a woman or two men, who are much more inclined to accept, even endorse, both relational and political hierarchy.

This analysis will be dismissed as an endorsement of lesbian political theory and strategy (see Fuss 1991). I am simply saying that sexual orientation can be political and that it represents an excellent example of ways in which feminists attempt to restructure the power relations of their lifeworlds by resisting male-supremacist heterosexuality as an instance of the more generic notion of heterotextuality (with the text of male supremacy reproducing women's subordinated lives). Perhaps more than any other group, lesbian feminists "live" their political and social theories, connecting everyday choices to larger institutional issues. I would suggest that a great deal of feminist theory, no matter how radical in intent, misses this crucial aspect of the politics of gender and sexuality by sidestepping the politics of sexual orientation as somehow irrelevant to other, more ostensibly political, issues (see Meese 1992). This is especially true now that AIDS has further demonized homosexuals. But lesbian feminists well understand that sexual orientation, because it drives the sexual division of labor and thus a host of sexual-political hierarchies, is the most fundamental dimension of heterotextuality—here, the way in which women reproduce their subordination to men in their intimate lives by marrying them and taking their last names via the text of the marriage contract, hence losing their own liberty and identity.

Must a feminist postmodern critical theory endorse lesbian feminism? At the very least, it would incorporate lesbian-feminist insights into the politics of sexual orientation as a paradigmatic example of the generic logic of lifeworld-grounded hierarchies of value over valuelessness (see Fuss 1991). Here, women have value only in light of their utility for men, an asymmetry that straight women reproduce by coupling with men. Ours is a heterosexist and heterotextist society. It is very difficult to escape the centrifugal pull of discipline and social control. In my own case, I and my partner "had" to get married in order to adopt a child. Interestingly, in most parts of the United States single people can adopt but unmarried cohabitors cannot. The very notion of choice derives from liberalism, frequently exaggerating people's autonomy in the face of daunting social forces that, as structures, take on lives of their own. Thus, although I and my partner wanted to avoid the married state, opposing it on political grounds, our desire to adopt a child contextualized our pure political preferences, which were sacrificed to the unpleasant reality of adoption law.

I am deliberately using the strong discourse of lesbian feminism in order to make my point about the lifeworld grounding of the feminist valorization of reproductive activities as a way of smashing heterotextuality, which I have identified as the civilizational logic of domination. Better than postmodernism and even German critical theory, feminist theory understands the importance of everyday life as a political venue in which production is routinely hierarchized over reproduction as texts like the marriage contract become lives. Feminism recognizes very clearly that *women do this to themselves*, as well as have it done to them by men (who promote marriage and make family law). Reproduction reproduces itself where women make self-defeating "choices," which by definition could have been made differently. Although I just argued against the liberal discourse of choice as an adequate representation of a contextualized autonomy or agency, lesbian feminism draws dramatic attention to the power of feminist subjectivity either to empower itself or to be disempowered (Jay and Glasgow 1990; Hoagland and Penelope 1988). Women who define themselves in terms of their relations to men necessarily lose, and contribute to further losses for other women, who are overwhelmed with the seemingly inescapable everydayness of compulsory heterosexuality and hence submit to the male-supremacist sexual division of labor (see Darty and Potter 1984).

This is abundantly clear when we examine images of lesbians in our society. Dykes (Lesbian Writing and Publishing Collective 1990) are women who are supposedly anti-men, anti-children, anti-family. They are necessarily failures in the marriage marketplace—too unattractive, too strident, too political, too uncompromising to "get" a man. These images run very deep (see Kitzinger 1987). Women university students in my classes regularly deny their feminism, even when they clearly hold a host of feminist views about the family, work, and politics. Feminism is conflated with lesbianism and thus demonized now that the 1960s have run their course and we have returned to an extraordinarily repressive era of sexual politics (see Myron and Bunch 1975). The right has successfully stigmatized the women's movement, capturing both the discourse and agenda of sexual politics in our time. This happens largely by branding feminists as lesbians, a remarkably effective strategy in the AIDS and pro-family era. Every politician must run for office in defense of what is called "family," representing a constellation of values and practices surrounding a heterotextist, male-supremacist version of the politics of gender.

As I remarked earlier, heterosexuality is a particular local example of heterotextuality. Heterosexuality is the fundamental norm constituting gender relationships in our society. Its peculiar discourse involves the objectification and self-objectification of women as libidinal objects for men. Lesbian identity is fundamentally represented by women's refusal to be defined, and to define themselves, in terms of men. Lesbians resist their discursive formulation as objects for men. That is why some lesbians wear closely cropped hair and "mannish" clothes, purposely deobjectifying themselves with respect to the male gaze. This is not to say that all lesbians are lesbian feminists, or that lesbians necessarily eschew traditional modes of self-beautification like makeup. But there are clearly a particular discourse and style of lesbianism in the United States that break with heterosexual/heterotextual norms by valorizing women who shun male-identification as the source of their identities and lives.

Lesbian everyday life, in its absence of heterosexual norms, demonstrates the possibility of ground-up transformational activities that fit the framework of my critical theory of heterotextuality, framed by the production/reproduction hierarchy. Lesbians refuse the lives scripted for them by straight men and male-identified heterosexual women. But they do more than this. They also refuse to be measured by the yardstick of heterosexual culture, insisting that attractiveness-and-utility-to-men is not an adequate standard of women's value as human beings. They insist on a new order of value, which suggests a new order of social being in which women refuse the standards of beauty and nurturance against which they are found wanting by men and male-identified women.

The really important point here is that women must become lesbians in the sense that they refuse to define and adorn themselves in terms of their value to men. This exemplifies a politics of everyday life suggested by my generic critical theory, which holds reproducers at least partly responsible for reproducing their servitude inasmuch as they restrict themselves to roles and lives scripted for them by others who benefit from their subjugation. Short of blaming the victim (Ryan 1971) for her own predicament, this recognizes the transformational opportunities open to any efficacious human being. To be lesbian means to be alive to one's own world-making possibilities, which are not exhausted by heterosexual norms. In this sense, then, anticipating one of the themes of my concluding chapter, men can be lesbians, too—indeed, some are, especially gay men who politicize their own homosexuality in terms of its everyday resistance to heterosexism. It is facile to bio(onto)logize lesbianism, as it is currently fashionable to do, even among feminists who substitute the term *sexual orientation* for the term *sexual preference*, thus suggesting the naturalness of homosexual identity. But some men, too, prefer to live as feminists, which, according to my notion here, means to live as a lesbian—a reproducer who no longer participates in the reproduction of a subjugated gender identity defined in terms of its delectation for others, straight male masters. Importantly, one of the most interesting new social movements is the alliance between gay men and women galvanized by their demand for a more vigilant assault on AIDS, which is both a mortal and discursive threat to gays and straights everywhere and an occasion for the further marginalization of homosexual "others" (see Bristow 1992).

I will stop short of offering a critical theory of AIDS, although I have already noted that AIDS produces a certain homophobic discourse that is enormously important in fueling the neoconservative backlash against alleged sexual permissiveness left over from the 1960s. This spreading homophobia is harnessed in the neoconservative onslaught against rights earned by women, both straight and lesbian, and by gay men. There is a battle taking place over whether the discourse of AIDS should be mainstreamed so as to alert straights to its perils (e.g., the media spectacle of Magic Johnson's affliction with HIV-positive). Although the discursive heterosexualization of AIDS is useful in alerting straights to practice safe sex, this mainstreaming obscures the way in which the punitive discourse of AIDS contributes to the homophobic momentum of neoconservatism, which, as I suggested above in another context, defends "traditional family values" against which homosexuality is constructed as a dreaded (and now fatal) otherness. On the other hand, if the discourse of AIDS is mainstreamed and heterosexualized, the right loses the particular homophobic focus of its own AIDS discourse, which suggests that AIDS—death—is what faggots deserve. Homophobia is central to this neoconservative discourse, for it is a discourse defined by its commitment to heterotextuality, which wants reproducers willingly to reproduce their own victimhood (a paradigmatic example of which is the way women objectify themselves for men).

CRITICAL THEORY FOR AND AGAINST THE POPULAR

The Frankfurt School's particular substantive contribution to a generic critical theory is, on one level, very apparent. Their revision of Marxism, in works like *Dialectic of Enlightenment* and *One-Dimensional Man*, expanded Marx's critique of the logic of capital into a general critique of domination (see Schroyer 1973). I began this book by arguing that critical theory is my central theoretical noun, to be modified by named theories like feminism and postmodernism. I defended critical theory's totalizing tendencies as a necessary framework for emancipatory theory. In particular, Horkheimer and Adorno's (1972) discussion of the relationship between a Promethean civilizational subject, first narrativized by Homer, and objective otherness (nature, Jews, labor), is a central motif in my notion of the domination of production over reproduction, which is the way in which I extend the Frankfurt critique of domination to address topics, notably including women, unforeseen or ignored by them. As well, I make central use of the Frankfurt culture-industry thesis, suggesting that domination in postmodern capitalism is reproduced through an everyday life littered with discourse/practices of adjustment and consumption, which redouble old-fashioned ideological textuality. These original texts of religion and economic theory were susceptible to being deconstructed through rigorous critical work, whereas it is much more difficult to decode the dispersed "texts" of sense and sentience—cities, fashion, media, science.

In another sense, though, the Frankfurt culture-industry thesis does not comport with my own critical theory of heterotextuality, which wants to valorize the devalued activities of millennial otherness. Indeed, a transcoded version of critical theory reverses Horkheimer and Adorno's own hierarchy of mandarin culture over popular culture, thus producing a version of critical theory as cultural studies. The Frankfurt theorists recognized the political importance of mass culture in late capitalism but rejected out of hand the possibility that mass culture could be reconstructed, along with the everyday life it saturates. As I observed in Chapter 2 Adorno's (e.g., 1945, 1954, 1974b) own empirical research on mass culture is fine-grained and informative, showing that he paid careful attention to the culture industry that he and Horkheimer theorized in *Dialectic of Enlightenment*. Indeed, as I indicate in *Cultural Studies as Critical Theory*, the project of cultural studies is simply impossible without the inspirations of both the Marxist sociology of culture (Lukacs, Goldmann) and the Frankfurt School's culture-industry theory. Unfortunately, the Frankfurt theorists could not overcome their own aversion to mass culture sufficiently to formulate alternative modes of quotidian discourse and expression appropriate to a free society. They recognized the hegemonizing function of the culture industry but could not theorize their way around it.

Subsequent students of cultural studies, including the Birmingham School (Hall, Willis), postmodernists (Baudrillard), and feminists (Lauretis, Mulvey), have reformulated the popular, recognizing that cultural counterhegemony could reverse the spin of Hollywood mainstream culture, which, as Horkheimer and Adorno recognized, has become such an important political factor in late capitalism. It is almost as if the Frankfurt theorists threw up their hands in despair once they decamped from Nazi Germany to Los Angeles, where they spent part of their World War II exodus (see Zaret 1992 on the relationship between the sociology of culture and critical theory). The totalizing, commodifying power of MGM led Horkheimer and Adorno (1972) to characterize enlightenment as "mass deception" in postwar capitalism. Nearly everything they wrote about the simulating sweep and scope of mainstream cultural conglomerates has been proven correct. Any version of literary economy, like my (1990) *Decline of Discourse* or Schiller's (1989) *Culture, Inc.*, must reckon with the discursive as well as economic power of the gigantic media outlets that script, and hence reproduce, a certain version of the American way of life through heterotextuality.

What the Frankfurt theorists missed, blinkered by their own high-European mandarinism, was the potential for creating new cultural practices and products at the level of everyday life. These efforts are deliberately positioned outside of the mainstream in order to survive and even thrive. Small presses, journals, magazines, galleries, studios, newspapers, and even television stations harbor counterhegemonists devoted to writing and figuring an alternative quotidian life. There is a vital cultural life off the beaten path, and hence ample political possibilities for creating a populist culture in which cultural producers have much more control over their product, and hence their reception, than on the cultural Main Streets today. The Frankfurt theorists so detested the banalities of American hegemony that they did not credit the possibility that intelligent public citizens could transform the culture from below. For Adorno, there were no unsung Schoenbergs, Becketts, or Kafkas, merely the Muzak of the quotidian, which reduces Beethoven to background noise.

It is imperative that we transcode the Frankfurt theorists' aversion to the popular in light of their own understanding that the popular greatly matters in postmodern capitalism. Postmodern discourse theory can give critical theory a sharper perspective on the deceptive dispersal of texts into the sentient environment, helping them read and rewrite the simulations freezing experience into self-reproducing social fate via the heterotextual. Derrida shows that the popular can be strongly engaged, giving rise to a critical postmodern cultural studies that not only reads but reformulates the culture. Feminists (e.g., Walters 1992) for their part develop a feminist cultural studies grounded in the deconstruction of the male gaze in art and literature. They interpret "against the grain," suggesting that the codes of social control can be cracked if we reauthorize cultural practices and products as the ontological arguments they really are. Adorno knew a great deal about this. He recognized that Hollywood movies, like the *Los Angeles Times* astrology column (1974b), disclose a worldview dedicated to alienated labor and commodity consumption. Yet he could not foresee the deconstructive possibilities of aesthetic and cultural theory (see Adorno 1973b, 1984), which not only reads against the grain but becomes an author-ity itself, a new social text suggesting an alternative lifeworld in which people create beauty, truth, and justice.

In reversing Adorno's disdain for the popular as a ground of oppositional cultural and political projects, we should not transcode critique into apology. Too many cultural studies people celebrate MTV and "Twin Peaks," using the deconstructive method on whatever comes into their interpretive viewfinder. Cultural studies (see Grossberg, Nelson, and Treichler 1992) runs the risk of losing its theoretical and political intent, reifying mass culture where, in fact, it should be deconstructing it politically. There are good examples of a theoretically oriented cultural studies to be found (see Miller 1988; Ryan and Kellner 1988; Luke 1992). These people all steer a careful course between Frankfurt mandarinism, which denounces the popular, and an affirmative cultural-studies program (e.g., the Bowling Green group), which replaces ideology critique with episodic, objectivist readings of the popular. The Bowling Green journal, *Journal of Popular Culture*, is filled with such readings, which have neither theoretical direction nor political impact (see Browne 1989). There is a striking contrast between these pedestrian analyses of Stephen King novels and Adorno's Apollonian music criticism, which treats the relationship between music and society in extremely abstract terms.

Thus, I draw upon the Frankfurt *theory* of the culture industry as a crucial factor in late capitalism, but I reject their mandarin cultural *readings* and *taste*. I do not deny that Kafka's *Castle* may disclose a great deal of value about what a Foucaultdian (e.g., O'Neill 1986) might call the disciplinary society. Yet it is hard to accept Adorno's rejection of popular culture as a possible site of critique and resistance. Ryan and Kellner's (1988) important *Camera Politica* suggests ways of reading mainstream film that neither compromise critical theory's relentless negativity nor view Hollywood's films monochromatically, as unrelieved deception (also see Denzin 1991). Of course, both Ryan and Kellner were New Leftists open to posttraditional modes of radical politics and theory. They came of age politically at a time when it was very difficult not to be affected by the cultural politics of the 1960s.

There are few, if any, Adornoian acolytes in U.S. universities! To derive from Adorno is almost a contradiction in terms, given his own unsparing attitude toward orthodoxy (see Jay 1984a). Amazingly, Adorno's (1984) *Aesthetic Theory* is out of print, suggesting his obsolescence for contemporary students of culture. My effort in this book has been to defend and prolong the legacy of the original Frankfurt theorists, who are responsible for giving a theoretically oriented cultural studies much-needed political direction. Yet we need to transcode critical theory into a perspective on the liberation of the popular that is consistent with its critique of popular culture's narcotizing effects. I submit that we can do extraordinarily useful close readings of culture from an Adornoian perspective if we abandon the disdainful Frankfurt mandarinism, which was largely a product of the Frankfurt theorists' own cultural formation as high-modernist European intellectuals. Miller's (1988) book on television, *Boxed In: The Culture of TV*, comes close to being an Adornoian version of cultural studies, suggesting ways of doing media theory that harness the culture-industry thesis to actual readings of hegemonizing cultural practices. Luke's (1992) *Shows of Force* is also a Frankfurt-inspired reading, although Luke shares my view that Frankfurt cultural theory needs to be inflected with discourse-theoretic phrasings from postmodernism, as his readings of art exhibitions amply demonstrate. In this sense, Luke's transcoding of critical theory into a generic theory of discipline and domination with practical applications is close to my own.

Unfortunately for people of my and Luke's theoretical persuasion, studies like these are relatively rare. Few who pursue cultural studies derive from German critical theory. Virtually all of the theoretically oriented cultural-studies action derives from French theory, especially from Baudrillard, whose profile in North America continues to rise. Kroker's (see Kroker and Cook 1986) journal, *Canadian Journal of Political and Social Theory*, reflects this Baudrillardian agenda, although it began as a more eclectic, if offbeat, theoretical journal. Kroker and Cook's (1986) *Postmodern Scene*, as well as Kroker's Baudrillardian notion of panic (Kroker, Kroker and Cook 1989) as emblematic of our times, reflects the ascendant influence of New French Theory on cultural studies. Baudrillardians are especially touchy about their hero, who functions as a leftish alternative (antidote?) to Marxism, which is disdained by most people who pursue cultural studies (thus fatally ignoring the roots of cultural studies in Lukacs, Goldmann, and the Frankfurt School). Although, as I said above, Baudrillard is not without merit for critical theory, especially his claim that a good deal of our social experience is "simulated" by advertisers and other cultural copywriters, his (1983) exaggerated notion that we now inhabit "hyperreality" regresses behind materialism.

I blame Adorno as much as Baudrillard for the displacement of critical theory's own version of cultural studies. The Germans were too mandarin to bother with the sort of interpretive detail work done by Baudrillardians interested in particular cultural products and practices. This is exactly why we need to transcode critical theory into a critique, not a celebration, of the hierarchy of mandarin culture over mass culture. In no way does this require us to view the popular uncritically. Indeed, a critical theory reformulated as cultural studies relentlessly attacks the dissimulations of quotidian culture as false consciousness's forms of life today. One does not have to go overboard and endorse Jay Leno or Ninja Turtles simply because one takes the popular seriously enough to offer nuanced, differential readings of it. One must, though, distinguish between hegemonic and counterhegemonic cultural practices in a way that debunks ideology, which is now encoded in the various dispersed social texts of fast capitalism, *and* fosters resistance and reconstruction, both of which can sometimes proceed through culture and not in spite of it.

It is simply inconceivable for any theoretically inclined baby boomer to neglect the possibility of cultural critique and enlightenment arising from everyday life. We yuppies are awash in a sea of ink and buried under a mountain of celluloid, to which we contribute our own literary work in the hope of not only making our name but changing the world. Gitlin's (1980) *The Whole World Is Watching* suggests the way in which baby boomers at the Chicago Democratic Convention in 1968 already recognized the transformational power of the media—the same baby boomers whose identities were formed by sitcoms that taught us how to be men, women, and citizens as well as by the broadcast of President Kennedy's assassination, which changed our world in one afternoon.

Cultural studies reflects the intellectual and political interests of academic baby boomers, who have always known to take popular culture seriously. Whether a program of cultural studies can emerge from a latter-day version of critical theory remains to be seen. I believe that it can if critical theory overcomes the cultural preferences and prejudices of its founders. There needs to be a critical theory of television (Kellner 1990; Miller 1988), journalism (Hallin 1985; Rachlin 1988), and advertising (Wernick 1991; Harms and Kellner 1991; Goldman 1994). These topics are not ephemeral but reflect structural developments in capitalism since Marx. For cultural studies people to ignore social and economic structures impoverishes, indeed disqualifies, their appreciations of mass culture, which cannot be abstracted out of the institutional contexts of production, distribution, and reception. Yet the case needs to be made vigorously that Horkheimer and Adorno's theory of the culture industry has enduring relevance today, *especially* where their own cultural taste blocked an applied cultural-studies program. Imagine Adorno devoting critical attention to Guns 'n Roses, *People* magazine, or *Batman*. But an Adorno-inspired cultural studies must engage with the popular at this level, especially if it wants to function politically.

TRANSCODING THE TRANSCODER

My theory of the domination of production over reproduction, which amplifies and organizes postmodern, feminist, and critical-theoretical insights into domination and emancipation, itself must be transcoded lest it become a formulaic structuring device replacing thought. In this book I am suggesting a way to think about the integration, synthesis, and overcoming of three theoretical traditions that address many salient features of postmodern patriarchal capitalism. My transcoding exercises, which resolve their theoretical differences and nuances into a common theoretical logic, are only suggestive. They do not solve intellectual problems definitively but merely suggest new ways of thinking about problems. It is important to remember that transcoding itself is an undecidable activity, in Derridean terms, that needs to incorporate an acknowledgment of its own corrigibility reflexively in order to prevent its ossification or simply sheer wordiness.

We need a totalizing, comprehensive social theory that explains the complexly interrelated world system in terms of a singular theoretical logic, which I have called the domination of reproduction, or heterotextuality. Apparent differences are in fact similar if we look closely enough at what I have termed structural primacy. In particular, German critical theory needs to be infused with discourse-theoretic insights from New French Theory and with sexual-political insights from feminism. I recognize that this infusion necessarily changes all three theories in the process, thus challenging conventional assumptions about their separability. In challenging these assumptions I think we make important theoretical headway. For example, it is important to argue not only that men can be feminists and write feminist theory but that most men in a sense *are* women in that they, too, are oppressed by the hierarchies of value over valuelessness that rob their surplus labor and humanity.

To say that men are women, women are texts, or labor is capital invites scorn by nominalists, positivists, and realists. These conceptual identities are said to oversimplify, just as it might be said that I egregiously conflate postmodernism, feminism, and critical theory. In risking these simplifications, I am trying to reverse the momentum of certain assumptions about theory and practice, a momentum greatly accelerated by the neoliberal political agenda of multiculturalism and its articulation as postmodern difference theory. These assumptions pervade the left: Academics as well as tacticians assume that race, gender, and class are separate realities to which certain agitational interests and factions correspond. Above, I argued against this nominalist approach to social theory where I criticized postmodern difference theory and its academic articulation in the pedagogical politics of multiculturalism. Lest it be said that I "oppose" multiculturalism in the sense of preferring ethnocentrism, one can oppose multiculturalism as a transformational strategy, as well as the neoliberal pluralism that underlies it, without being a racist, sexist, or capitalist. Too many left academics are on the defensive because they fear censure by multiculturalists who accept the inviolability of their own categories and of the reformist strategy deriving from them. Although I have already acknowledged that the right greatly exaggerates the "political correctness" phenomenon on university campuses for their own devious purposes, it behooves the left not to allow slogans to do our own thinking for us, especially when some of these slogans have unfortunate unintended consequences such as the notion of the separability of dominations.

This notion of the separability of dominations, discussed earlier in the context of my comments about the relationship between postmodern Lacanian feminism and the curricular agenda of multiculturalism, is addressed by Russell Jacoby (1992) in his review of a book on political correctness in *The Nation*. This extends a theme unifying Jacoby's oeuvre since his discussion of the politics of subjectivity in his 1975 *Social Amnesia* and continuing through *The Last Intellectuals* (1987). Jacoby's position is very similar to my own in the sense that we both interrogate the nearly universal academic-leftist trinity of class/race/gender for its hidden assumptions about the nature of domination. That is, postmodern difference theorists as well as neoliberals assume that we should allow people occupying separable class, race, and gender fractions to "speak for themselves" in developing both social theory and agitational strategies devised to achieve plurality and equality. This discloses a postmodern difference-theoretic narrativization of suffering according to which people from outside the relevant fraction should not speak "for," or even theorize about, occupants of that fraction, who should instead be encouraged to tell their own "stories" about what ails them. Of course, these are to be Lyotardian small stories and not the universalizing sagas of the Enlightenment and Marx.

In his inimitable fashion, Jacoby attacks both the right for conjuring up a political-correctness conspiracy nearly out of whole cloth in order to suit its own neo-McCarthyist ends and the left for capitulating to neoliberalism and multiculturalism. Like me, Jacoby thinks that we need totalizing social theory in the form of grand narratives in order to comprehend and then transform axial structures of domination. Like me, Jacoby understands his own theoretical agenda to be Western Marxist, heavily influenced by Adorno but rejecting Adorno's totalization of negativity as lacking nuance. As I indicate in *Fast Capitalism* (1989a) and in *The Decline of Discourse* (1990), I owe a great deal to Jacoby's formulation of the decline of the American left in terms of structural forces like the academization and professionalization of critical theory (Jacoby 1987) as well as in terms of the Marxist dialectic of defeat (Jacoby 1981). No optimist, Jacoby nevertheless debunks the postmodernization of left discourse as a betrayal of the transformational aims of Western Marxism, critical theory, and the New Left.

Jacoby formulates the critique of difference-theoretic multiculturalism carefully in order to avoid contributing to the powerful global momentum of neoconservatism, which celebrates the end of communism as if that said anything about the rationality and viability of capitalism. His plague-on-both-your-houses tone, perhaps reflecting deep-seated temperamental characteristics that explain both his and my affinity for Adorno, who was also thoroughly disaffiliated, is a useful rhetorical strategy. It prevents readings of the critique of multiculturalism, with its embedded assumptions about the separability and fractional narrativization of dominations, from being read as reactionary. The critique of multiculturalism can be conducted from the vantage of radicalism, as this book and Jacoby's work demonstrate.

My transcoding of postmodernism applies postmodernism politically in ways rejected by Foucaultdians and Derrideans. I spend so much time on postmodernism because academic left (better, postleft) theory has become so saturated with postmodernist assumptions and formulations. Jacoby in his *Nation* review connects postmodernism to the celebration of the university among leftists, postleftists, and feminists, many of whom have reduced politics to textuality. Postmodernism as a theoretical practice epitomizes what Jacoby in *The Last Intellectuals* called the "academization" of theory. This postmodern academization of intellectual activity reflects not so much the love of texts but a liberal retreat from the political. The fetish of textuality, as I called it in *Fast Capitalism*, endeavors to transcend politics, which, in these dismal times, never appears to lead anywhere anyway.

The postmodern fetish of textuality challenges neither the university as an institution nor the sinecures of the academic leisure class. Jacoby is totally correct that tenured theorists love the university, which nurtures them *and* allows them to feel good about supporting the "voices" of the various incommensurable fractions whom they sponsor under the rubrics of multiculturalism and pluralism. There are now courses and conferences on "American pluralism," enriching the old-fashioned liberal-arts canon neoliberally. Anyone over the age of thirty-five should immediately recognize that pluralism, even more than multiculturalism, is a noun used by cultural hegemonists to define "America" itself, conjuring up images of the Statue of Liberty and Ellis Island. There is absolutely nothing subversive about the word *pluralism*, especially when preceded by the adjective *American*.

Academic neoliberals love a simulated America as well as the university. It is crucial to fight these tendencies, even if this means opposing multiculturalism in the name of real difference, which can only come about if the global totality is restructured (and recognizing that global restructuring requires simultaneous transformations of everyday life—precisely the theme of a feminist critical theory). The risk of opposing difference theory, albeit in the name of real difference—ever an appropriate goal since Marx's *Economic and Philosophical Manuscripts*—is that we fuel the right, not just the left's right. The right is powerful enough not to need the help of a few Jacobys! The people who read *The Nation*, let alone this book, are not the people who script hegemony and reap capital gains. If they have heard of multiculturalism and postmodernism, it is perhaps by reading David Lodge's send-ups of the decon crowd. Dinosaur leftists' books scarcely matter. We must reverse the momentum of post-Marxist, postmodernizing academic neoliberalism at a time when the right benefits from the left both because it affords a target, always the purpose of otherness (see Sartre's 1948 *Anti-Semite and Jew*), and because multiculturalism cools out people on the margins, especially women and ethnic minorities who attend the university. Multiculturalism tells them that *they belong to the American dream*, even when empirical evidence (e.g., Feagin and Sikes 1993; Faludi 1991) suggests otherwise.

A transcoding of my transcoding reveals that I am not, after all, a very literal Marxist. Marx offers guidance, little more. Indeed, to defend oneself for writing another grand narrative says a lot about the times. My own story has a stage-setting beginning and a plot but no dramatic resolution. Derrida is correct that every writing deconstructs itself, suggesting new versions of its version, even from within the text's own logic. This does not mean that my story lacks a certain logic and direction of meaning. The "plot" is the trinitarian play of postmodernism, feminism, and critical theory, which constitute the dramatis personae. I relieve, if not resolve, dramatic tension through what I call theoretical transcoding, transposing the three theories into an overarching critical theory that focuses on the hierarchy of value over valuelessness. There is action aplenty, even a few theoretical car chases.

But, alas, the whole text unravels into a loosely knit texture of claims and glosses. Aggressive readers will see through these tropes, posing to me the question of my answer, which will set them off on their own versions of comprehensive social theory. Like every textual attempt, my version contains omissions and inconsistencies; it is an essay. I anticipate these criticisms by engaging in a self-transcoding that draws attention to the moves of my own theoretical artifice, giving the reader extra insight into what brought me to where I am. It is important to disclose that every tightly drawn argument is in fact an act of caprice and craft, corrigibly dissolving into the possibilities of other versions of itself and hence into dialogue. Only in this way do we create community, Habermas's ideal speech situation.

Few Marxists write this way, fearing that the pleasure of the text will prove too intoxicating. Many deconstructors lose the distinction between poetry and science, essay and oeuvre. Marxists can learn a great deal from Derrida's logic of presentation about the way in which literary gestures constitute political institutions. Wittgenstein (1953) called these gestures forms of life, making way for a transcoding of Derrida and Wittgenstein that suggests that texts are nucleic societies through which power is transacted. They are what people call social texts, inflected by both power and desire. My desire here is to generate a social theory that recognizes its own undecidability and hence builds community by acknowledging its corrigibility and soliciting corrections. Most Marxists have been too Promethean to confess their limitations. They have been obsessed with the establishment of their own scientificity, accepting the Enlightenment's standard of validity. Yet I would argue that the most valid text is the one that transcodes itself, although not preempting other versions of it.

A self-transcoding suggests how that text could be different in light of different authorial choices. It does not relegate this circumspection to footnotes but builds it into the body of the text itself. I need to recognize the limitations of my argument for certain identities that drive my case for a new critical-theoretical logic. One could just as easily deny that Marxism, feminism, and postmodernism belong to the same class of emancipatory theories, branching out from a central structure best described by the hierarchy of production over reproduction. Having denied these identities, one could then proceed to demonstrate constructive points of intellectual and political overlap among the differentiated theories, a more conventional strategy when dealing with my topic. My point here is that there is no right or wrong way to deal with this. By emphasizing the transcodability of each of the three theories under discussion I am working against the assumption of the separability of dominations, which I believe courts certain regressive neoliberal and difference-theoretic agendas such as multiculturalism. But in emphasizing transcodability, I realize that I risk overdetermining my argument for commonality, playing with texts to such an extent that we lose referents for making useful distinctions. I am not against distinctions. I merely want to raise questions about distinctions among categories and classes of oppression made by many leftists.

A deconstructive text-within-a-text needs to anticipate the criticism that the text in question could have been written differently, either with a different slant or coverage of ignored topics. For the most part, these quite typical readings are not constructive; they state the obvious: A book could have had a different author, hence becoming a different book. Books write authors, not the other way around, in the sense that they position the author within a certain logic or language game that somehow dictates its own plot, resolution, and aporias. This is not to deny authorial choice, which enters into the literary production process at every step along the line, especially in versions (like the New Fiction) that eschew traditional narrative structures. Indeed, postmodern literary strategies are characterized by these unconventional tropes. But Derrida was profoundly correct that every textual choice constrains, and sometimes obfuscates, meaning as well as creates it.

In a future book I will consider these notions of literary and social overdetermination more fully in developing a social theory of the text. To date, my oeuvre has been dedicated to developing a theory of social texts, which extends the Marxist critique of ideology into the era of fast capitalism using transcoded insights from feminist theory and postmodernism. A social theory of the text considers the ways in which the logic and sociologic of exposition strain against linear literary plans, which we are taught to outline before we begin our narratives, and thus change the nature of writing as well as its reception. I am working toward a notion of postmodern texts, albeit with ample reservations about the apolitical direction of most such attempts to conflate cultural criticism and cultural performance (see Agger 1992a). The transcoding of transcoding is an important dimension of my notion of postmodern literary work, which acknowledges the powerful positioning influences of both the logic of texts and of their social con-texts. In the realm of social theory, a transcoding that transcodes itself helps to humble and ironize comprehensive social theory so that its Promethean energy does not get the better of its concern for the liberties of readers and other citizens. A postmodern theoretical text transcodes itself in order to ensure that theoretical practice does not produce canons that stand in the way of creative reinterpretation and hence public discourse—democracy, by another name.

Chapter Six

Critical Theory and Everyday Life 2: Desire, Discourse, and Domination

DESIRE: CAN MEN BE FEMINISTS (AND WRITE FEMINIST THEORY)?

In the preceding chapter, I outlined my transcoding of critical theory, postmodernism, and feminist theory in a way that grounded critical theory directly in everyday life, eschewing a fatalistic economism. In this sense, I rearticulated the Western-Marxist critique of orthodox Marxism (see Lichtheim 1961; Agger 1979; Jacoby 1981) by way of postmodernism and feminist theory, which add vital theoretical resources to Marxism (see Hekman 1990). I also deconstructed the Frankfurt School's critical theory, suggesting lifeworld-relevant strategies of cultural studies formulated as critique of ideology in the society of the spectacle (see Agger 1992a). Here, I want to approach critical theory's grounding in everyday life from a somewhat different perspective, emphasizing that the abandonment of economism does not require the abandonment of all structural analysis. I deal with three potential pitfalls of feminist theory, postmodernism, and German critical theory in terms of the exclusion of men, apolitical obscurantism, and the hidden determinism of negative dialectics, respectively. In order successfully to transcode these three theories into a useful generic critical theory, we must theorize the politics of desire, discourse, and domination. This will ensure that a feminist postmodern critical theory does not remain an aestheticist, pessimistic exercise conducted only by women.

I formulate the first section of this chapter as a critique of the postmodern-feminist politics of subjectivity, which tends to ignore the relationship between feminist identity and affiliation, on the one hand, and structural analysis, on the other. Although I heartily embrace a lifeworld-grounded politics of subjectivity and intersubjectivity as the central contribution of a transcoded critical theory that functions as an ideology-critical cultural studies in fast capitalism, informing German critical theory with feminist and postmodern insights, it is important to disentangle this politics of subjectivity sufficiently from the feminist project (without abandoning feminism) so that subjectivity becomes a generic mode of counter-hegemony. This is not an act of disentangling but a transcoding ensuring that all of our lifeworld-transforming activities are feminist in the sense of challenging production's primacy over reproduction. Men, too, must theorize and engage in everyday strategies of resistance and reconstruction. My transcoded feminist postmodern critical theory suggests lifeworld-transforming activities that include, but are not limited to, issues surrounding the gendered division of labor, which is a paradigmatic form of the hierarchy of production over reproduction. It is important to conceive of *all* everyday emancipatory practices as feminist, but in a way that also suggests linkages with structural issues of political economy.

I have argued that feminism addresses not only women but all hierarchies of value over valuelessness, making possible this linkage between production and reproduction. To the extent to which women have been responsible for the realms of reproduction, both in domestic and market labor, they are obvious topics of feminist theory. But as I have argued above, it is important to check the bio(onto)logizing tendencies of a postmodern feminism that endorses the notion of separate spheres and thus relegates women to the realm of subjectivity and intersubjectivity. It is important to break the link between women and subjectivity, intersubjectivity, domesticity. Accordingly, I develop the argument that men can be feminists and compose feminist theory—indeed, risking hyperbole, that men *are* women to the extent to which they, too, are reproducers, as most men are.

The risk of feminizing feminist theory, allowing it to remain or become an activity pursued only by women, about women, for women, is that we thus ensure the reproduction of the sexual division of labor, which, as I just noted, is the paradigmatic form of production's hierarchy over reproduction. We reproduce the sexual division of labor on the level of social theory, even where feminist critical theories might profess the desire to destroy male supremacy. We also require that feminist theory must be "about" women narrowly and not about all instances of the hierarchy of production over reproduction which, I contend, should be targets of the critique of heterotextuality. Where feminist theory is given the more generic formulation by virtue of its transcoding, it not only links up with other emancipatory interests but is *already* about those interests—class, race, the domination of nature.

A feminist theory that stresses the historicity of the sexual division of labor must attend to its own historicity, notably its academic and intellectual ghettoization. There is no reason why feminists should want to reproduce the sexual division of theoretical labor, or restrict feminism to women's issues. Feminist theory must totalize itself, both admitting men as writers and political activists and addressing issues not ostensibly about women. It is in this sense that I insist on the identification of feminism with Marxism and a critical version of postmodernism in terms of the universality of its emancipatory interests. It is imperative for men to be "allowed" to write feminism and to act and live as feminists, just as they must "allow" themselves these opportunities, in order to give transcoded feminism a generic, totalizing formulation.

It is sometimes argued that men cannot be feminists because they have a vested interest in oppressing women (see Di Stefano 1991). This is an empirical question: Do men oppress women? Better, *which* men oppress women? (or, which men oppress which women?) Many radical feminists argue that *all* men necessarily oppress all women. I can accept this formulation in a general sense, especially where it draws attention to crucial structural features of the hierarchy of production over reproduction, although, when applied to the sexual division of labor, it lacks nuance. I would take the opposite rhetorical approach and argue that *men are women*, just as I would eliminate the dichotomous hierarchies littering our civilization. Actually, both things could be said to be true: All men oppress all women, just as all men are women (and women men) in the sense that they participate in the dialectic of production and reproduction. There is no necessary contradiction between these positions if we are clear that the argument that men-oppress-women reflects the structural arrangement of production over reproduction, while the notion that men-are-women speaks to the heteronomous situations of nearly everybody on the planet. It is crucial for a feminist critical theory to join common cause between men and women, especially since we recognize that we are pitted against each other in order to deflect attention from the large structures enveloping all of us.

This becomes an epistemological issue when French feminists, following Lacan, argue that men cannot write feminism because they inhabit a different realm of symbolic expression from women. I have already criticized this biologism as counterproductive. It is especially so when it becomes the basis for establishing a gendered theoretical division of labor. The postmodern decentering of big narrative into plural little narratives tends to assume that women will have their own "story" to tell (see, e.g., Reinharz 1992). Moreover, they alone should tell this story, just as African-Americans should tell their story (e.g., see hooks 1984). Lacanian feminism suggests that *only* women can know and tell what it means to be a woman. There are two problems with this. First, some men might understand better than some women what it means to be victimized as a woman, that is, a reproducer. Second, it is extremely dubious that feminist theory is, or must be, about the experience of being a woman (as opposed to being a critical theory of all heterotextuality). Postmodern feminists might respond that it does not matter whether feminist theory tells the story of women's experience because, even if it does not, only women can write feminism.

This is perhaps the most relevant issue for my transcoding of feminist theory into a generic critical theory. Can I as a male say anything, let alone do anything, feminist? The answer may be no if, indeed, feminism must be spoken in a woman's voice, resonating with women's experiences of the world. But this assumes that all men are somehow denied the experience of womanhood. This depends on what it means to experience the world as women, and then to write about it from that vantage. If the experience of womanhood is equivalent to the experience of heteronomy, modeled on women's relegation to the valueless sphere of reproduction, then some men can be said to be women in this sense. Or, it could be argued that women have privileged access to the realm of the literary inasmuch as literary work, like housework, also belongs to the sphere of reproduction—traditionally "women's work."

The argument that men cannot be feminists and write feminism may stem from resistance to male territoriality as much as from certain Lacanian notions about women's access to the realm of the imaginary and radical-feminist notions about men's inability to understand the world as women experience it. These reasons form a gestalt of sorts: By now, it is conventional wisdom among radical, cultural, and postmodern feminists that men "cannot" be feminists and write feminism and should not try, except to lend political and personal support to the women's movement where appropriate. This follows less from a self-conscious man-hating posture characteristic of certain radical feminisms (see Dworkin 1974) than from an emerging theoretical consensus about how feminism is about, for, and by women—off limits to men. Men who "try" to be feminists and write feminism are rebuffed for their desire to dominate women, even in their own backyard.

To be sure, most men are not feminists—that is, they profit from and defend male supremacy. At the very least, most men feel extraordinarily threatened by the women's movement, especially in its more radical formulations. The neoconservative backlash against the women's movement is led by men and male-identified women who want to turn back the clock to a time when women did not work outside the home for wages or expect men to participate in egalitarian gender relations in the household. Men are massing to defeat the women's movement; they have a rising degree of gender consciousness in these dismal times. Yet there is a real need not only for room to be made for men politically in the women's movement but for men to write feminist theory as well as to live feminist lives. This is not a right "granted" to men by women but a reality to be forged by men themselves, who prove themselves worthy of being called feminists and feminist theorists. Men have to demonstrate that they are worthy of being called women!

This is important because male supremacy can only be undone through, not around, men. Just as 1960s feminists recognized that women had to raise their consciousnesses about their participation in their own victimization, so, too, must men both change themselves and help liberate women. To deny men feminist political, personal, and literary opportunities simply retards the effort to enlist men in their, and women's, own liberation. After all, my transcoding of feminist theory suggests a universal perspective on the domination of production over reproduction, an issue that affects most men as well as most women. Men have an objective interest in destroying male supremacy (once we reformulate male supremacy as the hierarchy of value over valuelessness). Feminist theory needs to demonstrate this interest by transcoding male supremacy into the more generic hierarchy of production (value) over reproduction (valuelessness).

Men can think, live, and write as feminists if they understand feminism to be a universal theory of human liberation. By the same token, feminists can become Marxists once they understand that a transcoded Marxism explains and challenges the subordination of (women's) reproduction to (men's) production. These transcodings require us to relinquish the simplistic notion that "all men" are objectively interested in oppressing "all women." Most men are reproducers and, as such, exploited. And some men do not oppress women, just as some women in fact oppress men by virtue of their class and race positions. I am not saying that women should "go easy" on men, many of whom objectify and subordinate women, but only that liberation must universally liberate both men and women. To accomplish this necessarily involves men and women in their own self-liberation, as well as in the liberation of others. For men-as-reproducers to be pitted against women-as-reproducers, no matter how falsely conscious many of these men are when it comes to issues of gender equality, only perpetuates the structural logic of domination that underlies all subordinations and hierarchies, according to my feminist postmodern critical theory.

It is generally accepted among liberal feminists that radical feminists have been "too hard" on men, who are portrayed as caught between harsh feminist expectations and their own inertia when it comes to changing their gender roles. I am skeptical about this apologia for men, especially since it assumes the model of the heterosexual nuclear family, albeit with more companionate/egalitarian gender roles. Radical feminist theory is especially sharp where it questions heterosexual norms as part of its overall critique of heterotextuality, which reflects the tendency of discourse/practices to reproduce certain hierarchies of value over valuelessness—here, men over women. For women to be overly concerned with the hearts of men (see Ehrenreich 1983) somehow misses the point: It is not men's hearts that matter but rather their structural positioning in the politics of everyday life. "Men matter" to feminist theory and the women's movement not because they are necessarily coupled with heterosexual women but because men-as-reproducers occupy the same structural location as women-as-reproducers and can thus join common cause with women in fighting the hierarchization of production/value over reproduction/valuelessness.

To be sure, individual men frequently neglect their own objective interests. Patriarchy leads individual men to assume and even defend the inviolability of male-supremacist gender relations. But, as Chodorow (1978) and Pleck (1981) demonstrate, patriarchy is bad for men inasmuch as it reproduces heterotextually the domination of production over reproduction, which victimizes men, too. I am not debating the issue of whether women are "more" exploited than men. It is easy to demonstrate that most women are more economically disadvantaged than most men. But there is a larger issue here: Men and women are *both* victimized, and self-victimized, by reproducing heterotextually quotidian discourse/practices that reproduce the global hierarchy of value over valuelessness, albeit in differential ways.

Admittedly, it is very difficult to view men-in-general and women-in-general as allies when individual men objectify and subordinate individual women. This difficulty must be overcome if we are to make headway in establishing theoretical and political commonality between men-as-reproducers and women-as-reproducers. I believe that we can overcome this difficulty in large measure by reconceptualizing patriarchy as an instance of a more generic logic of hierarchy that is manifested in a host of other, apparently nongender, ways. Although it is extraordinarily difficult to think of patriarchy, let alone violence against women and pay inequality, as transcending gender, we must transcode patriarchy into a more generic theory of domination, as I have tried to do in this book. Only by doing that can we begin to understand that men-as-reproducers and women-as-reproducers have common objective interests.

I risk obscuring the specificity of patriarchy or male supremacy by suggesting that men-as-reproducers and women-as-reproducers have common interests and should combine to fight their common opponent. But I am not convinced that patriarchy is specific in the sense that it can be differentiated out from other versions of the same root cause, namely the hierarchy of value over nonvalue. The sexual division of labor, which conceals hierarchy underneath naturelike differentiation, is no different in kind from other divisions/hierarchies of labor. Women are heteronomous in the sexual division of labor simply because they have been assigned naturelike roles of subordination on the basis of their capacity for biological reproduction. By the same token, Jews have been assigned subordinate roles within a Christian society in which Jews are necessarily viewed as a minority. The notion that male supremacy represents a plot of men-in-general against women-in-general misses the fact that male supremacy was not conceived by men in a state of nature and then deliberately foisted upon women.

Indeed, I am convinced that feminism should stress the numerous ways in which men, like women, fall blindly into male supremacy, accepting the sexual division of labor as second nature on the basis of what Chodorow (1978) calls the reproduction of mothering and fathering. Boys learn misogyny, according to her, by virtue of their need to individuate themselves with reference to their primary caretakers, usually their mothers. And our culture reinforces misogyny by objectifying women, which circularly justifies men's advantage over women with reference to the supposedly natural inferiority of women. By the end of adolescence, young men have not made conscious choices to subordinate women but simply learned the norms of their culture as well as grown egos formed in reference to present mothers and absent fathers. Chodorow's sensible feminist suggestion that we begin to undo male supremacy by involving fathers in childcare, providing boys male role models and not pitting them against "suffocating" mothers, liberates *both* boys and girls, hence future men and women. She appears convinced that men-in-general and women-in-general suffer the sexual division of labor, although she does not engage in the scholastic exercise of computing who suffers "more." Few would deny that women get the short end of the stick in patriarchal societies, although this is largely a difference in quantity and not quality.

It is very important to stress that men, too, can be feminists and write feminist theory if we are to forge bonds between men-in-general and women-in-general. These bonds are necessary in order to challenge the structuring logic of our civilization, which hierarchizes valued over valueless people, groups, and activities. This by no means requires women and men to adhere to a heterosexual norm, nor to accept the nuclear family as an ideal. Heterosexism and familism are significant artifacts of male supremacy and need to be opposed in the interest of universal human liberation. Nor does this mean that we should ignore the specificity of patriarchy as an epochal form of the hierarchy of production over reproduction. But we need to recognize that women are not in their nature denizens of the realm of reproduction, endlessly reproducing everyone but themselves. Women are reproducers with respect to men and children only because of an accident of nature, which gives them species-reproducing responsibility. This accident of nature becomes the basis for structured social inequality, which makes sexual differentiation the basis for social and economic stratification, ever the ruse of ideology. A universalistic feminist critical theory must oppose bio(onto)logy just as it opposes every other confusion of nature and history.

DISCOURSE: CRACKING THE CODE

Postmodernism becomes critical theory when we use its discourse theory to unpack ideologies dispersed as social texts into the sense and sentience of the public environment. It becomes a critical way to read ideologizing texts against themselves, exhuming their secret authorship and contesting their facile assumptions, which, as in the case of bio(onto)logy discussed above, confuse history and nature in the interest of domination. But postmodernism regresses when it is reduced to interpretive method, accepting with Derrida that the text has no outside. Although he may not have meant what is often heard by that remark—sheer idealism—Derrida's deconstructive program obscures the possible political contribution of a postmodern critical theory that uses discourse-theoretic insights in order to debunk new forms of ideology in fast capitalism.

In rejecting orthodox Marxism, postmodernism threatens to abandon all Marxist historicity, forgetting that the struggle over the validity of consciousness does not end with the dismantling of the Soviet Union. Although it was crucial to debunk Stalinist Archimedeanism, we must not give up truth, reason, or justice as reconstructive ideals. Although Habermas's attempt to revalidate critical theory with reference to certain universal pragmatics of communicative action is unconvincing, ignoring both discourse and gender, he is right to salvage Enlightenment notions of rationality in the face of irrationalists and antirationalists, who thrive in these times. The postmodern assault on positivism founders where it equates positivism and rationalism, precisely the claim of the Vienna Circle, which replaced speculative philosophy with mathematics and hence eviscerated reason altogether. I agree with Derrida that all texts are undecidable, hence puncturing the balloon of scientists who pretend to represent the world presuppositionlessly. But undecidability does not mean that we should (or can) avoid decisions about the good life, even where we recognize that these decisions are subject to deconstructive interrogation or, simply, doubt.

Postmodernism comes so close to being critical theory, and yet remains so far from having attained a coherent political program. Either postmodernists celebrate the present as the end of history, or they busily deconstruct the myriad different texts that litter the landscape and divert attention from more important problems, namely the abolition of injustice. Against these depoliticizing tendencies, I want to put deconstruction to work in the project of the critique of ideology, having theorized a distinctive new phase of postmodern capitalism. Deconstruction interrogates the flimsy boundary between textuality and the world, helping draw attention to social texts that are no longer found between covers, susceptible to a distancing reading. For this version of deconstruction to do its work in cracking the code of ideology today, we need to decommodify and politicize postmodernism, an uphill struggle at best given the co-optability of key postmodern insights.

It is easy to see why postmodernism serves the neoconservative project so well, even if Habermas (1981a) exaggerates the doctrinal conservatism of New French Theory. Although postmodernism originally positioned itself against the French Communist Party, New French Theory has inflated into a wholesale attack on all grand narratives. The deconstruction of Marxism has attained planetary proportions, with the demise of the Soviet empire both fueled by and fueling the postmodern critique of orthodox leftism. Virtually no one defends Marx against both his former statist followers and his Lyotardian detractors. Postmodernism inflects a flashy, insubstantial intellectual culture in which it is customary to view Marxism as a relic from the dustbin of history, belonging, at best, to the pantheon of moribund intellectual movements interesting only to archaelogists of our civilization. As Jacoby indicated in *Last Intellectuals* (1987), the academization of Marxism relates inversely to its political fortunes. One does not need to be postmodern to recognize the ample political failures of the left.

There is a certain relationship between postmodernism's rejection of Marxist narratives and its devotion to groundless close readings. Reading exhumes secret authorial perspective and hence amplifies opportunities for reauthorizing social texts that lead us to reproduce the world out of a belief in its naturelike permanence. But reading remains simply an academic career move where it is unhinged from transformational political theory. Jacoby's observation that erstwhile New Leftists busy themselves in the establishment of academic careers via vita building suggests a certain causality: The abandonment of leftist political practice is replaced by technical scholarship, which reproduces itself. Indeed, the humanities crowd resonates with "good" political motives, which are seldom subjected to scrutiny but simply assumed as universalistic values. The professional academics who apply Derrida and Foucault in their own interpretive practices proclaim all sorts of leftish values about curriculum as well as the overall state of the world.

I want postmodernism to become a vehicle for cracking fast-capitalist codes of acquiescence and adjustment, including those of academic neoliberals. This requires that postmodernists not reject all Marxist possibilities, especially where Marxism is transcoded into a generic critical theory targeting hierarchy and heterotextuality and not simply capital. This also requires that postmodernism not become a code to surpass all codes, even more involuted than the discourses it deciphers. The obscurity of postmodern interpretive theory frequently gets in the way of public discourse, defeating the postmodern attempt to read underneath texts for the secret authorship animating them. This is not to say that we possess one-for-one principles of translation whereby we can replace difficult words with transparently simple ones. Translations are themselves undecidable and thus must be translated. But postmodern critical theory needs to create a viable public sphere within which citizens can carry on intelligible discussions about societal purposes. Postmodern critical theory can help create this public sphere by decoding ideological claims wherever they may appear, in advertising as well as in organized religion. It is in this sense that I characterize postmodern critical theory as code-cracking work, albeit recognizing that decoding itself must be decoded lest we suggest or imply the possibility of a positivist language to end all languages—e.g., sheer mathematics.

A technically compulsive postmodernism reads culture without political direction, having abandoned what it purports are Archimedean criteria with which to assess texts' validity. But, as I argue in *Cultural Studies as Critical Theory* (1992a), one can retain the distinction between true and false human needs without endorsing a timeless truth. Marx balanced the historicity of needs against the notion of truth as reason. That is, with Marcuse (1964) in *One-Dimensional Man*, we can debunk the falsehood of needs with reference to a criterion of their heteronomy without stipulating definitive needs—opera over rock and roll, for example. Marcuse avoided mandarinism without endorsing an utter relativity, which dispenses with the distinction between truth and falsehood.

Postmodernism takes the undecidability of texts as license for relativism. Although tempting in an age well acquainted with the corruption of politicians, this relativism does not derive from the critique of totalitarianism, which people like Lyotard confuse with Marxism. Some narratives are "grander," that is more impervious to their humbling undecidability, than others. It is very important to make these distinctions lest we fall into a relativism, with Nietzsche, that abandons all judgment. I would argue that we need a rationalist standard of truth and value more than ever, when so much is going wrong. We need to reclaim textuality by gaining distance from the dispersed texts and codes cluttering the quotidian. This is precisely where a critical discourse theory can do its best work, first identifying social texts and then authorizing them by disclosing the busy literary artifice underneath claims that soft drinks and running shoes represent the good life.

Athletic apparel companies proclaim ontology: "Just do it" and "life is short, play hard." These are the secret political theories of our time. By cracking their codes for what they recommend about the commodification of experience, we take a halting step away from an enveloping quotidian, which would have us live our lives through these simulations, as Baudrillard calls them. The various Nike campaigns vividly suggest shoe and apparel acquisition designed to fill the vacuum of postmodern meaninglessness. With Beatles music and sophisticated editing, these campaigns insinuate themselves into our lives, suggesting commodity acquisition as a mode of aestheticist cultivation. Shopping is almost an afterthought, an automatic response from people convinced by advertising's simulations to view posturban life as an open road.

It is not enough for postmodern cultural theory simply to produce readings, both playful and pyrotechnic. Anyone can translate anything into something else. Derrida's influence on literary and cultural criticism has been positive inasmuch as he liberated us from the myth of positivist close readings (e.g., the New Criticism), which pretended that works or oeuvres admit of singular interpretive triangulations. These definitive readings were to be spiritually elevating, on the model of traditional Leavis-era aesthetic criticism (see Eagleton 1983). Derrida's influence has been negative to the extent that he has given license to the proliferation of readings unconstrained by criteria of judgment. This is not to say that snooty critics should find Nike ads wanting according to certain mandarin aesthetic criteria but that we need to read advertisements *in terms of their embedded truth claims*.

These truth claims are brought to light by deconstructive readings that demonstrate the busy literary artifice underneath glossy print and celluloid performances. Advertisements position consumers in deliberate ways, enticing them to live their lives in terms of their own reflected representations in the campaigns. Nike understands that the best way to sell sneakers to yuppies is to represent people like themselves attempting to deal with life on the road, which is potholed but also pregnant with the possibility of individual accomplishment, ever the yuppie grail. Just-doing-it inflects the quotidian with pursuits-of-meaning characteristic of baby boomers now dealing with hair loss and perfidious bosses.

One of Nike's most distinctive campaigns involves text lifted from a woman's diary. It is about coming to grips with contemporary womanhood, full of pathos and travail. In the end, of course, the woman culture hero evidences her newfound self-confidence by becoming athletic, just-doing-it a decision arrived at through new-age introspection (probably supported by therapy). This youthful everywoman is a deliberate textual outcome; indeed, the campaign is virtually all narrative, suggesting its own deconstructibility. We need to attend critically to the way in which this fake circumspection encodes a theory of self and society, recommending a certain adaptive posture on the part of yuppie women everywhere. In this case, it is suggested that the best way to deal with the denigration of women, and particularly the assaults on their self-esteem from adolescence into working womanhood, is through athleticism as an urban survival strategy. It does not really matter whether the everywoman in the campaign is a "real" athlete, running a certain number of miles per week. Her picture suggests a fit body and practiced stride. Nikes signify or simulate a certain way of dealing with women's experiences of degradation. Only a small fraction of people who buy athletic shoes actually use them for athletic purposes. It is by now well known how expensive basketball shoes bear certain cultural significances among young African-Americans, who, lacking largesse, sometimes commit crimes in order to obtain them. Just as Nike positions its yuppie everywoman as the protagonist in the social text of the quotidian, so Nike positions Michael Jordan and Bo Jackson as protagonists in the social text of African-American everyday life. The beauty of Jordan and Jackson is that they are transracial, selling shoes to whites as well. The Nike everywoman has a more limited appeal to those who read the texts of ads self-referentially, as a telling piece of autobiography.

Deconstructive work needs to be done on "what" these social texts are "saying" to people about the relationship between self and society. Nike and Reebok, like beer companies, depoliticize personal problems, which are to be remedied through elaborate processes of identification with the lives scripted in their campaigns. In a sense, this is nothing new: Advertising has always worked this way (see Ewen 1976, 1988). But now deconstructive interpretive techniques exhume the secret authorship behind these campaigns, reading advertising as political and social recommendation that can be challenged. Such readings help us resist these campaigns, interrogating the reasonableness of lives scripted by the companies dominating airtime, billboards, and the print media.

Advertisements can be read for their validity. We must ask whether it is really true that labeled shoes and clothes afford meaning and control. But to ask this question requires us to translate campaigns into the secret claims they are making about our world. Does beer make us sexy? Do cars enable us to escape workaday alienation? Can cigarettes bring us into harmony with the great outdoors? Advertising is not the only venue of deconstructive work. We can read buildings, fashion, science, movies, television, newspapers, and magazines in much the same way. We need to authorize them, bringing their assumptions to light and then contesting their silent advocacy. Packard was ahead of his time to understand that advertising is hidden persuasion. He lacked a methodological apparatus for doing deconstructive readings of these deceptions. Similarly, the Frankfurt theorists could not closely read movies or music as contentious social texts but only assert theoretically that popular culture is an industry crucial to late capitalism, both in its commodifying and reifying aspects.

We can authorize advertisements as discourse/practices secretly advocating a certain world, in the case of Nike a world in which people solve their problems by running around in circles expensively attired in labeled outfits. One can contest these versions of the world only if they are recognized as literary artifices achieved by the copywriters of the quotidian. Although it should be obvious to cultural theorists that advertising is a literary fiction, the most successful campaigns deploy a kind of cinema verité in order to simulate realist validity. These campaigns represent the flux and flow of "life itself"—people wearing Levi's (see Goldman and Papson 1991), drinking Coke and driving Hondas. Like other simulations, advertising conceals its own artifice in order to simulate a credible reality—hence reproducing it.

All of these readings identify postmodern textuality, and its advocacy, in surprising places. Textuality abounds as argument, although this is hard to detect since discourse makes its case by way of immersion in everyday experience, losing a certain distance from reality that makes critical reading, and hence evaluation, possible. Few read, except in the university world. Even the explosion of academic books is not matched by a busy readership. Academic publishers publish books with print runs of a few hundred. People write to get published, hence ahead. The postmodernism explosion adds to this busyness, lengthening curriculum vitae but not deepening social insight. Where the most relevant "texts" are those of concealed and congealed discourse like advertising, few readers gain enough distance from these texts in order to recognize the worlds they secretly recommend.

Texts today are everywhere and nowhere. There are many books, few readers, and perhaps even fewer writers. I have already suggested that books increasingly write authors and not the other way around in the sense in which the editorial, production, and even drafting processes are out of authorial control. Trade books are made to order—for the market. And yet textuality is increasingly important politically, albeit the disguised textuality of postmodern capitalism. Smart young college students no longer yearn to write the Great American Novel, let alone critical theory, but aspire to work for advertising agencies and television stations. They are the scribes of the culture industry, who simulate reality in order to reproduce it. They work in what McLuhan called "hot" media, by comparison to which the traditional literary and academic industries are stone cold.

Postmodern discourse theory enables us to read these simulations as the authorial acts they are, disgorging the secret textuality underneath the slick metaprose of advertising, television, movies, journalism. By *metaprose* I am referring to a textuality that, in concealing its own deliberate literary artifice, recommends lives surreptitiously. I am not suggesting that individual cultural producers purposely conceal the rhetoricity of their own writing. Rather, institutions of textuality determine literary outcomes through the elaborate scripting and screening processes of mass-market fiction, textbooks, movies, television, journalism, and even academic books and articles. The death of the reader is paralleled by a Barthesian death of the author. It is crucial to understand the process of deauthorization as an institutional outcome of the culture industry and of academia—books writing authors. In this sense, the postmodern critical agenda is both to translate metaprose into advocacy that can be rebutted and to empower authors to reclaim textuality as their own, thus rebuilding the public sphere in late capitalism.

Postmodernism suggests a public intellectuality that refuses literary overdetermination and specialization as well as the death of reader and writer. Postmodernism suggests a public standard of discursive accessibility that rests not simply on stylistic simplification but rather on the democratization of what Habermas calls dialogue chances—opportunities to read and write, hence to participate publicly. In cracking the code of fast-capitalist dispersed texts, postmodernism suggests the possibilities of demystifying, deconstructing readings and thus lives. It is ironic that postmodern discourse theory contributes to the decline of discourse. Alternatively, postmodern theory could function as a mode of public speech and critique that involves a perpetual questioning humbling all transformational and textual attempts, which are now viewed merely as essays—strong attempts to live intelligent lives.

The ironism of postmodernism in face of Archimedean narratives can be coupled to an agenda of social change, as I have demonstrated above. For this to occur requires us to turn postmodern interpretive techniques back upon postmodernism itself lest textual-critical efforts bog down in obscurantism. We should not mystify anew as we demystify, a real risk at a time when discourse theory is so academized as to have lost touch with the public project of discourse. That is, discourse theory, owed to people like Derrida, must check its own tendency to become so academic—ponderous, technical, self-referential—that it only contributes to the problem it intends to resolve, notably the closure of the public sphere. Where modernity is characterized by expert cultures and language games (see Bernstein 1971), postmodernity in its best sense should be typified by counterhegemonic, self-deconstructing discourse/practices that subvert the disciplinary society. Postmodern discourse should be dedisciplining, not the epitome of discipline. Postmodernism can not only crack the code of dispersed ideology in fast capitalism, but it can suggest a mode of code cracking that applies to itself, frustrating the efforts of academic postmodernists to transform deconstructing, decanonizing literary strictures into an unassailable edifice of ritual postures and dense prose. Only in this way can postmodernism work toward a democratic polity in which people realize their strength as readers and writers, ever the promise of Marxist political and social theory.

DOMINATION: NEGATING NEGATIVE DIALECTICS

Although this book has been formulated within the frame of reference of the Frankfurt School's critical theory, we must transcode German critical theory into a nonmandarin cultural studies that produces emancipatory readings and new cultural practices. Adorno's mandarinism is not a viable posture, if it ever was. He paints with too broad a brush in declaring administration total. In fact, oppositional projects and oeuvres fall through the cracks, making a difference. Although his negative dialectics is a powerful antidote to a cheerful liberalism that empowers subjectivity at a time when subjectivity is in serious decline, negative dialectics itself must be negated toward a more positive formulation of critical theory. For me, following but diverging from Habermas, this reformulated critical theory needs a lifeworld grounding in the contested terrains of gender, culture, and power.

The Frankfurt theorists set impossibly high standards for political resistance and cultural expression. They seem to have envisaged a proletariat tutored in Beckett as well as Marx. Thus, they failed to detect glimmers of resistance that did not conform to their high-modernist conception of total transformation. The absence of this elevated, edified collective subject led Adorno in *Negative Dialectics* to conclude that the opportunity to realize a new world had irrevocably passed. Although there is a great deal of empirical evidence to suggest that Adorno's pessimism is justified today, given the globalization of domination coupled with the successful neoconservative blockage of new social movements, negative dialectics must not be allowed to become ontology, which it nearly did in Adorno. The major failing of Frankfurt theory was its inability to engage with popular, populist insurgency in the venues of gender and discourse, preventing them from theorizing the possibility of new social movements capable of destabilizing administered society.

As I indicated above, Adorno failed not simply because his cultural tastes prevented him from engaging with the popular as a ground of political contest, contradictorily vitiating the ideology-critical promise of the culture-industry thesis presented in *Dialectic of Enlightenment*. Adorno was so far removed from the quotidian that he could not grasp the significance of the politics of gender and discourse that marked a variety of new social movements in the 1960s. Indeed, Adorno and Horkheimer were intensely threatened by the student movement and counterculture, which they recognized as irrationalist, anti-modernist forces inimical to high-modernist values. In no way am I suggesting a postmodern Luddism but am rather pointing out that Adorno's negative dialectics went wrong where it prevented him from developing a differentiating reading of everyday life that focuses on counterhegemonic developments in the realms of gender, culture, and power. This was not mainly because he was a pessimist; that was more outcome than cause. It was rather because he did not theorize gender, culture, and power as politically significant moments in late capitalism, succumbing to a variety of blindspots and prejudices characteristic of high-modernist critical theorists.

Had Adorno-generation critical theorists managed to detect the politics of everyday life in the venues of gender, culture, and power, they could have transcoded their own critique of domination into the more generic hierarchy of value over valuelessness, applying their critique of civilization to a host of practices traditionally ignored by Marxists. Inasmuch as Adorno's critique of identity theory paralleled that of Derrida, it is not unimaginable that Adorno could have become postmodernist *avant la lettre*, anticipating discursive themes in postmodernism that reformulate critical theory in fast capitalism. It is less imaginable that Adorno could have anticipated feminist themes. This is not because he was male per se, a fatal error of biologism. Rather, his sexual politics prevented him from recognizing male supremacy as a problem, indeed, the *same* problem as the alienation of labor. There is nothing about critical theory that makes it "male" apart from demonstrably male-supremacist biases (e.g., the Frankfurt work on paternal authority) or blindspots (e.g., their inattention to the women's movement). I have already declared my opposition to the grafting of feminism onto critical theory, thus preserving their differentiation. Instead, I transcode them into each other, producing a generic critical theory that not only has room for the critique of male supremacy and the alienation of labor but develops these critiques out of common theoretical resources.

Adorno was far from identifying this common theoretical logic. It was enough for him to debunk orthodox Marxism as an Enlightenment project, an important theoretical advance at a time when capitalism, fascism, and Stalinism were combining into impregnable postwar "total administration." Adorno brilliantly analyzed total administration as a conjuncture of liberal and illiberal forces, producing an analysis of the Holocaust that was fully continuous with his analysis of authoritarianism. Adorno understood the depravity of liberalism more deeply than almost anyone else, debunking liberal strains in Marxism that threaten to turn Marxism into yet another human disaster. Unfortunately, he did not theorize beyond the consolidated capitalism of the 1950s which, he correctly understood, integrated the fascist conquest of otherness. Adorno's hesitancy about the new social movements of the 1960s followed from his premise that it was impossible to undo the self-reproducing, hence totalizing, tendencies of late-capitalist total administration.

I cannot refute Adorno's apparently metaphysical pessimism metaphysically. The only way to challenge his negativity is with evidence of positive social movements. There is little evidence of this kind today. Indeed, Adorno's totalizing negativity makes a good deal of sense on empirical grounds, even if he did not take a sufficiently close look at everyday life in order to detect the faint pulse of dissent and reconstruction. Adorno was highly skeptical that microlevel opposition could resist its integration. This approached an ontological negativity in books like *Minima Moralia* and *Negative Dialectics*. Although Adorno deeply understood capitalist total administration, Adorno leaves us no method with which to prevent his negativity from hardening into a metaphysical posture, hence defeating political projects today. Suffice it to say that there is no Adornoism, no Adornoian program—there was only Adorno, an encyclopedic intellectual who chastened cheerful liberals for their optimism and reformism. We should learn from him but not duplicate him (assuming that duplication is even possible).

This presents a real problem for people like me, who drink deeply of German critical theory. I am saying that we must transcode critical theory into lifeworld-relevant themes, including those of gender and discourse. Although that project is not inconsistent with Adorno's (1973a: p. 406) insistence that we must escape "the objective context of delusion . . . from within," the critical theorists were nearly allergic to lifeworld resistances, insisting that they were eminently co-optable by hegemonic interests, discourses, and practices—the theme of Marcuse's (1964) *One-Dimensional Man*. But we must ground critical theory squarely in everyday life in order to foster the new social movements identified by Habermas. We must build on the politics of the personal, much as feminists have tried to do, although keeping in mind that simply because projects originate in everyday life does not somehow mean that they are invulnerable or charmed. Indeed, everyday life is very much a site of heteronomy, threatening to eclipse subjectivity and intersubjectivity, as the Frankfurt theorists recognized. But the lifeworld is a contested terrain, never entirely losing the dynamic dialectical possibilities found everywhere people confront oppression with imagination. In fact, critical theory, perhaps because of its relentless negativity, stimulates imagination at a time when most agendas of social change are either neoliberal or postmodern, thus promising no change at all.

Critical theory can refract domination in quotidian experience and practice. The Frankfurt critique of domination sheds ample light on the way in which domination is both imposed and self-imposed, "chosen" in the false needs (see Marcuse 1964) that damage lives and wreck the environment. People can break their surplus repression, as Marcuse (1955) called it in his Freud book, *Eros and Civilization,* by adopting counterhegemonic modes of existence (I hesitate to call them lifestyles, endorsing their self-commodification as modes of happy consumerism). Marcuse recognized the possibility of these embryonic, prefigurative choices in his 1969 *Essay on Liberation,* which took seriously New Left politics and Dionysian youth culture for their transformational impact on the bourgeois quotidian. The Frankfurt School itself indicated the ways in which these oppositional modes are quickly commodified and co-opted, Woodstock Nation becoming a movie and album. Marcuse's sympathy for the politics of the personal constitutes a positive example of the possible grounding of critical theory in everyday life, both identifying and amplifying ongoing struggle.

On the one hand, the Frankfurt theorists traced domination's invasion of lived experience and the body. On the other hand—and noncontradictorily—they argued that the overcoming of domination must proceed from this ground in experience and the body. Self-transformation can lead to full-blown societal transformation via the process of what Marcuse calls prefiguration: The choices we make today constitute social movements and societies of the future, ensuring that we do not postpone liberation until a distant future time (and hence justifying all manner of sacrifices, even atrocities, in the meantime). In demonstrating convincingly that the late-capitalist person is incredibly manipulated by external and internal imperatives of discipline, the Frankfurt theorists add sobriety, even skepticism, to millenarian Marxist optimism. But they also suggest reasons for optimism inasmuch as they ground politics in subjectivity and intersubjectivity, thus rooting political dynamics in the quotidian choices people make about their lives. This strategy avoids liberalism precisely where human needs are depicted as social and not private. Marcuse's conception of needs resembles early Marx's in its stress on their communitarian character. Marcuse argues that people can choose work and intimate lives embodying nonauthoritarian power dynamics and thus help bring about optimally nonauthoritarian societies.

My version of critical theory owes a great deal to this Marcusean formulation of a political subjectivity grounded in the lifeworld. Marcuse plays a central role in my (1992b) *Discourse of Domination: From the Frankfurt School to Postmodernism,* in which I retrieve and revive critical theory for the 1990s, a project extended in this book. I add feminism and postmodernism to Marcuse where they provide important perspectives on gender and discourse largely ignored by the Frankfurt theorists. Tellingly—given the times—Marcuse is now largely ignored (but see Lukes and Bokina 1993). He is dismissed as a period philosopher of the 1960s—a mistake, given the origins of his Freudian Marxism in the 1950s. Although Marcuse was flexible enough to adapt the lifeworld grounding of his critical theory to new social movements during the 1960s, this brief affiliation with the New Left was in no way essential for his theory. It is very important that we avoid sentimentality about the original Frankfurt School's versions of critical theory, however instructive. It is necessary to adapt their analysis of domination to a postmodern stage of capitalism, especially with the aid of feminism and postmodernism, which together refocus critical theory on everyday life, a grounding it lost with Adorno.

The legacy of negative dialectics is important in the sense that Adorno, Horkheimer, and Marcuse explained why late capitalism survives Marx's expectation of its demise (see Buck-Morss 1977). They acutely dissected domination. But their legacy frustrates attempts to reground critical theory in oppositional practices and social movements that avoid the fate of total administration. Are there in fact people and groups who resist their own integration? The nearly metaphysical posture of negative dialectics is insufficient to answer this question. We need to develop a perspective on the possibility of new social movements that answers to the lifeworld grounding of critical theory without appearing romantic or gullible. After all, Adorno was correct that critique tends to be absorbed by the very system it attacks, perversely strengthening it by suggesting its openness. Facile optimism about new social movements should be discounted, especially at a time when the right flourishes and all sorts of neoliberal gains have been reversed. It is extremely difficult to find evidence of leftist vitality in these grim times. My argument is that feminism and postmodern discourse theory help us locate this evidence in places that would surprise even the sophisticated skeptics of the Frankfurt School.

WHO'S LEFT?

My transcoding of German critical theory, New French Theory, and feminist theory into an overarching theoretical logic appropriate to fast capitalism seeks political purchase at a time when people everywhere lament and/or celebrate the declared end of politics. Who among us on the left does not wonder whether the demise of the Soviet Union seals the fate of organized leftism once and for all? Indeed, the very phrase "on the left" trades on a notion of ideological bipolarity increasingly rejected by postmodernists, neoconservatives, and neoliberals everywhere. Who's left on a left that is increasingly off the political map?

My book has attempted to answer this question, providing a new perspective on critical theory that focuses our transformational attention on everyday life by understanding hegemonic and counterhegemonic pressures in the venues of gender, culture, and power—the respective foci of feminism, postmodernism, and German critical theory. By elaborating a generic theoretical logic focusing on the hierarchy of valued over devalued activities, a feminist postmodern critical theory can identify and then amplify resistances to this hierarchizing structural tendency at the level of everyday life. These resistances include but are not limited to the valorization of housework (feminism), the deconstruction of discourse/practices of quotidian modernity (postmodernism), and the liberation of popular culture from a suffocating mandarinism (critical cultural studies). All of these activities, and more, reflect people's attempts to claim value for their lives—a version of Marcuse's Great Refusal. Theory can add momentum to these lifeworld-grounded struggles, orchestrating them into full-blown social movements. It is important to insist on the *leftishness* of these struggles precisely in order to oppose the postmodern, neoconservative, and neoliberal dismissals of the left-right continuum. All of these voices join the chorus of the end-of-Marxism, which makes leftist discourse seem archaic today. My transcoded theoretical logic—the critique of value's hierarchy over alleged valuelessness—has grounds in Marx, although it pays no canonical debt to Marx. I consider myself and my theoretical logic Marxist, although, as I said earlier, what it means to be a Marxist is up for grabs. Marxism weighs heavily on those who revise Marxism in Marx's name, shamelessly adapting Marx's theoretical logic to social, economic, political, and cultural circumstances that Marx could scarcely have foreseen. The issue of whether my transcoding of critical theory is "really" Marxist is wrongly posed: I prefer to inquire whether Marx was a critical theorist—I am convinced that he was—in the sense that he offered a theoretical framework within which to situate labor's effort to claim value for itself.

The cult of theoretical personality defeats attempts to adapt critical theory to new historical circumstances. At the same time, we must not abandon the claim to leftishness given the chorus of post-Marxism in the voices of postmodernism, neoconservatism, and neoliberalism. At a time when unions, people of color, and the women's movement are fighting for their political lives, it is more than ever necessary to claim Marxism proudly, acknowledging that we must reinvent it on the ground of people's everyday lives. To shelve Marxism in a dusty university library neglects the fact that Marxist theory was always deeply invested in political struggles. Marx's every sentence reflected the passion and program of radical social change, just as everything critical theorists write today must resonate with the possibilities of personal and collective liberation. Marx did not adequately understand the lifeworld ground of his own theory, producing the peculiar lack of reflexivity noted by Habermas (1971) in *Knowledge and Human Interests* as the occasion for a reconstruction of Marx's theoretical logic making way for the activity of his own critique (thus halting the slide of Marxism into economism and determinism).

In this context, we need "more" Marxism—more politics, engagement, theory. Post-Marxism disguises anti-Marxism, now as before. The postulate of the end of ideology *ends* ideology self-servingly, as Bell (1960) intended. (Of course, Bell wants to disguise his true political intentions: He recently sent me a note scolding me for unmasking his apparent neoliberalism as neoconservative. I clearly struck a nerve!) The neoconservatives misunderstand American academia: Political correctness is liberal, not Marxist. Academic Marxism is dead, or nearly so. Liberalism takes a postmodern and feminist turn, disqualifying Marxist totality theory. This is no threat to universities' positioning in the state apparatus: College curricula that have a place for "difference" help produce human capital capable of dealing with our increasingly diverse cultural and gender mosaic. These curricula do not produce revolutionaries, especially where academic neoliberals decry Marxism as a modernist male power trip.

I am not confident that we can invigorate the left, especially under neoconservatism, which thrives in these times. We should begin, as I have done in this book, by theorizing what it means to *be left*. We should then identify and nurture people's attempts to reconstruct their own lives, connecting these efforts both theoretically and practically. My version of a feminist postmodern critical theory contributes to a generic critical theory that theorizes apparently heterogeneous resistance movements attacking the generic hierarchy of valued over valueless activities.

There is no magic in my theoretical transcodings. I have solved few problems, especially practical ones. At most, I have raised the question of what it means to be left at a time when it is either an enigma or an embarrassment to be identified with the left project, whatever that might mean. At times like these, we must insist on our Marxism, as well as on our feminism and postmodernism. I am Marxist, but I lament the way in which an inflexible Marxism has allowed the right to disqualify Marxism as dogma. We must interrogate the text of our leftism lest the left classics that inspire us become our tombstones. We must write leftist texts with an eye toward their inherent ambiguity and undecidability, recognizing that texts are language games within which we solve all arguments self-referentially, in terms of the falsely impregnable logics of our own positions. What we cannot do is compare our logics with those of others in terms of criteria of external validity, assessing the extent to which different theories mirror a one-true-world out there.

Marxism remains the most compelling emancipatory theory of our time, even if it misses nonproletarian people and groups. My point in this book is that Marxism does not have to miss these groups if its theoretical logic is expanded considerably beyond, and beneath, what Marx intended in the mid-nineteenth century. Feminism and postmodernism enrich Marxism by changing it perhaps beyond the point of recognizability. Scholastic Marxists may lament my lack of textual grounding in the canonical literature of Marx and his epigones. So much the worse for Marxism. By now, it should be clear that Marxism is not a canon to be defended against the apostate but a way of life, a language game, a mode of social being. To lead a Marxist life or feminist life or postmodern life requires one to interrogate all canons deconstructively, seeking out their weak points, inconsistencies, omissions—all in the name of theoretical and political fidelity to the core logics of those positions. I would argue that it is very much in the nature of critical theory to engage in rigorous revisionism, continually confronting Marxist theoretical logic with societal developments that challenge Marxism to reinvent itself.

It is necessary at once to defend Marxism's contemporary relevance and interrogate Marxism's insufficiencies in light of feminist and postmodern challenges, which I interpret not as attacks but as sympathetic readings. We must get beyond the either/or of dualist society (see Jacoby 1975), transcending the notion that one cannot have coexisting theoretical and political identities that are in fact a singular identity, once understood deeply enough at the level of their common logic. Today, unfortunately, interest-group politics holds sway: One cannot simultaneously "be" Marxist, feminist, and postmodernist. Identities are so narrow that they exclude nearly everything outside the ambit of one's personal experience, biography, commitments. We are all on the defensive at a time when selfhood has become minimal (Lasch 1984) and must jealously defend itself against external challenges.

This is extremely unfortunate in that it prevents a real catholicity of theoretical, political, and personal affiliations. The increasingly refined academic division of labor also plays a part in the balkanization of the left into feminist theory, postmodernism, and Marxism. Academic specialization dooms the left to fragmentation, which is redoubled by the fragmentation of identity in postmodern capitalism. It is difficult to separate these two influences, which together undercut the possible theoretical and political unity of various new social movements. The fragmentation of the left reflects and reproduces the fragmentation of personality and academia, reproducing discipline and domination. Swimming upstream against the powerful current of hegemony, people struggle to reinforce their own precarious singularity, thus diminishing the possibility of collectivity.

Left collectivity has traded off against liberty and autonomy. The price of affiliation has been freedom, too steep a price by any reckoning. To preach collectivity today is especially problematic given the disasters of state socialism. But people need to find ways out of their embattled subjectivities, which, without collectivity and organization, inevitably fall prey to hegemony. The transcoding of the special interests of class, race, and gender into a unified theoretical logic launches this structured intersubjectivity. By uniting the oppressed—including ourselves—under a common theoretical logic, we move a step closer to political unity. In turn, this requires the establishment of a common theoretical logic that explains a variety of apparently differentiable oppressions as moments of the same heterotextual hierarchy.

One must use words like *collectivity* unashamedly, especially in this postmodern era, where commonality is viewed skeptically. It is possible to salvage one's individuality while joining common cause. Indeed, the only way to achieve autonomy is through community—early Marx's notion of social freedom. It is symptomatic that these notions are highly threatening. That they are threatening says much about both the depravity of our political culture and the decline of our theoretical discourse. We tend to assume that freedom is equivalent to subjectivity, especially now that subjectivity is administered both externally and internally. Although freedom cannot be attained without passing through subjectivity, it is meaningless without a ground in community, which, I have argued, requires theoretical commonality above all else. In this book, I have attempted to demonstrate that theoretical commonality does not have to be achieved at the expense of difference, the typical victim of what Adorno called identitarian thinking. Indeed, it is only through community that we can protect difference against its betrayal by neoliberals and neoconservatives alike.

Bibliography

Ackerman, Bruce (1980) *Social Justice in the Liberal State*, New Haven: Yale University Press.
Adorno, Theodor W. (1945) "A Social Critique of Radio Music," *Kenyon Review* 9, 208–17.
―――― (1954) "How to Look at Television," *Quarterly of Film, Radio and Television* 3, 213–35.
―――― (1967) "Sociology and Psychology I," *New Left Review* 46, 67–80.
―――― (1968) "Sociology and Psychology II," *New Left Review* 47, 79–97.
―――― (1973a) *Negative Dialectics*, New York: Seabury Press.
―――― (1973b) *Philosophy of Modern Music*, New York: Seabury Press.
―――― (1974a) *Minima Moralia*, London: New Left Books.
―――― (1974b) "The Stars Down to Earth: *The Los Angeles Times* Astrology Column: A Study in Secondary Superstition," *Telos* 19, 13–90.
―――― (1984) *Aesthetic Theory*, London: Routledge and Kegan Paul.
Adorno, Theodor; Frenkel-Brunswik, Else; Levinson, Daniel; and Sanford, R. N. (1950) *The Authoritarian Personality*, New York: Harper.
Agger, Ben (1976) "Marcuse and Habermas on New Science," *Polity* 9, 151–81.
―――― (1979) *Western Marxism: An Introduction*, Santa Monica, Calif.: Goodyear.
―――― (1983) "Marxism 'or' the Frankfurt School?" *Philosophy of the Social Sciences* 13, 347–65.
―――― (1989a) *Fast Capitalism: A Critical Theory of Significance*, Champaign, Ill.: University of Illinois Press.
―――― (1989b) *Reading Science: A Literary, Political and Sociological Analysis*, Dix Hills, N.Y.: General Hall.
―――― (1989c) *Socio(onto)logy: A Disciplinary Reading*, Champaign, Ill.: University of Illinois Press.
―――― (1990) *The Decline of Discourse: Reading, Writing and Resistance in Postmodern Capitalism*, London: Falmer Press.

—— (1991) *A Critical Theory of Public Life: Knowledge, Discourse and Power in an Age of Decline*, London: Falmer Press.
—— (1992a) *Cultural Studies as Critical Theory*, London: Falmer Press.
—— (1992b) *The Discourse of Domination: From the Frankfurt School to Postmodernism*, Evanston, Ill.: Northwestern University Press.
—— (1994) *Do Books Write Authors?: A Social Theory of the Text*, Durham, N.C.: Duke University Press.
Altheide, David (1985) *Media Power*, Beverly Hills: Sage.
Althusser, Louis (1970) *For Marx*, London: Allen Lane.
—— (1971) *Lenin and Philosophy and Other Essays*, New York: Monthly Review Press.
Althusser, Louis, and Balibar, Etienne (1970) *Reading Capital*, New York: Pantheon.
Andersen, Margaret L., and Collins, Patricia Hill, (eds.) (1992) *Race, Class and Gender: An Anthology*, Belmont, Calif.: Wadsworth.
Arendt, Hannah (1958) *The Human Condition*, Chicago: University of Chicago Press.
Aronowitz, Stanley (1990) *The Crisis in Historical Materialism*, 2d ed., Minneapolis: University of Minnesota Press.
Barthes, Roland (1975) *The Pleasure of the Text*, New York: Hill and Wang.
Baudrillard, Jean (1975) *The Mirror of Production*, St. Louis: Telos Press.
—— (1981) *For a Critique of the Political Economy of the Sign*, St. Louis: Telos Press.
—— (1983) *Simulations*, New York: Semiotext(e).
—— (1985) *Just Gaming*, Minneapolis: University of Minnesota Press.
—— (1988) *America*, London: Verso.
Beauvoir, Simone de (1953) *The Second Sex*, New York: Knopf.
Bell, Daniel (1960) *The End of Ideology*, Glencoe, Ill.: Free Press.
—— (1973) *The Coming of Post-Industrial Society*, New York: Basic Books.
—— (1976) *The Cultural Contradictions of Capitalism*, New York: Basic Books.
Benhabib, Seyla (1992) *Situating the Self: Gender, Community and Postmodernism in Contemporary Ethics*, Cambridge: Polity Press.
Benjamin, Jessica (1988) *The Bonds of Love: Psychoanalysis, Feminism and the Problem of Domination*, New York: Pantheon.
Bernstein, Basil (1971) *Class, Codes and Control*, London: Routledge and Kegan Paul.
Best, Steven, and Kellner, Douglas (1991) *Postmodern Theory: Critical Interrogations*, London: Macmillan.
Block, Fred (1990) *Postindustrial Possibilities: A Critique of Economic Discourse*, Berkeley: University of California Press.
Bloom, Allan (1987) *The Closing of the American Mind*, New York: Simon and Schuster.
Blumstein, Philip, and Schwartz, Pepper (1983) *American Couples: Money, Work, Sex*, New York: Pocket Books.
Bourdieu, Pierre (1984) *Distinction: A Social Critique of the Judgement of Taste*, Cambridge, Mass.: Harvard University Press.
—— (1988) *Homo Academicus*, Cambridge: Polity Press.
Bristow, Joseph, ed. (1992) *Sexual Sameness: Textual Differences in Lesbian and Gay Writing*, New York: Routledge.

Bibliography

Brodkey, Linda (1987) *Academic Writing as Social Practice*, Philadelphia: Temple University Press.
Brodribb, Somer (1992) *Nothing Mat(t)ers: A Feminist Critique of Postmodernism*, North Melbourne: Spinifex Press.
Brown, Richard Harvey (1987) *Society as Text*, Chicago: University of Chicago Press.
Browne, Ray B. (1989) *Against Academia: The History of the Popular Culture Association, 1967–1988*, Bowling Green, Ohio: Bowling Green University Press.
Buck-Morss, Susan (1977) *The Origins of Negative Dialectics*, New York: Free Press.
───── (1989) *Dialectics of Seeing: Walter Benjamin and the Arcades Project*, Cambridge, Mass.: MIT Press.
Butler, Judith P. (1990) *Gender Trouble: Feminism and the Subversion of Identity*, New York: Routledge.
Chodorow, Nancy (1978) *The Reproduction of Mothering*, Berkeley: University of California Press.
Cixous, Helene (1986) *Inside*, New York: Schocken Books.
───── (1988) *Writing Differences: Readings from the Seminar of Helene Cixous*, edited by Susan Sellers, Milton Keynes, England: Open University Press.
Cleaver, Harry (1979) *Reading Capital Politically*, Austin, Texas: University of Texas Press.
Colletti, Lucio (1973) *Marxism and Hegel*, London: New Left Books.
Collins, Patricia Hill (1991) *Black Feminist Thought: Knowledge, Consciousness, and the Politics of Empowerment*, New York: Routledge.
Connell, Robert (1987) *Gender and Power: Society, the Person and Sexual Politics*, Cambridge: Polity Press.
Cowan, Ruth (1983) *More Work for Mother: The Ironies of Household Technology from the Open Hearth to the Microwave*, New York: Basic Books.
Daly, Mary (1978) *Gyn/Ecology: The Metaethics of Radical Feminism*, Boston: Beacon Press.
Dandaneau, Steven (1992) "An Immanent Critique of Post-Marxism," Current Perspectives in Social Theory 12, 155–77.
Darty, Trudy, and Potter, Sandee, eds. (1984) *Women-identified Women*, Palo Alto, Calif.: Mayfield.
Debord, Guy (1970) *The Society of the Spectacle*, Detroit: Black and Red Press.
Deleuze, Gilles, and Guattari, Felix (1977) *Anti-Oedipus: Capitalism and Schizophrenia*, New York: Viking.
Dalla Costa, Mariarosa, and James, Selma (1973) *The Power of Women and the Subversion of the Community*, Bristol, England: Falling Wall Press.
Delphy, Christine (1984) *Close to Home: A Materialist Analysis of Women's Oppression*, London: Hutchinson.
Denzin, Norman (1991) *Images of Postmodern Society: Social Theory and Contemporary Cinema*, London: Sage.
DeVault, Marjorie (1991) *Feeding the Family: The Social Organization of Caring and Gendered Work*, Chicago: University of Chicago Press.
Dews, Peter (1984) "Power and Subjectivity in Foucault," *New Left Review*, 144, 72–95.
───── (1987) *Logics of Disintegration: Post-Structuralist Thought and the Claims of Critical Theory*, London: Verso.

Diesing, Paul (1991) *How Does Social Science Work? Reflections on Practice*, Pittsburgh: Pittsburgh University Press.
Di Stefano, Christine (1991) *Configurations of Masculinity: A Feminist Perspective on Modern Political Theory*, Ithaca, NY: Cornell University Press.
Donovan, Josephine (1985) *Feminist Theory*, New York: Ungar.
D'Souza, Dinesh (1991) *Illiberal Education: The Politics of Race and Sex on Campus*, New York: Free Press.
Dworkin, Andrea (1974) *Woman Hating*, New York: Dutton.
Eagleton, Terry (1983) *Literary Theory: An Introduction*, Minneapolis: University of Minnesota Press.
Ehrenreich, Barbara (1983) *The Hearts of Men: American Dreams and the Flight from Commitment*, Garden City, NY: Anchor Press/Doubleday.
Eisenstein, Zillah, ed. (1979) *Capitalist Patriarchy and the Case for Socialist Feminism*, New York: Monthly Review Press.
Evans, Sarah (1979) *Personal Politics: The Roots of Women's Liberation in the Civil Rights Movement and the New Left*, New York: Knopf.
Ewen, Stuart (1976) *Captains of Consciousness: Advertising and the Social Roots of the Consumer Culture*, New York: McGraw-Hill.
—— (1988) *All Consuming Images: The Politics of Style in Contemporary Culture*, New York: Basic Books.
Faludi, Susan (1991) *Backlash: The Undeclared War against American Women*, New York: Crown.
Faurschou, Gail (1987) "Fashion and the Cultural Logic of Postmodernity," *Current Perspectives in Social Theory* 11, 68–82.
Feagin, Joe, and Sikes, Melvin (1993) *Modern Racism: On Being Black and Middle Class*, Boston: Beacon Press.
Fekete, John (1978) *The Critical Twilight: Explorations in the Ideology of Anglo-American Literary Theory from Eliot to McLuhan*, London: Routledge and Kegan Paul.
Finke, Laurie (1992) *Feminist Theory, Women's Writing*, Ithaca, N.Y.: Cornell University Press.
Firestone, Shulamith (1970) *The Dialectic of Sex*, New York: Morrow.
Fish, Stanley (1980) *Is There a Text in This Class?: The Authority of Interpretive Communities*, Cambridge, Mass.: Harvard University Press.
—— (1989) *Doing What Comes Naturally*, Durham, N.C.: Duke University Press.
Fiske, John (1987) *Television Culture*, New York: Methuen.
Flax, Jane (1990) *Thinking Fragments: Psychoanalysis, Feminism and Postmodernism in the Contemporary West*, Berkeley: University of California Press.
Forester, John, ed. (1985) *Critical Theory and Public Life*, Cambridge, Mass.: MIT Press.
Foucault, Michel (1977) *Discipline and Punish*, New York: Pantheon.
—— (1978) *The History of Sexuality*, New York: Pantheon.
Fraser, Nancy (1989) *Unruly Practices: Power, Discourse and Gender in Contemporary Social Theory*, Minneapolis: University of Minnesota Press.
Fraser, Nancy, and Bartky, Sandra Lee, eds. (1992) *Revaluing French Feminism: Critical Essays on Difference, Agency, and Culture*, Bloomington, Ind.: Indiana University Press.
Friedan, Betty (1963) *The Feminine Mystique*, New York: Norton.

——— (1981) *The Second Stage*, New York: Summit Books.
Fuss, Diana (1989) *Essentially Speaking: Feminism, Nature and Difference*, New York: Routledge.
Fuss, Diana, ed. (1991) *Inside/Out: Lesbian Theories, Gay Theories*, New York: Routledge.
Giddens, Anthony (1984) *The Constitution of Society: Outline of the Theory of Structuration*, Cambridge: Polity Press.
Gilligan, Carol (1982) *In a Different Voice*, Cambridge, Mass.: Harvard University Press.
Gitlin, Todd (1980) *The Whole World Is Watching: Mass Media in the Making and Unmaking of the New Left*, Berkeley: University of California Press.
——— (1987) *The Sixties: Years of Hope, Days of Rage*, New York: Bantam.
Goldman, Robert (1994) "Contradictions of a Political Economy of Sign Value," *Current Perspectives in Social Theory* 13.
Goldman, Robert, and Papson, Steven (1991) "Levi's and the Knowing Wink," *Current Perspectives in Social Theory* 11, 69–95.
Grossberg, Lawrence; Nelson, Cary; and Treichler, Paula A., eds. (1992) *Cultural Studies*, New York: Routledge.
Habermas, Jurgen (1971) *Knowledge and Human Interests*, Boston: Beacon Press.
——— (1975) *Legitimation Crisis*, Boston: Beacon Press.
——— (1981a) "Modernity versus Postmodernity," *New German Critique* 22, 3–14.
——— (1981b) "New Social Movements," *Telos* 49, 33–7.
——— (1984) *The Theory of Communicative Action*, Vol. 1, Boston: Beacon Press.
——— (1987a) *The Philosophical Discourse of Modernity*, Cambridge, Mass.: MIT Press.
——— (1987b) *The Theory of Communicative Action*, Vol. 2, Boston: Beacon Press.
Hall, Stuart (1980a) *Culture, Media, Language: Working Papers in Cultural Studies, 1972–1979*, London: Hutchinson.
——— (1980b) "Cultural Studies: Two Paradigms," *Media, Culture and Society* 2, 57–72.
——— (1988) *The Hard Road to Renewal: Thatcherism and the Crisis of the Left*, London: Verso.
Hallin, Daniel (1985) "The American News Media: A Critical Theory Perspective," in *Critical Theory and Public Life*, edited by John Forester, Cambridge, Mass.: MIT Press.
Harding, Sandra (1986) *The Science Question in Feminism*, Ithaca, N.Y.: Cornell University Press.
Harms, Douglas, and Kellner, Doug (1991) "Critical Theory and Advertising," *Current Perspectives in Social Theory* 11, 41–67.
Hartmann, Heidi (1979) "The Unhappy Marriage of Marxism and Feminism: Towards a More Progressive Union," *Capital and Class* 8, 1–33.
Harvey, David (1989) *The Condition of Postmodernity*, Oxford: Blackwell.
Hegel, G. W. F. (1966) "Preface to *Phenomenology of Mind*," in *Hegel: Texts and Commentary*, edited by Walter Kaufman, Garden City, N.Y.: Anchor Books.
Heidegger, Martin (1962) *Being and Time*, New York: Harper.
Hekman, Susan J. (1990) *Gender and Knowledge: Elements of a Postmodern Feminism*, Oxford: Polity Press.

Hennessy, Rosemary (1993) *Materialist Feminism and the Politics of Discourse*, New York: Routledge.
Hoagland, Sarah Lucia, and Penelope, Julia, eds. (1988) *For Lesbians Only: A Separatist Anthology*, London: Onlywomen.
Hochschild, Arlie (1989) *The Second Shift: Working Parents and the Revolution at Home*, New York: Viking.
hooks, bell (1984) *Feminist Theory: From Margin to Center*, Boston: South End Press.
Horkheimer, Max (1972) "Traditional and Critical Theory," in his *Critical Theory*, New York: Herder and Herder.
—— (1973) "The Authoritarian State," *Telos* 15, 3–20.
—— (1974) *Eclipse of Reason*, New York: Seabury Press.
Horkheimer, Max, and Adorno, T. W. (1972) *Dialectic of Enlightenment*, New York: Herder and Herder.
Huyssen, Andreas (1986) *After the Great Divide: Modernism, Mass Culture, Postmodernism*, Bloomington, Ind.: Indiana University Press.
Hymes, Dell (1974) *Foundations in Sociolinguistics: An Ethnographic Approach*, Philadelphia: University of Pennsylvania Press.
Irigaray, Luce (1985) *This Sex Which Is Not One*, Ithaca, N.Y.: Cornell University Press.
Iser, Wolfgang (1978) *The Act of Reading: A Theory of Aesthetic Response*, Baltimore: Johns Hopkins University Press.
Jacoby, Russell (1975) *Social Amnesia: A Critique of Conformist Psychology from Adler to Laing*, Boston: Beacon Press.
—— (1976) "A Falling Rate of Intelligence?" *Telos* 27, 141–46.
—— (1981) *Dialectic of Defeat: Contours of Western Marxism*, New York: Cambridge University Press.
—— (1987) *The Last Intellectuals: American Culture in the Age of Academe*, New York: Basic Books.
—— (1992) Review of *Debating P.C.: The Controversy over Political Correctness on College Campuses*, edited by Paul Berman, in *The Nation*, March 9, 307–309.
Jaggar, Alison (1983) *Feminist Politics and Human Nature*, Totowa, N.J.: Roman and Allenheld.
Jameson, Fredric (1971) *Marxism and Form: Twentieth-Century Dialectical Theories of Literature*, Princeton: Princeton University Press.
—— (1981) *The Political Unconscious: Narrative as a Socially Symbolic Act*, Ithaca, N.Y.: Cornell University Press.
—— (1984) "Postmodernism, or, the Cultural Logic of Late Capitalism," *New Left Review* 146, 53–93.
—— (1991) *Postmodernism, or, the Cultural Logic of Late Capitalism*, Durham, N.C.: Duke University Press.
Jay, Karla, and Glasgow, Joanne, eds. (1990) *Lesbian Texts and Contexts: Radical Revisions*, New York: New York University Press.
Jay, Martin (1973) *The Dialectical Imagination*, Boston: Little, Brown.
—— (1984a) *Adorno*, Cambridge, Mass.: Harvard University Press.
—— (1984b) *Marxism and Totality*, Berkeley: University of California Press.
Keller, Evelyn Fox (1985) *Reflections on Gender and Science*, New Haven: Yale University Press.

Kellner, Douglas (1989a) *Critical Theory, Marxism and Modernity*, Cambridge: Polity Press.
―――― (1989b) *Jean Baudrillard: From Marxism to Postmodernism and Beyond*, Palo Alto: Stanford University Press.
―――― (1990) *Television and the Crisis of Democracy*, Boulder, Colo.: Westview Press.
Kitzinger, Celia (1987) *The Social Construction of Lesbianism*, Newbury Park, Calif.: Sage.
Kristeva, Julia (1980) *Desire in Language: A Semiotic Approach to Literature and Art*, New York: Columbia University Press.
Kroker, Arthur, and Cook, David (1986) *The Postmodern Scene: Excremental Culture and Hyper-Aesthetics*, New York: St. Martin's.
Kroker, Arthur; Kroker, Marilouise; and Cook, David (1989) *Panic Encyclopedia: The Definitive Guide to the Postmodern Scene*, New York: St. Martin's.
Lacan, Jacques (1977) *Ecrits: A Selection*, New York: Norton.
―――― (1982) *Feminine Sexuality*, New York: Norton.
Laclau, Ernesto, and Mouffe, Chantelle (1985) *Hegemony and Socialist Strategy*, London: Verso.
Lasch, Christopher (1977) *Haven in a Heartless World: The Family Besieged*, New York: Basic Books.
―――― (1984) *The Minimal Self*, New York: Norton.
Lather, Patti (1991) *Getting Smart: Feminist Research and Pedagogy with/in the Postmodern*, New York: Routledge.
Lauretis, T. de (1984) *Alice Doesn't: Feminism, Semiotics, Cinema*, Bloomington, Ind.: Indiana University Press.
―――― (1987) *Technologies of Gender: Essays on Theory, Film and Fiction*, Bloomington, Ind: Indiana University Press.
Lentricchia, Frank (1980) *After the New Criticism*, Chicago: University of Chicago Press.
Lesbian Writing and Publishing Collective, eds. (1990) *Dykewords: An Anthology of Lesbian Writing*, Toronto: Women's Press.
Lewis, Lionel S., and Altbach, Philip G. (1992) "Political Correctness, Campus Malaise," *The Times Higher Education Supplement* 1008 (February 28), 17.
Lichtheim, George (1961) *Marxism: An Historical and Critical Study*, London: Routledge and Kegan Paul.
Lodge, David (1984) *Small World: An Academic Romance*, London: Secker and Warburg.
Lorraine, Tamsin E. (1990) *Gender, Identity and the Production of Meaning*, Boulder, Colo.: Westview Press.
Lukacs, Georg (1971) *History and Class Consciousness*, London: Merlin Press.
Luke, Timothy W. (1989) *Screens of Power: Ideology, Domination and Resistance in the Informational Society*, Urbana, Ill.: University of Illinois Press.
―――― (1992) *Shows of Force: Power, Politics and Ideology in Art Exhibitions*, Durham, N.C.: Duke University Press.
Lukes, Timothy, and Bokina, John (1993) *Marcuse Revisited*, Lawrence, Kans.: Kansas University Press.
Lyotard, J-F. (1984) *The Postmodern Condition: A Report on Knowledge*, Minneapolis: University of Minnesota Press.

McCloskey, Donald (1985) *The Rhetoric of Economics*, Madison: University of Wisconsin Press.
McLuhan, Marshall (1967) *The Medium Is the Massage*, Harmondsworth, England: Penguin.
——— (1968) *The Gutenberg Galaxy*, Toronto: University of Toronto Press.
——— (1989) *The Global Village*, New York: Oxford University Press.
Macpherson, C. B. (1962) *The Political Theory of Possessive Individualism*, Oxford: Clarendon Press.
Man, P. de (1986) *The Resistance to Theory*, Minneapolis: University of Minnesota Press.
Mandel, Ernest (1975) *Late Capitalism*, London: New Left Books.
Mannheim, Karl (1936) *Ideology and Utopia: An Introduction to the Sociology of Knowledge*, New York: Harcourt, Brace and Company.
Marcus, George, and Fischer, Michael, eds. (1986) *Anthropology as Cultural Critique: An Experimental Moment in the Human Sciences*, Chicago: University of Chicago Press.
Marcuse, Herbert (1955) *Eros and Civilization*, New York: Vintage.
——— (1958) *Soviet Marxism*, New York: Vintage.
——— (1960) *Reason and Revolution: Hegel and the Rise of Social Theory*, 2d ed., Boston: Beacon Press.
——— (1964) *One-Dimensional Man*, Boston: Beacon Press.
——— (1968) *Negations*, Boston: Beacon Press.
——— (1969) *An Essay on Liberation*, Boston: Beacon Press.
——— (1972) *Counterrevolution and Revolt*, Boston: Beacon Press.
——— (1978) *The Aesthetic Dimension*, Boston: Beacon Press.
Meese, Elizabeth A. (1992) *(Sem):Erotics: Theorizing Lesbian: Writing*, New York: New York University Press.
Merleau-Ponty, Maurice (1964a) *Sense and Non-Sense*, Evanston, Ill.: Northwestern University Press.
——— (1964b) *Signs*, Evanston, Ill.: Northwestern University Press.
Miller, Mark Crispin (1988) *Boxed In: The Culture of TV*, Evanston, Ill.: Northwestern University Press.
Mitchell, Juliet (1974) *Psychoanalysis and Feminism*, New York: Pantheon.
Moi, Toril (1985) *Sexual/Textual Politics: Feminist Literary Theory*, London: Methuen.
——— (1990) *Feminist Theory and Simone de Beauvoir*, Oxford: Blackwell.
Mulvey, Laura (1988) *Visual and Other Pleasures*, Basingstoke, England: Macmillan.
Myron, Nancy, and Bunch, Charlotte, eds. (1975) *Lesbianism and the Women's Movement*, Baltimore: Diana Press.
Nestle, Joan, ed. (1992) *The Persistent Desire: A Femme-Butch Reader*, Boston: Alyson.
Neumann, Franz (1942) *Behemoth*, London: Gollancz.
Newman, Charles (1985) *The Post-modern Aura: The Act of Fiction in an Age of Inflation*, Evanston, Ill.: Northwestern University Press.
O'Brien, Mary (1981) *The Politics of Reproduction*, Boston: Routledge and Kegan Paul.
——— (1989) *Reproducing the World: Essays in Feminist Theory*, Boulder, Colo.: Westview Press.
O'Neill, John (1970) *Perception, Expression and History: The Social Phenomenology of Maurice Merleau-Ponty*, Evanston, Ill.: Northwestern University Press.

_____ (1972) *Sociology as a Skin Trade*, New York: Harper and Row.
_____ (1974) *Making Sense Together: An Introduction to Wild Sociology*, New York: Harper and Row.
_____ (1982) *Essaying Montaigne*, London: Routledge and Kegan Paul.
_____ (1986) "The Disciplinary Society: From Weber to Foucault," *British Journal of Sociology* 37, 42–60.
Paci, Enzo (1972) *The Function of the Sciences and the Meaning of Man*, Evanston, Ill.: Northwestern University Press.
Packard, Vance (1957) *The Hidden Persuaders*, New York: McKay.
Parsons, Talcott (1951) *The Social System*, Glencoe, Ill.: Free Press.
Parsons, Talcott, and Bales, Robert (1955) *Family, Socialization and Interaction Process*, Glencoe, Ill.: Free Press.
Piccone, Paul (1971) "Phenomenological Marxism," *Telos* 9, 3–31.
_____ (1976) "Beyond Identity Theory," in *On Critical Theory*, edited by John O'Neill, New York: Seabury.
Pleck, Joseph (1981) *The Myth of Masculinity*, Cambridge, Mass.: MIT Press.
Portoghesi, Paolo (1983) *Postmodern, the Architecture of the Postindustrial Society*, New York: Rizzoli.
Poster, Mark (1975) *Existential Marxism in Postwar France*, Princeton: Princeton University Press.
_____ (1989) *Critical Theory and Poststructuralism*, Ithaca, N.Y.: Cornell University Press.
_____ (1990) *The Mode of Information: Poststructuralism and Social Context*, Cambridge: Polity Press.
Rachlin, Allan (1988) *News as Hegemonic Reality*, New York: Praeger.
Reinharz, Shulamit (1992) *Feminist Methods in Social Research*, New York: Oxford University Press.
Rosenau, Pauline (1992) *Post-modernism and the Social Sciences*, Princeton: Princeton University Press.
Ryan, Michael (1982) *Marxism and Deconstruction*, Baltimore: Johns Hopkins University Press.
Ryan, Michael, and Kellner, Douglas (1988) *Camera Politica: The Politics and Ideology of Contemporary Hollywood Film*, Bloomington, Ind.: Indiana University Press.
Ryan, William (1971) *Blaming the Victim*, New York: Pantheon.
Sartre, Jean-Paul (1948) *Anti-Semite and Jew*, New York: Schocken.
_____ (1956) *Being and Nothingness*, New York: Philosophical Library.
_____ (1963) *Search for a Method*, New York: Knopf.
_____ (1976) *Critique of Dialectical Reason*, London: New Left Books.
Sawicki, Jana (1991) *Disciplining Foucault: Feminism, Power and the Body*, New York: Routledge.
Scheler, Max (1961) *Ressentiment*, New York: Free Press of Glencoe.
Schiller, Herbert (1989) *Culture, Inc.: The Corporate Takeover of Public Expression*, New York: Oxford University Press.
Schroyer, Trent (1973) *The Critique of Domination: The Origins and Development of Critical Theory*, New York: Braziller.
Sennett, Richard (1977) *The Fall of Public Man*, New York: Knopf.

Shelton, Beth Anne (1992) *Women, Men and Time: Gender Differences in Paid Work, Housework and Leisure*, New York: Greenwood Press.
Shelton, Beth Anne, and Agger, Ben (1992) "Shotgun Wedding, Unhappy Marriage, No-Fault Divorce?: Rethinking the Feminism-Marxism Relationship," in *Theory on Gender/Feminism on Theory*, edited by Paula England, New York: Aldine de Gruyter.
Slater, Phil (1977) *Origin and Significance of the Frankfurt School*, London: Routledge and Kegan Paul.
Steinem, Gloria (1986) *Outrageous Acts and Everyday Rebellions*, New York: New American Library.
Walby, Sylvia (1990) *Theorizing Patriarchy*, Oxford: Blackwell.
Walters, Suzanna (1992) "Material Girls: Toward a Feminist Cultural Studies," *Current Perspectives in Social Theory* 12, 59–96.
Weedon, Chris (1987) *Feminist Practice and Poststructuralist Theory*, Oxford: Blackwell.
Wernick, Andrew (1991) *Promotional Culture: Advertising, Ideology and Symbolic Expression*, London: Sage.
Williamson, Judith (1978) *Decoding Advertisements: Ideology and Meaning in Advertising*, London: Boyars.
Willis, Paul (1977) *Learning to Labour*, Farnborough: Saxon House.
―――― (1978) *Profane Culture*, London: Routledge and Kegan Paul.
Wittgenstein, Ludwig (1953) *Philosophical Investigations*, Oxford: Blackwell.
Wolfe, Alan (1977) *The Limits of Legitimacy: Political Contradictions of Contemporary Capitalism*, New York: Free Press.
―――― (1981) *America's Impasse: The Rise and Fall of the Politics of Growth*, New York: Pantheon.
―――― (1989) *Whose Keeper? Social Science and Moral Obligation*, Berkeley: University of California Press.
Wright, Erik Olin (1985) *Classes*, London: Verso.
―――― (1987) "Reflections on *Classes*," *Berkeley Journal of Sociology* 23, 19–49.
Young, Iris Marion (1990) *Justice and the Politics of Difference*, Princeton: Princeton University Press.
Zaret, David (1992) "Critical Theory and the Sociology of Culture," *Current Perspectives in Social Theory*, 12, 1–28.

Index

Adorno, Theodor W., 3, 4, 6, 7, 19, 60, 73, 127, 129, 150; application of cultural theory of, 47; on displacement of politics, 23; essays of, 99–100; identity theory of, 97, 120–121, 151; on importance of non-identical, 25; on logic of domination, 22; as mandarin modernist, 44, 50, 113, 127; pessimism of, 151, 152; political optimism of, 113–114; postmodern themes of, 32; on totalization of negativity as lacking nuance, 133; view of domination, 154
Advertising: positioning of consumers by, 147–148; postmodern campaigns in, 92, 93; sociology of, 73; validity of, 148
Agency, determinism vs., 88–90
Agger, Ben, 16
AIDS, 126
Althusser, Louis, 32, 88
Authoritarianism, 52

Barthes, Roland, 73, 92
Baudrillard, Jean, 6, 19, 33, 130; fast capitalism and, 17–18; hyperreality of, 11, 12, 14; simulation theory and, 15, 116; on sociology of advertising, 73
Behemoth (Neumann), 28
Bell, Daniel, 21, 55–56
Benjamin, Walter, 100
Birmingham School, 111, 127
Bloom, Allan, 104, 118
Blumer, Herbert, 73
Buchanan, Pat, 61
Buck-Morss, Susan, 100
Bush, George, 61

Capitalism: fast, 11–18; late, 7, 41, 129; theories of patriarchal, 78–79; transitions in postmodern, 7–11
Chodorow, Nancy, 142, 143
Cixous, Helene, 57
Commodity fetishism, 13
Cook, David, 130
Critical theory: Agger's perspective on, 95–96; applied to contemporary social problems, 8–9; domination and, 153; essaying, 98–104; inaccessibility of, 49; lifeworld grounding of, 41–42; parallels between feminism and, 2; for and against the popular, 126–131; postmodernism as, 143–144; require-

ments of, 112; rhetoric of, 100–101; third-generation, 1–7; working-class politics and, 77–78
Cultural studies: critical theory's version of, 130, 131; intent of, 129; modernism, postmodernism, and, 46–51

Daly, Mary, 61
Deconstruction, as critical social and political theory, 118
Democratization, 49–50
Derrida, 73, 91, 144; Foucault, Baudrillard, Frankfurt School and, 42–46; influence of, 146–147; on literary undecidability, 101, 103; parallels between Adorno and, 50; political theory of, 61; postmodern discourse theory and, 46, 93–94
Determinism, agency vs., 88–90
Dialectic of Enlightenment (Horkheimer and Adorno), 3, 7, 15, 17, 22, 26, 151
Dialectic of nature, 20–21
Difference theory: celebration of feminine, and end of politics, 66–73; postmodern feminist, 61–62
Discipline, 43–44
The Discourse of Domination: From the Frankfurt School to Postmodernism (Agger), 84, 153–154
Discourse theory: politics and, 50; postmodern, 46, 75, 143–144, 149; tendency to become academic, 150
Domination: Habermas' attempt to retheorize, 5; logic of, 22, 83; and negative dialectics, 150–154; and production over reproduction, 95–96; of reproduction, 8, 9, 81–82, 95; as structural, 92; transcoding logics of, 109–116
Donovan, Josephine, 57
Dukakis, Michael, 61
Duke, David, 61

Economism: effects of, 112, 113; failure of, 114; and politics of everyday life, 110
Enlightenment, 119, 120, 128

Fast capitalism: Baudrillard and, 17–18; and new theory of ideology, 11–16
Feminism: challenge to male critical theory, 1–3; conflated with lesbianism, 125; and hierarchies of values over valuelessness, 138; Lacanian, 57–66; Marxism and, 13, 59, 65, 156–157; theorizing, 77–82; and valorization of reproduction, 121–126; written by men, 3. *See also* Postmodern feminism
Feminist postmodern critical theory: incorporation of feminism, postmodernism, and critical theory into, 4; logic of, 1
Feminists: cultural vs. capitalist-patriarchy, 79–80; Lacanian, 80–81; men as, 137–143; problem of, 73–77
Feminist theory: ability of men to write, 70; in academia, 72; decoupling of feminist practice and, 78; difference theory and, 69–70; heterotextual hierarchies of production addressed by, 81–82; written by men, 139–143
Fonda, Jane, 62
Foucault, Michel, 6, 73, 112; rejection of project of modernity by, 35; on traditional Marxism, 14; view of power, 9; writings on discipline and sexuality, 43–44, 75
Frankfurt School: aesthetic theory of, 47; critical theory of, 2, 3, 29–30, 77, 126–130; Derrida, Foucault, Baudrillard, and, 42–46; on duality of agency and structure, 91; and engagement with student movement or feminism, 53; failing of, 151; high-culture theory of, 19; postmodern themes in, 116, 117; and understanding of ideology, 111
Fraser, Nancy, 2
Freud, Sigmund, 59–60

Giddens, Anthony, 90
Gitlin, Todd, 131
Gramsci, Antonio, 49

Index

Grand narratives: aversion to, 31–36; Lyotard's view of, 55, 84, 89; structural primacy and, 89

Habermas, Jurgen, 1, 2, 4, 21, 22, 42, 97, 102, 144, 155; attempt to retheorize domination, 5; and empirical social science, 56; on historical materialism, 102–103; ideal speech and, 117, 119; new social movements theory of, 54; and paradigm of communication, 27; system and lifework of, 83; view of communication theory, 7–8, 54; view of postmodernism, 31, 34, 53–54; writing on oral communication, 44
Hegel, G.W.F., 42
Heidegger, Martin, 90
Heterosexuality: compulsory, 123; resistance to, 126
Heterotextual hierarchies: of production, 81–82; productivist, 16–17
Heterotextuality, 122, 132
Horkheimer, Max, 3, 4, 6, 7, 14, 19, 22; on displacement of politics, 23; view of domination, 154
Household labor, 86
Huyssen, Andreas, 116
Hyperreality, 11, 12, 14, 18

Ideal speech, 117, 119
Identity theory, 97, 120–121, 151
Ideology: postmodernism and end of, 52–56; toward new theory of, 11–16
Imagination, postmodernism and discourse of, 116–121
Informationalism, 40–41
Intellectuality, 13
Irigaray, Luce, 57

Jacoby, Russell, 13, 49, 62, 112–113, 132–133, 145
Jaggar, Alison, 57
Jameson, Fredric, 2, 7, 21, 97–98
Janowitz, Tama, 50

Kristeva, Julia, 57
Kroker, Arthur, 130

Lacan, Jacques, 57
Lacanian feminism: difference theory and, 67; discussion of, 57–66, 79; explanation of, 57–58
Late capitalism, 7, 41, 129
Lenin, V. I., 31
Lesbians: images of, 124–125; men as, 126
Luddism, 20
Lukacs, Georg, 77
Luke, Timothy W., 130
Lyotard, J-F., 17, 31, 146; rejection of project of modernity by, 35, 39; view of grand narratives, 55, 84, 89

Mandel, Ernest, 7
Marcuse, Herbert, 2, 28, 113, 152–154; critical theory of, 26, 116; Freudianization of Marx, 19; new science and technology advocated by, 49–50; on subjectivity in late capitalism, 41; view of domination, 154; view of one-dimensionality, 18, 116
Marx, Karl: canonization and demonization of, 24–25; critical theory's relationship to, 4, 5; as modernist, 6; and notion of truth, 146; revision and revitalization of theoretical logic of, 86–87; and structural primacy, 86–88; view of structure, 94
Marxism: abandonment of, 33–36; conclusions regarding, 155–157; economism as basis of orthodox, 114; feminist view of, 75–76; and hierarchy of production over reproduction, 10, 80–81; as identity theory, 120–121; nature of, 85; postmodernism and postwar existential, 119; and theories of patriarchal capitalism, 78–79; translated into feminism, 13, 59; view of household labor, 86
McCarthyism, 14, 37
Mead, George Herbert, 73
Merleau-Ponty, Maurice, 32, 101, 118
Modernism: postmodern, 24; postmodernism, cultural studies, and, 46–51

Multiculturalism: as academic manifestation of difference theory, 69; difference-theoretic, 133; opposition to, 132

Named theory, 2
Neoliberalism: clash between neoconservatism and, 63; of French feminist difference theory, 61; postmodernism, and post-Marxism, 36–42
Neumann, Franz, 28
New French Theory, 29; characteristics of, 31, 58, 144; Derrida, Foucault, Baudrillard, the Frankfurt School and, 42–46; and discourse of imagination, 116; Nietzsche and, 120; postmodernism, post-Marxism, and neoliberalism and, 36–42, 112; postmodernism and end of ideology and, 52–56
Nietzsche, Friedrich Wilhelm, 119–120
Nixon, Richard, 76
Neoconservatism, 63

O'Neill, John 102
Ontology, 26

Paci, Enzo, 102
Perestroika, 27, 28
Piccone, Paul, 102
Pleck, Joseph, 142
Politics: aversion to, 91; difference theory and end of, 66–73; discourse theory and, 50; displacement of, 23; of totality, 21–27, 91
Positivism: and concept of social universe, 25–26; vs. empirical social science, 83
Poster, Mark, 41
Postmodern capitalism: nature of era of, 86; transitions in, 7–11. *See also* Fast capitalism
Postmodern feminism: effects of, 57; neobiologism of, 60–62; problem of subject and, 73–77. *See also* Feminism

Postmodernism: aversion to grand narratives, 31, 32; and concept of social universe, 26; critical social science and, 74; depolitization and, 77; and discourse of imagination, 116–121; levels of, 35–36; Marxism and, 31, 156–157; modernism, cultural studies, and, 46–51; and pluralist affirmation of capitalism, 10; post-Marxism, and neoliberalism, 36–42; postwar existential Marxism and, 119; as radical moment of modernism, 6; theorizing, 27–30
Postmodernism (Jameson), 97
Poststructuralism: beyond, 88–94; French, 89; nature of, 93–94
Production: heterotextual hierarchies of, 81–82; over reproduction, 10, 80–81, 94–98, 104–106
Productivism, 4–5
Productivist heterotextual hierarchy, 16–17
Psychoanalysis, 58

Reading Science (Agger), 103, 104
Reagan, Ronald, 76
Relationality, 104–107
Relativism, 146
Reproduction: domination of, 8, 9, 81–82; feminism and valorization of, 121–126; Marxism and hierarchy of production over, 10, 80–81; production over, 94–98, 104–106

Sartre, Jean-Paul, 32, 90
Science: democratization of, 49–50; essaying, 102, 103
Sexual orientation, 123–124
Simulation theory, 15
Slater, Phil, 112
Social science: dialectical, 84–85; empirical, 56, 84; positivism vs. empirical, 84; postmodernism and critical, 74
Socio(onto)logy: A Disciplinary Reading (Agger), 98–99
Soviet Marxism (Marcuse), 28

Soviet Union: collapse of, 28, 76, 144–145; function of Communist Party in, 32
Stalinism, 31–32, 52
Steinem, Gloria, 62
Structural analysis: economism and, 110; and production over reproduction, 94
Structural primacy: and Derridean poststructuralism, 88; retaining concept of, 83–88
Structuration theory, 90
Subjectivity: in late capitalism, 41; politics of, 133

Technology, democratization of, 49–50

Tel Quel group, 32–33, 38
Theory of Communicative Action (Habermas), 7
Third-generation critical theory, 1, 8
Totality: approaches to in, 99; politics of, 21–27, 91; relationality, transformationality and, 104–107
Totality theory: inadequacy of, 91; possibility of, 16–21
Transcoding: logics of domination, 109–116; self-, 135–136; the transcoder, 131–135
Transformationality, 104–107

Women's study programs, 67

About the Author

BEN AGGER is Professor of Sociology at State University of New York, Buffalo. He has authored ten books and specializes in social theory and neo-Marxism.

ADC-3461

DATE DUE